Lauer Series in Rhetoric and Composition
Series Editors, Catherine Hobbs and Patricia Sullivan

LAUER SERIES IN RHETORIC AND COMPOSITION
Series Editors, Catherine Hobbs and Patricia Sullivan

The Lauer Series in Rhetoric and Composition honors the contributions Janice Lauer Hutton has made to the emergence of Rhetoric and Composition as a disciplinary study. It publishes scholarship that carries on Professor Lauer's varied work in the history of written rhetoric, disciplinarity in composition studies, contemporary pedagogical theory, and written literacy theory and research.

Other Books in the Series

1977: A Cultural Moment in Composition by Brent Henze, Jack Selzer, and Wendy Sharer (2007)

Untenured Faculty as Writing Program Administrators: Institutional Practices and Politics, edited by Debra Frank Dew and Alic Horning (2007)

Composing a Community: A History of Writing Across the Curriculum, edited by Susan H. McLeod and Margot Soven (2006)

Historical Studies of Writing Program Administration: Individuals, Communities, and the Formation of a Discipline, edited by Barbara L'Eplattenier and Lisa Mastrangelo (2004).

Rhetorics, Poetics, and Cultures: Refiguring College English Studies (Expanded Edition) by James A. Berlin (2003)

Networked Process

Dissolving Boundaries of
Process and Post-Process

Helen Foster

Parlor Press
West Lafayette, Indiana
www.parlorpress.com

Parlor Press LLC, West Lafayette, Indiana 47906

© 2007 by Parlor Press
All rights reserved.
Printed in the United States of America.

SAN: 254-8879

Library of Congress Cataloging-in-Publication Data

Foster, Helen, 1950-
  Networked process : dissolving boundaries of process and post-process / Helen Foster.
    p. cm. -- (Lauer Series in Rhetoric and Composition)
  Includes bibliographical references and index.
  ISBN 978-1-60235-019-9 (pbk. : alk. paper) -- ISBN 978-1-60235-020-5 (hardcover : alk. paper) -- ISBN 978-1-60235-021-2 (adobe ebook)
  1. English language--Rhetoric. 2. Report writing. I. Title.
  PE1404.F67 2007
  808'.042071--dc22
                                    2007026549

Cover design by David Blakesley.
Cover background "Magma Share" © 2005 by Eva Serrabass. Used by permission.
Printed on acid-free paper.

Parlor Press, LLC is an independent publisher of scholarly and trade titles in print and multimedia formats. This book is available in paper, cloth and Adobe eBook formats from Parlor Press on the World Wide Web at http://www.parlorpress.com or through online and brick-and-mortar bookstores. For submission information or to find out about Parlor Press publications, write to Parlor Press, 816 Robinson St., West Lafayette, Indiana, 47906, or e-mail editor@parlorpress.com.

For Kate and Janice

Contents

Illustrations	ix
Acknowledgments	xi
Introduction	xiii
1 Profiling Process and Post-Process	3
Post-Process	4
Entrance of Post-Process Theory into the Discourse of Rhetoric and Composition	6
Post-Process Moniker and the Discourse of Rhetoric and Composition	9
Post-Process Scholarship and the Social/Cultural Turn	13
Critiques of Process within Strand Two Post-Process	19
Calls for Reform within Strand Two Post-Process	23
Repercussions for a Post-Process Profession within Strand Two Post-Process	27
Post-Process Scholarship that Positions Itself Beyond That of the Social/Cultural Turn	28
A Few Rejoinders to Thomas Kent's Edited *Post-Process* Collection	29
Process: A Rebuttal	31
Process Profile	31
Process, Post-Process: A Point of *Stasis*	36
Writing Process/Post-Process Unbound: Networked Process	38
2 Exploring Networked Process in James Berlin's Cognitive Maps	42
Berlin's Cognitive Maps	43
"Current-Traditional Rhetoric: Paradigm and Practice"	46
"Contemporary Composition: The Major Pedagogical Theories"	48
Writing Instruction in Nineteenth-Century American Colleges	51

*Rhetoric and Reality: Writing Instruction
  in American Colleges, 1900–1985* — 54
"Rhetoric and Ideology in the Writing Class" — 58
The Platform That Berlin Built — 61

3 Networked Subjectivity — 70
  Subjectivity: Entering the Network — 71
  Articulating Networked Process:
    Mapping Networked Subjectivity — 79
  Space/Time/History — 81
  Language/Discourse — 82
  Self — 89
  Alterity/Other/Horizon — 99
  Addressivity/Answerability — 104
  Networked Process:
    Networked Subjectivity and Writing Process(es) — 107

4 Situating Networked Subjectivity — 112
  Discursive Relations — 114
  Multiple Epistemologies/Multiple Subjectivities — 130
  Multiple Literacies/Classroom — 136

5 Textbooks, Writing Program Reforms,
  Institutionality, and the Public — 141
  Audience, Self, and Alterity — 143
  Understanding — 148
  Language/Discourse — 151
  Context and Horizon — 153
  Purpose: Addressivity and Answerability — 156
  Introduction to "Basic Work and Material Acts:
    The Ironies, Discrepancies, and Disjunctures
    of Basic Writing and Mainstreaming" — 166

6 Networked Process and the Long Revolution — 180
  Institutional Place(ment) — 185
  The Writing Major — 190
  Re-visioning Rhetoric and Composition — 191
  Disciplinarity — 193

Notes — 199
Works Cited — 227
Index — 245
About the Author — 251

Illustrations

Figure 1. Early Process/Post-Process/ Radical Post-Process Continuum	*38*
Figure 2. Networked Subjectivity	*80*
Figure 3. Space/Time/History	*81*
Figure 4. Language/Discourse	*86*
Figure 5. Self	*90*
Figure 6. Space of the Self	*95*
Figure 7. Alterity/Other/Horizon	*102*
Figure 8. Addressivity/Answerability	*105*
Figure 9. Networked Subjectivity	*113*
Figure 10. Multiple Epistemologies / Multiple Subjectivities	*135*
Figure 11. Multiple Literacies/Classroom	*139*

Acknowledgments

As any book is, this one is likewise thoroughly intertextual, for every graduate professor I've studied with along with some intellectually formidable colleagues has influenced the scholarly journey that culminated in this book. My thanks go to all for the challenges and discussions. However, special consideration goes to the interlocutor who inspired the dissonance of this inquiry. Although he was gone before I had the chance to study with him, his passion, inspiration, and keen intellect live on in his work. Thank you Jim Berlin, wherever you are.

Without the patience and good humor of David Blakesley at Parlor Press, this book would literally not have been possible. Dave is a terrifically hard-working editor, whom I'm convinced rarely sleeps. And to Lauer Series' editors Catherine Hobbs and Patricia Sullivan go my appreciation for careful readings and insightful comments.

For material support of my work, I am indebted to the University of Texas El Paso for a research grant, as well as to the English department for a course release.

My thanks extend to Claudia Rojas for contributing her talents in graphic design and to Scott Lunsford and Paul Lynch for their skills in manuscript editing. Thanks, too, for the thoughtful manuscript reading and questioning offered by Brian McNely. Although he's convinced me that we use the notion *intertextuality* to our own detriment, I'm consigned to using it until he coins a more appropriate term, an event I eagerly anticipate in the not so distant future.

My love and appreciation go to my family who have never quite understood why I want to do this but who support and encourage me, nevertheless. To my children—Katy, Blair, and Hailey—thank you for tolerating me and my scholarly baggage. To my five-year old granddaughter Kaitlyn, who recently asked me to read aloud a scholarly article only to stop me mid-sentence after about three pages to announce that "I know stuff, too!" thank you for the concrete reminder that all "stuff" has value. Finally, for the inexhaustible encouragement and inspiration, along with the occasional timely reminder that this line of work was my choice, I can never accurately measure my gratitude for the tolerance and understanding of my husband and best friend, Don.

Introduction

Rhetoric and composition emerged some forty years ago in response to a variety of institutional and cultural pressures occasioned by perceived crises in student writing and the inadequacy of prevalent writing curricula to successfully address them. As the teaching and learning of writing became the focus of study, the term writing process came to represent not only a material, curricular approach to the teaching of writing, but also a significant, symbolic representation of the field itself.

Dedicated faculty lines, thriving graduate programs, and field-specific scholarly journals and books have since created a dynamic knowledge base of writing studies that continues to benefit from and to be challenged by poststructuralist, feminist, critical, and postmodern theories. In the wake of these productive challenges, writing process has become increasingly suspect as a curricular approach and, particularly, as a symbolic representation of the field whose disciplinary interests now far exceed the boundaries of the traditional first-year composition course.

This turn has come to be labeled post-process, and, although not well defined as a position or school of thought, its general sentiment is gaining currency with those discontented with process. Many, however, do not comfortably identify with either position. Process today is not the process of the 1970s and early 1980s on which our disciplinary identity was based and post-process remains for many a nebulous concept that equally misses the mark. Thus, a tension ensues that either can polarize or productively challenge us to rethink our disciplinary identity and mission.

A prerequisite to meeting this challenge, however, is an engagement of dialogue among the process and post-process positions, as well as with the many who do not comfortably identify with the extremes of either position. A potential mutual point of departure for a dialogue between the two discourses can be identified using the classical theory of *stasis*. As a heuristic, *stasis* would pose questions regarding existence, quality, and procedure/policy as a method by which to assess *the* point of departure at which an ensuing conversation between process and post-process could commence.[1] Effectively, these questions would address the issues of "what is," "what is good," and "what is possible." It is obvious that *stasis* would be located at the level of existence or the issue of "what is." However, given that post-process posits itself in definitional opposition to process, it is considerably less clear what value the two positions share at this level that could serve as the actual point of *stasis*, that is, the point at which productive dialogue could commence. It is not hyperbolic, I believe, to say that in the absence of productive dialogue between the two, each might increasingly exhibit its own will to power, which would then hold potentially negative repercussions for students, for us, for the spaces of teaching writing, for the larger culture, and for the very nature of our disciplinary identity.

Thus, the goal of this book is to explore process and post-process for the point of *stasis* from which we might begin, anew, a conversation that would honor our past, recognize the exigencies of our present, and anticipate the future to which the conversation could lead us. An equally important goal is a conceptualization of some of the various institutional sites with which writing overlaps. Such a conceptualization could maintain the conversations that ebb and flow within and among these sites as a complex network in which the past, the present, and the future co-exist in a web of genuine organic simultaneity.

Because post-process is so ill-understood, Chapter 1 profiles post-process in an attempt to answer the first question of *stasis* theory: What is? This profile illuminates the heterogeneous nature of the post-process position and gauges the nature of its criticism aimed at process. I then compile a process profile that demonstrates the heterogeneous nature of writing process, along with its material and metaphoric roles in forming our early disciplinary identity. Ultimately, I map the process and post-process profiles along a continuum to assess how they differ and how they resonate. The point of resonance is identified as the point of *stasis*, the place at which both share some degree of common value, the place at which productive dialogue might create material and conceptual spaces that exceed the limitations of both positions.

I name this material and conceptual space *networked process*. As a metaphor for rhetoric and composition's contemporary disciplinary identity, networked process evokes both the growing number of sites and the relational loops that characterize the discipline, a discipline of ever-increasing complexity.[2] Materially and conceptually, networked process encompasses a variety of sites, including multiple notions of writing processes, spaces/places, epistemologies, literacies, disciplinary artifacts, and subjectivities. But a proverbial and fundamental conundrum common to both process and post-process, and thus to the sites with which they are networked, is subjectivity, or the individual who writes.

In Chapter 2, I explore historical scholarship that points toward the possibility of *stasis* between process and post-process, as well as the scholarly journey that eventually arrived at said *stasis*. James Berlin's scholarship, specifically his cognitive mappings of various classifications of writing, is the focus. Analysis of these cognitive maps illuminates how his work speaks to a theory of networked process: they provide (1) a panoramic view of the first half of the process/post-process continuum mapped in Chapter 1, (2) a complex representation of relations that culminated in the theory that would come to be characterized as post-process, and (3) a platform for further elaboration of networked process.

In Chapter 3, I take up the conundrum of subjectivity. First, I articulate a theory of networked subjectivity that describes the materiality of the individual who writes. Then, I posit the conceptual potential of networked subjectivity to function as a heuristic for curricular, pedagogical, and programmatic decision-making. Networked subjectivity describes the nature of the subject and its relation to the world, suggesting that while not a teleology, the subject is nevertheless the necessary analytical ground for entry into the complexity of networked process.

In Chapter 4, I situate networked subjectivity relative to specific discursive formations or webbed relations with which writing and the teaching of writing inevitably co-exist. These discursive formations include power relations, discourse communities, epistemologies, subjectivities, literacies, and classrooms, all of which can be productively considered as sites that exponentially increase the dynamic complexity of networked process. My description of these discursive formations does not exhaustively explore networked subjectivity. These formations represent the minimum networked sites we ought to consider in the pursuit of our educational enterprise.

In Chapter 5, I use networked subjectivity as a heuristic to assess various sites of a network. First, I consider the artifactual site of a well-known first-year composition textbook, and then I turn to the material and conceptual site of a published composition program reform effort. These analyses illustrate that a notion of subjectivity, whether tacit or explicit, influences a conception of what writing is and thus sets in motion a set of assumptions and practices regarding how it ought to be taught. These analyses also indicate the capacity of curricula, pedagogies, writing programs, local institutions, and state governments to convene in the complex site of a particular student subject position, a site that can easily undermine and frustrate the most well-intentioned educational goals and objectives.

I conclude in Chapter 6 with a discussion of the disciplinary ramifications of networked process, as I attempt to (re)imagine the possibilities for the space of networked process and what it could portend for our disciplinary identity. This space, along with others not yet imagined, might become an additional site in the complex educational and cultural network in which both we and student-writer-subjects are enmeshed. Networked process can function as a nuanced and complex thermometer by which to measure the state of our disciplinary identity and health, as well as a dream-catcher for imagining what might be.

Networked Process

1 Profiling Process and Post-Process

That writing process continues to function as a metaphor for the disciplinary identity of rhetoric and composition is nowhere more apparent than in the coinage of *post-process,* a contemporary movement that arguably functions not to revise process so much as to insist that any hope ever attached to it was and is as futile as charging at windmills. The problem with making such a statement, however, is that it assumes that both process and post-process discourses are monolithic. Neither is, after all, nearly so tidy. But with its naming alone, *post-process* clearly does mean to substantively challenge process. The question is how, to what extent, and for what purpose. At stake in these questions is nothing less than where we teach, how we teach, what we teach, and even whether we teach, along with what answers to these questions might portend for rhetoric and composition's disciplinary identity.

All of us undoubtedly believe ourselves well versed in process theory and practice. With only a little exaggeration, it might be said that process constitutes the conceptual fabric of our disciplinary hegemony.[3] The very naming of *post-process,* then, brings this hegemony into relief, an event we ought to consider healthy and productive. But if we uncritically discard one organizing principle for the field only to uncritically adopt another, we risk not only capitulating to similar errors in our disciplinary history but also foregoing a dialogue that might allow us to (re)see process so that we can understand the challenge of post-process within the context of some shared value. Without such a context, the risk is that adherents of both positions will cling to their positions in a posture of recalcitrant self-defense. Certainly, disillusionment with process is not sufficient reason to discard it, but neither is allegiance to process sufficient reason to dismiss post-process. Indeed, disillusionment and allegiance are tricky warrants, offering little exigence for a context in which a genuinely engaged dialogue might occur. More is needed, then, to build a context that can produce dialogue. Minimally, this involves understanding the nature of the two positions and how they differ. It also involves identifying what value the two might share and at what point that value destabilizes. Therefore, a context for genuine dialogue requires at the very least that we determine the point of *stasis* at which productive disagreement might begin.

My purpose in this chapter is to identify this point of *stasis*. To accomplish this, I first construct post-process and process profiles to determine how they differ, and what they mutually value. I devote more space to post-process, simply because it is the less well understood perspective, and I ask a variety of questions. What characterizes the post-process position? What does post-process reject of the process position? Why? What is the nature of the disciplinary identity post-process rejects and would supersede? What characterizes process? What shared value might serve as an effective starting point for a productive dialogue? To answer these questions, I begin with post-process and examine process in light of what post-process critiques in process. Then, I consider the two positions against *stasis* theory to identify the point at which productive dialogue might ensue.

Post-Process

Although some are calling the present time in our history "post-process," it, "like its counterpart, *postmodern*," Lynn Bloom writes, "seems vague in comparison with its referent" (35). Many, undoubtedly, would agree, and while this vagueness is attributable in great part to an unclear understanding of the post-process position, it is also influenced by other factors. One is generational.[4] Many of those emerging from rhetoric and composition doctoral programs within the last decade or so may associate process with a seemingly remote watershed moment in the history of the field. Thus, they identify themselves as post-process because they perceive an evolutionary, disciplinary sensibility, which they happen to equate with post-process. There are also those disillusioned with what first-year composition accomplishes, with the labor issues that sustain it, and with the way first-year composition shapes rhetoric and composition's professional and disciplinary identity. Although these attitudes about post-process inform the scholarship of both process and post-process, they are not often translated, themselves, into a publishing focus. Thus, factors involving both the generational and the disaffected may indicate particular sensibilities more than any tangible scholarship, rendering it difficult to assess how the nature of post-process is constituted across these constituencies.

Even within explicit post-process scholarship, however, there is little to mitigate the vagueness of post-process. For example, one factor is the range of scholarship claimed. Some post-process theorists mark its advent with the social and cultural turn of the mid-1980s, effectively enveloping this scholarship within post-process. Others, however, most notably Thomas Kent, a leading theorist of post-process, direct their critique at expressivists, cognitivists, and social constructionists alike, thus situating post-process as following rather than encompassing these schools of thought. Furthermore, there are additional complications within these post-process groups, such as differences over what the adoption of a post-process position would or should lead to. Some, for example, argue for reform of first-year composition; some call for its abolition; some advocate programmatic change; and some hint at disciplinary and institutional changes so profound as to have us re-think the nature of education itself. Post-process is, then, no more homogeneous than process.

Therefore, to gauge post-process—to get some sense of what it is, how it is valued, and what it would portend—I profile post-process according to the following scheme:

1. Entrance of post-process theory into the discourse of rhetoric and composition

2. Entrance of the *post-process* moniker into the discourse of rhetoric and composition, along with a rejoinder

3. Post-process scholarship that lays claim to the scholarship of the social/cultural turn, which is divided into two strands:

   a. Strand One Post-Process, comprised of those who may self-identify as post-process but who do not necessarily partake of Kent's theory

   b. Strand Two Post-Process, comprised of those who explicitly self-identify as post-process but appropriate only specific concepts from Kent's theory of paralogic hermeneutics, concepts which they then repurpose

      1. Critiques of process within Strand Two Post-Process

2. Calls for reform within Strand Two Post-Process

3. Repercussions for a post-process profession within Strand Two Post-Process

4. Post-process scholarship that positions itself beyond that of the social/cultural turn

5. A few rejoinders to Kent's edited *Post-Process* collection

Entrance of Post-Process Theory into the Discourse of Rhetoric and Composition

As this post-profile unfolds, it becomes increasingly obvious that what constitutes post-process theory is arguable. For the moment, though, I want to focus on the theoretical grounding that some who both self-identify as post-process and who address post-process in their scholarship reference in their work. This is the theory of Thomas Kent.[5]

Kent began publishing work that articulated the theory now most closely associated with *post-process* in 1989, some six years before the term itself would actually be coined.[6] Indeed, Kent's theory, which eventually came to be known as "post-process," culminated in his book, *Paralogic Rhetoric: A Theory of Communicative Interaction*, published in 1993. Paralogic hermeneutics, as it is often called, is based on the theory of communicative interaction of analytic philosopher Donald Davidson.[7] This theory rests on two premises: the first, that "communicative interaction is a thoroughly hermeneutic act"; and the second, that this act "cannot be converted into a logical framework or system of social conventions that determines the meaning of our utterances" (x). In his formulation of paralogic hermeneutics, Kent argues that conventions of language do not "control" language use; rather, conventions of language are "established through the give and take of communicative interaction" (x). Further, he argues against "the claim that discourse production occurs in specific communities," along with "the related claim that ethnographers can account for the process of discourse production by disclosing the cultural conventions that define a community" (x). Kent suggests that "an externalist conception of language" such as Davidson's "can account for many of the inherent problems engendered by the assumption that meaning derives from a framework of normative conventions" (x). Paralogic hermeneutics rests on the assumption that "human subjectivity is all that we can know of the world" (100). No mediation is thus required between the individual and other individuals or between the individual and the world, for to make such a claim would be, according to Kent, paramount to endowing the particular "conceptual scheme" of mediation *sole* epistemological status (97–101).

Kent takes from Davidson four concepts, which are key to paralogic hermeneutics: triangulation, passing theory, prior theory, and the principle of charity. Briefly, *triangulation* is the organizing principle, enfolding the other three to arrive at what Jane Perkins calls a "baseline of communication and understanding," where understanding is, of course, understood to be interpretive (*Paralogic* 160). *Passing theory* is enacted when we communicate with another person and is constituted by the "unconscious adjustments" we make regarding our communicant's beliefs, values, and background knowledge in order to realize a more ideal communicative act. However, passing theory requires a concomitant enactment of *prior theory*, which is constituted by a person's background knowledge and which functions to improve the "guesses" of passing theory (160). Last, the *principle of charity* constitutes an assumption that (a) the ground of communication is a shared, common world in which we each assume others to be relatively rational beings and that (b) we unconsciously extend our best effort to understand others because we do *want/need* to communicate (161). Kent appropriates these concepts from Davidson's theory of communicative interaction to fashion his theory of paralogic hermeneutics, which he advocates as a theory for both discourse reception and discourse production.

But to fully understand Kent's theoretical formulation of paralogic hermeneutics, it is necessary to distinguish how he characterizes paralogy. According to Kent, *paralogy* is

> the feature of language-in-use that accounts for successful communicative interaction. More specifically, paralogy refers to uncodifiable moves we make when we communicate with others, and ontologically, the term describes the unpredictable, elusive, and tenuous decisions or strategies we employ when we actually put language to use, [. . .] *paralogy* should be distinguished from the rhetorical concept of *paralogism*, which refers to a sophism, an illogical argu-

ment, or an example of false reasoning. Unlike paralogism, paralogy is not a derivative of logic: paralogy is not faulty logic. Rather paralogy seeks to subsume logic. As the etymological origin of the term suggests, paralogy means "beyond logic" in that it accounts for the attribute of language-in-use that defies reduction to a codifiable process or to a system of logical relations. (3)

In Kent's theory, each instance of language-in-use is a radically unique act. I would add that Kent makes much of the word *codify* in both his theory and in his criticism of process. His reliance on this word warrants a dictionary explication. The first definition listed in the tenth edition of *Merriam Webster's Collegiate Dictionary* reads, "to reduce to a code," where code is then found to be defined as "a systematic statement of a body of law; *esp:* one given statutory force," "a system of principles or rules" ("Codify").

Kent is critical of traditional "logico-systemic approaches" that continue, he says, to "dominate" the field (*Paralogic* 24). These include expressive, empirical, and social constructionist approaches. According to Kent, expressive approaches, as represented in the work of Peter Elbow and Ken Macrorie, assume that all writers "share certain innate mental categories," which they access through "systemic processes," for example, freewriting and heuristics (24). Empirical approaches such as those of Linda Flower and John Hayes, H. H. Clark and Susan Haviland, and Barry Kroll assume that writing competence can be measured by the likes of protocol analysis or brain hemisphere research and the results systematized to accurately describe the "constitutive elements of effective writing" (24). Moreover, the social constructionist work of Kenneth Bruffee and M. K. Halliday assumes that writing is a "transactive social activity," that is, that writers and readers contribute equally to the construction of meaning. Moreover, the social constructionist work of Bruffee and Halliday assumes an equal contribution of writers and readers to the construction of meaning. This equal contribution represents both discourse production and reception as "conventional social processes" (25). All share, Kent says, a foundationalist assumption that discourse production and reception "can be reduced to systemic processes and then taught in classrooms in some sort of codified manner" (25). If, then, discourse production and analysis cannot be reduced to a logico-systemic process, Kent says we must concede that both our rhetorical tradition and our current notions of writing and reading need serious reconsideration. Paralogic hermeneutics is, of course, his recommendation.

As for the potential repercussions of paralogic hermeneutics, Kent says the theory would require us to re-think the student/teacher relationship and to "reimagine the curricular mission of composition and literature courses within the university" (*Paralogic* 158). We would give up our dependence on Plato and Aristotle; we would understand that while codifiable material—for example, grammar rules, syntax, paragraphing, modes of discourse, etc.—can be usefully taught through the dialectic method, dialectic is moot since knowledge is located in the subjective knower; we would also understand that writing and reading "cannot be taught, for nothing exists to teach" (161). Traditional writing and literature courses would thus cease to exist and we would work, instead, as mentors who co-construct meaning with students. Admittedly, he says, more teachers would be required, which would not only "be very costly" but also "create complex problems for the discipline of English" (169).

Again, not all or even most who may self-identify as post-process necessarily subscribe to Kent's theory. Indeed, when the term *post-process* entered the field, Kent's theory, which he had already begun to discuss in various articles, was not even addressed.

Post-Process Moniker and the Discourse of Rhetoric and Composition

John Trimbur is said to have been the first to coin the term *post-process*, in a review written in 1994 of Patricia Bizzell's *Academic Discourse and Critical Consciousness,* C. H. Knoblauch and Lil Brannon's *Critical Teaching and the Idea of Literacy,* and Kurt Spellmeyer's *Common Ground: Dialogue, Understanding, and the Teaching of Composition.*[8] All three books address literacy as a problem for democratic participation in terms of how difference is negotiated, how literacy is defined, and how civic discourse has been impoverished. Each is notable, according to Trimbur, for couching literacy arguments in a framework of politics rather than the usual framework of students' processes of reading and writing. Thus, Trimbur writes that

> taken together, the three books can be read as statements that both reflect and [. . .] enact what has come

> to be called the "social turn" of the 1980s, a *post-process, post-cognitivist* theory and pedagogy that represent literacy as an ideological arena and composing as a cultural activity by which writers position and reposition themselves in relation to their own and others' subjectivities, discourses, practices, and institutions. (emphasis added, "Taking" 109)

Trimbur then uses this clear and succinct concept of post-process to analyze how each of the three books distinguishes the result of "a crisis within the process paradigm and a growing disillusion with its limits and pressures" (109). This is not to say, however, that Trimbur dismisses the significance of process or the contributions that researchers of writing have made to our understanding of writing. He does take process to task, though, as he recounts its early, heady days, when teachers responded to the repressive "formalism" of current-traditional rhetoric and sought to empower students by giving them ownership of their learning and their writing. Effectively, this move to empower and to confer ownership to students not only simplified a very complex act, he says, but it also led teachers to assume that they could inhabit some culturally pristine space from which to bestow an authentic language upon their students. Equally destructive was an abdication of teacher authority, as teachers attempted to occupy the role of facilitator or co-learner. This led, Trimbur says, to genuine problems. Students recognized only too well the bottom line that their writing products would be exchanged for a grade. The more astute students also recognized the genuine currency of symbolic exchange to be "sincerity" and "authenticity." Ironically, then, even as teachers abdicated authority in the interest of freeing students' powers of authenticity, students were "learning a genre their teachers had failed to name" and for which they would be handsomely rewarded for (re)producing (110).

Trimbur's interest in the three books revolves around problems inherent in process, particularly with the issue of teacher authority and the utopian desire each work advocates as negotiation to the cultural politics of literacy and thus to a fuller notion of democracy. Knoblauch and Brannon, he says, realized that their attack on the classical tradition in a previous book and their subsequent subscription to process merely replaced one master narrative with another, the latter distinguished by its liberalism and focus on individuality. Now, paralyzed by a postmodern fear of master narratives, Knoblauch and Brannon, in Trimbur's estimation, succumb to the process fetish of relinquished teacher authority and eschew the engagement of rhetorical argument that would promote their own beliefs in radical social change. Trimbur suggests that Spellmeyer also capitulates to a preoccupation of process with the student-writer. Spellmeyer attempts to resolve the contradiction between educating students for mastery and educating them for citizenship by nominating the essay as his genre-of-choice and presuming that the essay resides in some privileged and unmarked social and political space that students can unproblematically appropriate for their own ends. Finally, Trimbur endorses Bizzell's self-understanding, which she achieves through a critical review of her own work, that no method and no meta-discourse can successfully bring students to critical consciousness. Trimbur agrees with Bizzell that we must recognize the limitations of the prison-house of language and unapologetically assume the attendant responsibility to promote what we ethically view as the common good.

Countering Trimbur and the many who adopted Trimbur's position, Debra Jacobs argues that regardless of its limitations, "losing sight of writing as a process can lead to impoverishing the process of critical inquiry" (673). She admits, however, her discomfort "with the risk I take in advancing an allegiance to what [process] has been so thoroughly critiqued that its limitations can readily be rehearsed by anyone who is even modestly acquainted with recent composition scholarship" (663–64). Nevertheless, Jacobs does take issue with Trimbur and his review, not for the critique and resolution he offers, but with his recommendation of the notion *post-process*, which is bought with what she views as an essentialist characterization of process theory and classroom practice. Furthermore, she admonishes those advocates of post-process who conflate process theory with expressivism and call upon dated process theory from the 1970s and early 1980s to construct a straw man merely for the sake of dismissing it.

In her 2001 essay published in *JAC*, Jacobs responds to three articles—Candace Spigelman's "What Role Virtue?," Thomas Rickert's "'Hands Up, You're Free': Composition in a Post-Oedipal World," and Anthony Petruzzi's "Kairotic Rhetoric in Freire's Liberatory Pedagogy." She concedes that she takes liberties in applying the ideas in these three articles, particularly those of Rickert, to pedagogy in general and to process theory in particular since the three do not share the same views. Nevertheless, she defends doing so on the grounds that unless we conceive the classroom only as a space for "happenings," we are forced to theorize classroom practice (666). The purpose of her response is to "reexamine process theory and pedagogy in light of some common characteristics of the liberatory pedagogy" all three writers, she says, "point toward" (663). In the estimation of Jacobs, the characteristics the writers identify in their formulations of a critical or liberatory pedagogy not only "resonate" with but also "enrich" her understanding of writing as process (663).

Both Spigelman and Rickert address the rub between emancipatory pedagogies and the disciplinary and institutional authority that undermines them. For Spigelman, problems occur as teachers attempt to intervene in students' critical and ethical development, but her position is that teachers still have a responsibility to exercise such interventions. Rickert advocates a post-pedagogy that promotes and values "transformative acts of transgression" (Jacobs 663). But Jacobs believes Rickert's post-pedagogy is actually a "non-pedagogy," since his post-pedagogy of the act would "refuse accommodation entirely in favor of a radical abandonment" (qtd. in Jacobs 666). Petruzzi, in his attempt to theorize a Freirean version of "critical consciousness as a *rhetorical* concept," understands passivity and accommodation from a phenomenological perspective, as comprising an individual's *doxa* (commonsensical, passive, and unexamined knowledge) to which new knowledge is added and subsequently assimilated. In his view, then, both quotidian (stream of consciousness) and critical consciousness are situated in the "same hermeneutic circle" and are thus "co-implicated with critical consciousness in processual acts of cognition" (663).

Jacobs believes all three writers strive for an emancipatory moment achieved through transvaluation. To achieve this, however, an intervention must occur. Jacobs says that process theory offers us the possibility for such disruptive interventions. If process theory has been reduced to disciplinary *doxa*, she says, then it is our responsibility to disrupt it through interventions such as asking "new and better questions" (617). Jacobs thus chooses to enlarge process to accommodate the goal of critical inquiry she shares with Trimbur and other social/cultural scholars.

The entrance of the post-process moniker into rhetoric and composition (1994) clearly did not reference the paralogic hermeneutic theory or paralogic rhetoric of Kent (1989–1993). Additionally, *post-process*, as originally coined, clearly assumed a provenance of scholarship synonymous with that of the social/cultural turn. This assumption did not go uncontested, as evidenced in Jacobs's contention that critical inquiry cannot be effectively practiced without a viable theory of process.

Post-Process Scholarship and the Social/Cultural Turn

This third space of post-process is where most who self-identify as post-process reside, making it the most heterogeneous of all post-process spaces. However, an examination of post-process scholarship that lays claim to the social/cultural turn of the mid-1980s forward reveals two major post-process strands. One includes those who may self-identify as post-process but who do not necessarily ground that identity in Kent's theory of paralogic hermeneutics. The other strand self-identifies as post-process but appropriates from Kent's theory only specific concepts, which are then mediated in degree from his strong version. In the following section, I consider these two strands in turn in order to clarify and contrast them.

Strand One Post-Process, Comprised of Those Who May Self-Identify as Post-Process but Who Do Not Necessarily Partake of Kent's Theory

This strand of post-process includes some of those who likely self-identify as post-process but whose scholarship does not foreground the term. They might be said, therefore, to harbor a post-process sensibility of the type described earlier: generational and/or disaffected. This sensibility is informed at the very least by a tacit critique of process, as well as by the assumption that the advent of post-process coincides with the mid-1980s scholarship of the social/cultural turn.

Designating scholarship into this category is problematic if only because some whose scholarship I include might well take issue with their inclusion. To mitigate this difficulty, I restrict coverage to one edited collection, with the assumption that the contributors share, to some degree, the sensibility if not the position of the collection's editor, Joseph Petraglia. The edited collection to which I allude is *Reconceiving Writing, Rethinking Writing Instruction,* published in 1995. It is in his introduction that Petraglia illustrates his particular post-process sensibility and position.

Petraglia writes that the focus of the collection is the acronym GWSI (general writing skills instruction), which he defines as "the general ability to develop and organize ideas, use techniques for inventing topics worthy of investigation, adapt one's purpose to an audience, and anticipate reader response" (xi). According to Petraglia, GWSI characterizes almost all contemporary writing curricula in most composition courses, with the exception of those such as basic writing, technical writing, writing-intensive content courses, and creative writing, all of which have their own "specialized content and limited rhetorical scope" (xii). These latter, content-rich, and rhetorically situated courses contrast sharply with the intention of the GWSI course, which, he says, is to give students skills that, ostensibly, teach them "'to write,'" with the assumption that these skills transcend any context or content (xii). Moreover, Petraglia says that GWSI is not any straw man since it is the curriculum taught by the majority of teachers, the curriculum that almost all composition textbooks endorse, and the curriculum for which English departments garner considerable resources. Because GWSI is synonymous with writing instruction itself for many in the discipline, Petraglia concedes that questioning the legitimacy of GWSI is tantamount to questioning the discipline itself.

As I have indicated, the degree to which contributors to the collection share Petraglia's view varies, but all offer some critique of GWSI. Broadly, these critiques revolve around a variety of queries regarding GWSI: whether it is "intellectually defensible," given what we now know about what it means to be a rhetor and a writer; whether it helps students perform effectively beyond the specific course in which it is taught; whether it can continue to secure a space for rhetoric and composition in the academy and, if not, whether we ought not begin to attempt to create spaces more congenial to current theory and research (xii).

Addressing the issue of the intellectual defensibility of GWSI, some suggest that there is a paradox in how the GWSI course is constructed and conducted in its disciplinary and institutional space and what we now commonly acknowledge as part of our disciplinary knowledge about writing. This disciplinary knowledge is abstracted by Lil Brannon:

> The act of writing is a complex sociocognitive interaction with the world that entails, beyond mechanical control, such subtle practices as establishing and

> maintaining social positions, adapting to variable discursive conventions, and constructing ideas and relationships for oneself and others. It is not separate from one's life or from one's culture. Our [. . .] responsibility then [is] to ensure not that students receive some essentially alien technology, some "correct" set of language practices, in order to proceed through the university, but rather that they learn to use, with greater subtlety and control, the language they bring with them, adjusting the register, the cadences, the vocabulary, the social codes, the nuances, and the intellectual moves, as they confront the demands of writing. (240–41)

In light of what this passage represents about our disciplinary understanding of writing, contributors find the GWSI classroom, as constructed in this edited collection, to be deficient.

For example, Dan Royer maintains that the rhetorical situation of the GWSI course cannot accommodate the range of student experience needed for a genuine practice of invention. He also believes, however, that the course can be improved with a new theory of invention as guided phenomenology, which he articulates. David Kaufer and Patricia Dunmire address the lack of content in the GWSI course and offer a course they developed and based on Sylvia Scribner's notion of knowledge design for teaching analysis and analytic writing. To address his criticism of the theoretical thinness of the GWSI course, David Jolliffe recommends we reconsider the multivocal and interreferential nature of discourse. With his critique that the GWSI course is not so much bad pedagogy as pedagogy effective at producing "the wrong results," Fred Kemp recommends a postmodern-informed pedagogy based on electronic texts, which he believes would offer us a way to literally rethink what it means to write (181).

Others, however, are not so optimistic regarding the potential of reform. David Russell studies the course as a paradoxical activity system that attempts to teach writing as part of activity systems of which neither teachers nor students are actually part. For writing to have genuine meaning and purpose, it must occur within the complexity and richness that can only be offered, he says, by a specific activity system ("Activity Theory and Its Implications"). Aviva Freedman's research on genre echoes this idea. Her findings indicate that students acquire the discipline-specific features of genres routinely taught in GWSI classrooms in their content courses without resort to either models or to explicit teaching. Furthermore, not only does the explicit teaching of the underlying rules of genre in the GWSI classroom fail to facilitate learning, Freedman says, it often impedes it. Petraglia concurs, writing that formal instruction of genre conventions and principles may well be "counterproductive." Such instruction may suggest to students that rhetorical situations are governed by rules and conventions. This impression diminishes the complexity and richness of rhetorical situations students will be expected to navigate in their futures. Petraglia maintains that evaluating students on their performance in the impoverished contexts of GWSI is not just "unrealistic" but is also "unethical" (90–91).

Criticism of GWSI also considers contexts that would better facilitate students' writing. "The combined evidence from many studies" Freedman reports, "pointed compellingly to the powerful facilitative effect of establishing a richly textured and finely managed discursive context" for students (141). This, she continues, "is what we saw typically in the disciplinary classes observed, where students did indeed learn to write, and learn to write extraordinarily well" (141). Her suggestion for an alternative to GWSI is "a specialized model of WAC" that might function in a variety of ways, for example, with writing centers, "sheltered courses," and/or writing-intensive courses (140). Suggesting that writing cannot be taught but that we can nevertheless locate environments for students in which writing "naturally occurs," Petraglia, too, suggests guidelines analogous to WAC (94). Lil Brannon, who reports on The University at Albany, SUNY's move away from compulsory first-year composition to a WAC model, along with their rationalization for doing so, says that first-year composition continued to function so long as they conceived of literacy and writing in strictly functional terms, as "something basic, a skill to be mastered, a technology to be applied" (239). Having critiqued that assumption, an assumption that constructs students in terms of lack and deficiency, they were able to "move away from ghettoized general writing skills instruction" and toward a model of literacy that views students as developing writers (240). This move was accomplished, she says, by a group of faculty across the curriculum understanding that the first-year composition requirement was based on a "'skills' concept of writing that was losing professional currency" that contradicted what those responsible for SUNY's composition program believed about writing and what "major researchers in the field found credible" (240). This vein of criticism of GWSI suggests programmatic changes that will provide students with more rhetorically sound environments. Such changes, of course, also have implications for disciplinarity.

Many in this collection advocate for reform in first-year composition; others call for its abolition. Many are sympathetic to Freedman's position that "in the end, I am arguing against stand-alone GWSI classes" (140). While they argue for reform rather than abolition, even Kaufer and Dunmire, write that "the question of a college writing program's goals and cultural legitimation has to be answered better than we have so far answered it" (218). In terms of activity theory, the writing done in GWSI courses must meet the objectives of *each* of the activity systems served by the course; the activity system of the GWSI course, on the other hand, simply does not exist beyond the confines of the course. Petraglia says, too, that the real question is not whether the GWSI course "could be doing something better but whether it is attempting to do something that needs to be done at all" (89). "Baldly stated," he writes, "general writing skills instruction—perhaps the very notion of the composition classroom—is an idea whose time has gone" (97).

This strand of post-process also distances itself from early process theory, as it tacitly envelops process theory and practice into its critique of the ubiquitous GWSI approach. It also presumes to envelop the scholarship of the social and cultural turn of the mid-1980s on as part of its domain. These scholars appropriate this scholarship as theoretical ground upon which they offer additional theoretical formulations to render the composition course more consonant and amenable to the social/cultural turn. Still, some within this post-process strand believe the course to be hopelessly compromised by its disciplinary and institutional context, and they call for its abolition ("The New").

Interestingly, Robert Connors opens this edited collection with a historical account of calls for both the reform and abolition of composition, so that we can, he says, better understand how the current abolitionist movement compares with those of the past. Historically, he says, calls for abolition have come from those outside the field, whereas the current one is being proffered by insiders. Because insiders do have knowledge of the local circumstances of our disciplinary situation, Connors suggests the current abolitionist movement warrants greater scrutiny and consideration on our part.

Strand Two Post-Process, Comprised of Those Who Explicitly Self-Identify as Post-Process but Appropriate from Kent's Theory of Paralogic Hermeneutics Only Specific Concepts, Which They Mediate

This strand of post-process theory includes those who explicitly self-identify as post-process but appropriate specific concepts from Kent's theory, which they then mediate. While Kent's position might be said to constitute a strong version of a particular concept, most in this group do not fully share Kent's conviction. Kent acknowledges this in the introduction to his edited collection, *Post-Process Theory: Beyond the Writing-Process Paradigm*, published in 1999.

In the introduction, Kent writes that "different incarnations" of post-process theory exists (1), and that while not all of the book's contributors agree about "the nature of 'post' in 'post-process' theory, all agree that change is in the air," regarding how we talk about writing and what writers do (5). It is with such a caveat, then, that we can reasonably expect this collection to reflect a broad range of consonance with Kent's theory as formulated and described in *Paralogic Rhetoric*. Kent distills three principle assumptions that he believes unite the scholarship of the book's contributors,: that writing is (1) public, (2) interpretive, and (3) situated.

The claim that writing is public implies two assumptions: (1) that writing is constituted by communicative interaction between individuals who share specific relations with others and the world at specific historical moments, and (2) that since these moments and relations are unique in each instance of communicative interaction, "no process can capture what writers do" in these ever-changing moments and relations (1–2). While it is advantageous for individuals to have a command of conventions, genres, and language use, or what Kent calls "codifiable shortcuts," these do not equate to a "Big Theory," as they cannot function as a repeatable process that would lead to success in every writing situation. The point, Kent says, is that a writer "cannot start from nowhere" (2). There is always a public dimension to writing.

The claim that writing is interpretive refers to an act that engages in "a relation of understanding" with others (2). Interpretation is thus equally involved in reception and production. Because it engages in perpetual hermeneutic acts, interpretation constitutes nothing less than our attempt to make sense of the world. Although hermeneutic acts are based on guesswork, Kent does concede that practice can render us "better guessers" (2–3) but insists that effective guessing resists codification to any process that might guarantee success. Because any degree of knowing is the result of interpretation, most post-process theorists maintain that interpretation "goes all the way down." Writing cannot occur, therefore, in a "vacuum," since the ground of interpretation is a relationship with others and the world (2–3).

That writing is situated simply indicates that "writers are never nowhere," a notion Kent concedes is as equally commonplace among process as post-process theorists. However, the latter put more emphasis on situatedness, he says, given their understanding of a communicative act as a fluid and indeterminate "hermeneutic dance" comprised of two simultaneous acts, prior theory and passing theory. From this perspective, situatedness assumes that we are always "somewhere" in relation to other language users, a positioning that influences not only the nature of our prior theory but also how we use a prior theory to formulate a passing theory. Importantly, these communicative instances "can never be reduced to a predictable process" (4).

Critiques of Process within Strand Two Post-Process

Again, the degree to which *Post-Process* contributors share these three basic concepts of writing varies, but all are united in their critique of process. From a historical perspective, George Pullman critiques the history of the process movement as a rhetorical narrative of "triumph of compassion and empiricism" over the current-traditional rhetoric of "tradition and prejudice" (16). This was accomplished with two moves: one from a focus on the teacher to the student and the other from a notion of writing as skill to writing as ontological, or as a way of being (23–25). This "triumph" constituted, he says, nothing less than a return to the "self-reflective, contemplative life," which Plato offered to Phaedrus as "an alternative to the life of political power that the young man thought he wanted" (25). Pullman thus employs these binaries to argue that many of the dichotomies constructed by process have cast long, pervasive, and detrimental shadows.

From a disciplinary perspective, Petraglia critiques the close association of process with the behaviorist model in psychology. Process theorists argued against a notion of writing as a single behavior and for a notion constituted by procedures and strategies that eventually coalesced into the complex system of process. This understanding then established a professional agenda that both resonated with the notion of rhetoric as practical art (*techne*) and propelled research and teaching. It rendered other methodologies viable, especially those including a scientific analytic component, which contributed, Petraglia argues, (1) to serve composition well as a field "dedicated to the *production* of rhetorical skills"; and (2) to "[discipline] writing in every sense of the word," imposing a coherence on lore (North) and providing "a catechistic structure through which writing could attain a distinct academic identity" ("Is There" 51). Cognitive models of process greatly contributed to the development of "a genuinely academic profile" that ultimately became the movement's "Manifest Destiny" (51). However, the empirical method objectified writing process and continued he says, a two-millennia tradition of "dissecting and redissecting the whole of rhetoric into manageable parts" (53). Thus, Petraglia argues that the current professional profile of the field remains entrenched in the impoverished pedagogy of GWSI.

Others also take process to task for its privileging of individuality. David Russell credits process with enacting an important shift from text to the individual writer, thus effectively rendering the student an object of study. The problem, he argues, is that process "remained with *the* individual" and attempted to generalize psychological processes across a broad range of students and settings ("Activity Theory and Process" 80). Along with this, process altered teacher/student relationships, but then exerted a normative influence on them. Teachers were taught, Russell says, to intervene strategically in students' process, using a normative process vocabulary to guide not only their verbal interaction with students but also their written responses and final evaluations. This pedagogy assumed that the stages of student writing constituted "legitimate stages of work in progress rather than failed attempts to produce a correct product"; teachers then responded with "transactional in-progress comments [. . .] rather than evaluative 'final' judgments" (150). Russell concludes, however, that the shifts made by process contributed to disciplinary legitimacy. These shifts provided English departments leverage to successfully bid for additional institutional resources, and they allowed some writing programs to successfully argue for separation from English departments, based on a body of knowledge created through strong research agendas and newly minted graduate programs.

Interestingly, this collection includes a voice that contradicts the lament over the focus of process on the individual writer. Barbara Couture critiques process precisely for having failed to translate process scholarship—which, she says, assumed that writing ought to develop and express the "subjective agent"—into effective classroom application. Composition relied on modeling technique rather than on the emulation of expression. Where the former relies on experts' writing, the latter relies on students' striving "to emulate others, to be like them, worthy of them, perhaps, even better than them." This attitude, she says, is partly to blame for the failure of process to translate process scholarship into practice (30–31). According to Couture, post-process can thus more effectively address the issue of students' self-development and self-expression.

Others critique process for the universality they believe process harbors. Gary Olson expresses this complaint in terms of a master narrative that results from the attempt to formulate a model that would apply in all writing situations and ignore the local (8). This attempt to systematize something that cannot be systematized, he says, is the gist of the complaint Thomas Kent and other post-process theorists offer. George Pullman agrees: speaking of the goal of process to reduce writing to "some step-by-step procedure with universal application" (27), Pullman argues that, had the process movement accomplished this goal, all writers in all situations would use the same process. That process has not thus proven adequate to this task indicates a need for change. Nancy DeJoy offers personal experience in her description of the "complexes" she experienced as a gendered student subjected to both expressivist and cognitivist writing process approaches. She says she was "accused more than once of being confused and/or hysterical, of not understanding, for example, the 'universal' quality of any or all of dominant process models' conceptualizations of audience, invention, and so forth" (164).

Pullman also objects to the universality of the classroom site. He contends there was no paradigm shift, that both writing process and current-traditional rhetoric share a limiting and disabling metaphor that defines both, namely, the classroom, whose nature is distinguished by the exigency of illiteracy mediated by abstracted, universalized conventions (27). Pullman concludes, however, that rhetoric is too complex to ever be codified; its teaching, therefore, "must serve only an introductory purpose and must never be mistaken for (or reconstructed as) real rhetoric as it is lived and practiced" (28-29). Russell, on the other hand, does not share Pullman's presumption regarding the goal of universality. He believes that process was commodified. Still, he contends that most process research focuses on the classroom, rather than on what is of more interest: the relation between the writing processes of school and those beyond school. Russell uses activity systems theory to argue that we look beyond how "*the* writing process" is taught within our own school activity systems to "the plural socio-*logics* of various networks of people and purposes and tools, including that most protean tool, writing, in the relation between school and society" (95). If our desire is to make substantive changes in writing, composition must broaden its "study of the microlevel circulation of discursive tools (and power)" between school and society and insinuate our own tools into those activity systems. "In doing so," Russell says, "the commodification of writing processes is not an irony to be lamented but a sign of composition's influence to be understood and used, one hopes, for good" (95).

The universality of process beyond the composition classroom is also a target of critique. Nancy Blyer reports that knowledge of writing in one situation does not ensure successful writing in another, nor can any pedagogy ensure such success (68). Russell critiques process in public schools with an anecdote regarding his and others' attempts to have NCTE make changes regarding the description of process in their curriculum standards document. Russell has passionately argued, to no avail, to change the phrase "'*the* writing process'" to the plural "'writing processes.'" "Early on," he writes, "researchers such as Applebee ("Problems") pointed to problems with notions of the writing process, as a unitary psychological process that would be somehow more 'real'—less school-bound—than previous ways of learning and teaching writing" (80). That a notion of "*the* writing process" has, indeed, become reified in public education is evidenced in Russell's narrative about entering his third-grade daughter's classroom to see four, large, commercially produced posters, each containing a one-word text: "PREWRITE. WRITE. REVISE. EDIT." (80). Both Blyer and Russell attest to the problems of individuality and universality in process as it is applied in institutional contexts other than first-year composition.

Strand two post-process critiques differ from those in strand one, where scholars maintain that neither GWSI nor process is theoretically or pedagogically defensible, that GWSI is actually detrimental to students' writing, and that it compromises our disciplinary security. In contrast, strand two advocates must explicitly critique process in order to self-identify as post-process. Their critiques, therefore, focus on aspects that process valued in its turn away from current-traditional rhetoric: (1) a focus on the student, which this group of scholars translates to the privileging of individuality over the social; (2) a focus on the cognitive models of process, which is maintained to have continued a two thousand year-old tradition of essentializing rhetoric as *techne;* (3) a focus on a universality that process is said to have valued but was unable to achieve; (4) and a critique of the value process placed on the teacher-student relationship, which is argued to have constituted a system of mediation inherently flawed by its overdetermined, always-already commodified epistemological assumptions. But it must also be said that while these critiques are, indeed, more specific and directed than those in strand one post-process, they nevertheless seem very familiar.[9]

Calls for Reform within Strand Two Post-Process

As anticipated, contributors to this edited collection use broad strokes to paint a post-process landscape. Many of these also resonate with great familiarity, while others call for more radical disciplinary (re)imaginings. All agree, however, that change is needed. Most familiar are calls for particular sorts of reform. These might be said to subscribe to a mild version of Kent's paralogic hermeneutic theory. For example, Couture writes that by treating writing as design, we can "fulfill the [process] movement's original promise" (31). This would be realized through the use of textual theory, with its deconstruction of foundationalism, along with critical genre theory. These complementary theories, she believes, are sufficient to help students understand writing as personal agency and as a way to become better people. Debra Journet also endorses genre theory as enabling us to rethink the relation of the social and cognitive in composing, the relationship between composing processes and composed products, and the extent to which composing is communal or individual. Focusing on disciplinary and interdisciplinary genre relationships, she argues, has implications for how we understand the intellectual factors involved in all composing practices.

John Schilb, who critiques the role of the essay, particularly the centrality of personal and exploratory essays in many composition courses recommends reform based on a reconceptualization of the essay. He contends that we and students ought to critique the signifying practices essay writers use to "simulate" experience in their writing. He is also concerned with the role of the social in the essayist's experiences, whether the experiences depicted in the essay itself or those that surround the writing of the essay. The circulation and reception of essays also merit critical attention. The point, Schilb says, is that we ought not view essays as virtual re-enactments of experience but as constructed representations. Such an understanding can lead students not only to better appreciate the craft of essay writing, he believes, but also to imaginings of how their own texts might influence different situations ("Reprocessing").

A stronger affiliation with Kent's concepts of writing as public, interpretive, and situated, is evident in Helen Rothschild Ewald's "A Tangled Web of Discourses: On Post-Process Pedagogy and Communicative Interaction." She articulates how post-process pedagogies steeped in the notion of communicative interaction might influence discourse away from a transmission model and toward the transactional, a move that might suggest ways for students and teachers to interact as subjects. The organizing principle she nominates for this pedagogy is discourse moves, that is, rhetorical strategies enhanced by students' prior knowledge and social differences. Because post-process places a high "exchange value" on teacher contributions to their student communicants, a writing class would explore writing studies' disciplinary content (e.g., "writing skills and pedagogical methodologies"), along with "the contingent nature of instructional advice" (129). This pedagogy would function, she says, to demystify both the explicit and tacit content students confront in the classroom, enabling more successful communicative interaction with the classroom, the teacher, and their fellow students. Ewald concludes, however, that the potential to realize this post-process classroom depends "in large part on our ability to research and re-envision the educational paradigms and speech genres that currently shadow our efforts" (130).

Sidney Dobrin most explicitly sympathizes with Kent's theory, even as he admits that paralogic hermeneutic theories fail to account for power and ethics. Therefore, his goal is to make these theories, if not consonant with, at least resonant with liberatory and radical pedagogies ("Paralogic"). Other contributors likewise recognize this need. Blyer, for example, advocates a critical research approach that rejects the process research mode and focuses on interpretation and meaning. In addition, her approach insists that a focus on domination and power is prerequisite to critique and social change. She says that while critical research may not be on the post-process agenda, such research is consonant both with post-process scholars' view of communicative interaction as hermeneutic and paralogic and their goal of communicants engaging in a "'hermeneutical journey of self-discovery'" (79). Just such a journey of self-discovery is illustrated in John Clifford and Elizabeth Ervin's account of their own moves to post-process. Though Clifford and Ervin do not share generation, gender, or geography, they do share the common experience of having embraced process, only later to become disaffected with it in favor of a post-process model that engages both teacher and student in public, civic work.

David Foster sees the pedagogical challenge of the post-process classroom in the diversity of ethnicity, culture, and socioeconomic status. He is not particularly optimistic about the possibility of meeting this challenge. Chronicling Kent's externalist posture, which views writing as radically contingent from situation to situation, Foster concedes that such "a thorough-going skepticism of this sort" dampens the "best-intentioned efforts" to formulate an acceptable writing pedagogy, threatens the very existence of traditional writing programs, and challenges our notions of appropriate research methods (153). In place of traditional writing programs, Foster therefore recommends WAC programs, which he views as enacting pedagogy more compatible with Kent's paralogy. In place of process research methods, he recommends more self-reflexive methods informed by concepts such as Sandra Harding's notion of strong objectivity. Although Foster does not articulate a specific pedagogy, he does interrogate and critique a variety of collaborative pedagogical models for their potential to avoid the collision that leads, he says, to genuine conflict when pedagogy explicitly values difference.

Vulnerable to charges of being "masculinist, phallogocentric, foundationalist, often essentialist, and, at the very least, limiting" (9), the ubiquitous rhetoric of assertion (asserting an argument of truth) in composition classes is, according to Olson, ripe for critique. To wage this postmodern critique, he suggests we look to Sandra Harding's notion of strong objectivity, Donna Haraway's notion of cyborg writing, and Jean-Francois Lyotard's notion of master narratives, all of which he believes would challenge us to reinvent writing and to reflect on how we translate our understanding of discourse into the post-process classroom. Writing in this view, Olson says, is "radically contingent" and "radically situational" (9).

Critical discourse and the strategies of feminist discourse merit a firm position in the post-process classroom, according to DeJoy, who articulates a notion of counterprocess that embodies these discourses and strategies. Counterprocess is distinguished, she says, by three moves: (1) from "mastery to analysis"; (2) from "identification" with the dominant to "alternative routes to subjectivity"; and (3) from "persuasion to participation" (164). To this end, she recommends heuristics that positively change the subject positions available to writers.

Again, what is most obvious in these calls for reform is the degree of affinity individual contributors exhibit with Kent's theory. Kent's theory, taken to its logical conclusion, raises the question of whether there is any reason to think that these calls for reform are any less susceptible than process to the charge of epistemological commodification. Can these reforms—writing as design, genre theory, critique of signifying practices, discourse moves, difference, liberatory and radical pedagogies, postmodernism, and/or critical/feminist discourse—avoid the "Big Theory" trap? This would not be an issue, of course, but for the fact that the people who are suggesting these reforms not only explicitly self-identify as post-process but also, by virtue of their inclusion in Kent's collection, share some affinity with his theory of paralogic hermeneutics. More troubling among these recommended reforms, however, are the calls for liberatory and radical pedagogies and the valuing of difference in the classroom, made without even a cursory nod toward a body of scholarship in the field regarding these issues. Finally, a certain degree of ambivalence toward process is exhibited in this collection: some appear to call for an enlargement or expansion of process, while others appear to so thoroughly disregard process that they advocate reinventing the wheel.

REPERCUSSIONS FOR A POST-PROCESS PROFESSION WITHIN STRAND TWO POST-PROCESS

Taking a historical approach to paint the broadest strokes for a post-process landscape yet, Petraglia speculates on a post-process profession. Indirectly dating post-process from about 1980 on, he says that the production of scholarship since this time has contributed to making post-process increasingly "hybridized and complex" (53). His own view of the "post" in post-process rejects what he views as a highly formulaic approach to writing. The observation that writers use a process to produce a text continues to inform our disciplinary reality even though we now consider "the mantra 'writing is a process' as the right answer to a really boring question" ("Is There" 53). Process has been critiqued and found wanting. In response, we have moved beyond it with the work of social construction and social-epistemic, whose tenets that writing is socially and culturally mediated are, according to Petraglia, as readily accepted today as the fact that a text is the outcome of writing (54).

Nevertheless, since, our current professional profile remains entrenched in the impoverished pedagogy of general writing skills instruction, Petraglia seeks to explore what being post-process would portend for empirical research and for the writing profession. Ultimately, he advocates for the "new social scientism," which situates writing "in physical and metaphysical spaces of time, place, culture, and identity" (56) and is more "epistemologically aware" and more self-reflexive than its predecessor (59). Such a rethinking would lead us away from *techne* and toward the development of rhetorical sensibilities. We need to deploy our efforts "to inculcate *receptive* skills" (62). Petraglia endorses David Russell's recommendation that, in addition to WAC classes, we offer introductory and interdisciplinary courses that would raise awareness about writing among students, other faculty, and the public. However, all of this depends upon the "ability and willingness of writing professionals to evolve not only post-process but post-composition" (63). In Petraglia's view, post-process research is likely "to suggest the ways in which the enterprise of composition is misguided and why the explicit teaching of writing—as rhetorical *production*—is a losing proposition" (60).

As for the future of a post-process profession, Petraglia suggests several scenarios. One is that we "will hunker down into the general writing-skills trenches" and continue to maintain a service role in the university (60). Another is that we will shun the very method of empirical research that could lend us greater disciplinary integrity (60–61). The last is that we will realize the need to study how writers write outside the composition classroom, an initiative currently addressed by writing-across-the disciplines (WAC) and writing-in-the-disciplines (WID) programs. WAC and WID do not, however, promote disciplinary security or prominence and, he argues, we can achieve such security and prominence only by rethinking the entire enterprise of teaching writing (61).

The degree to which Kent's contributors share the strong version of his theory depends on the extent to which they agree about the radical nature of writing as public, interpretive, and situated, along with what they believe this portends for teaching writing, much as the degree to which Petraglia's contributors share his strong version of GWSI depends on their view of the disciplinary and professional repercussions. These two edited collections share common values between the editors and a group of contributors whose sympathies mirror in kind, rather than degree, those values.

Post-Process Scholarship that Positions Itself Beyond That of the Social/Cultural Turn

Two scholars occupy this space, but only one rests comfortably here, and that is Thomas Kent, originator of this position. The other conceptual inhabitant is Sidney Dobrin. I have discussed Kent's theory earlier, so I will not belabor it again. Suffice to say that Kent maintains that expressive, empirical, and social constructionist approaches all share the same foundationalist assumption "that discourse production and analysis can be reduced to systemic processes and then taught in classrooms in some codified manner" (*Paralogic* 25). If, however, we concede that neither the production nor the reception of discourse can be reduced to a "logico-systemic" process, we must re-think all of our assumptions regarding writing and reading, along with the rhetorical tradition from which they are derived. We must also abandon writing instruction in any form that we know it today. This would inevitably entail forfeiting disciplinarity, since no body of knowledge regarding the acts of writing or reading could be assembled. No less problematic from an institutional standpoint would be the only alternative for student learning: the one-to-one mentoring relationship that would constitute an authentic communicative interaction.

While Dobrin shares an affinity with Kent's notion of paralogic hermeneutic theory, he critiques it to suggest that what is now needed are "*post-post-process* theories of paralogic hermeneutics" (emphasis added, "Paralogic" 133). Dobrin criticizes current attempts to derive post-process pedagogies from Kent's theory, and he nominates a different vision. Few attempts, he argues have been made to formulate a pedagogy derived from paralogic hermeneutics. Of the ones attempted thus far, however, Dobrin is critical, writing that they "tend to fall short of [paralogic hermeneutics'] agendas" (133). He also parses the field differently, based on his definition of post-process as "the shift in scholarly attention from the process by which the individual writer produces text to the larger forces that affect the writer and of which that writer is part" (132). Dobrin agrees with many of his fellow post-process scholars, but he disputes Kent's notion that the advent of post-process coincides with the social/cultural turn in the field.

Dobrin differs with all, however, in his advocacy of a yet more extreme remove from process, that is, *post-post-process* theories of paralogic hermeneutics. This post-post theory is required because regular theories of paralogic hermeneutics have failed to account for power and ethics: "triangulation, as it has been defined, denies that culture, race, class, or gender affect at all one's prior theories which determine one's passing theories, which affect the moment of triangulation and communication" (142). In order to correct this problem, he seeks effective resistance in the discursive moments of triangulation that are the heart of paralogic hermeneutic theories. Dobrin does not, however, actually offer a pedagogy of paralogic hermeneutics, as he believes the current educational environment would seriously compromise it and because he remains deeply ambivalent about even the possibility of formulating such a pedagogy. The challenge, he writes, "becomes not creating the uncreatable paralogic pedagogies but redefining how we envision the very *nature* of pedagogy with these theories in mind" (135).

The space of this post-process version is the most extreme of all post-process positions. Indeed, its most positive note for a discipline as we currently know it is a strong ambivalence about this possibility: were the field to accept these theories, it might well cease to exist.

A Few Rejoinders to Thomas Kent's Edited *Post-Process* Collection

Responses to Kent's edited collection reflect a certain degree of dismay as to how process has been constructed, what the differences between the two really are, and what the adoption of a post-process model would mean for the field. Richard Fulkerson maintains that post-process advocates have offered a "straw person" argument similar to the one process constructed for current-traditional rhetoric; however, the price of this new fallacy is the disparagement of three decades of thoughtful work in composition as "scientific, cognitivist, and universalistic" ("Of Pre-" 111). "[E]ven among those that use the [post-process] term with confidence," there appear to be few shared "assumptions, concepts, values and practices," except for their agreement with Kent's "industrial strength definition" that the process of writing cannot be systematically codified (Bloom 35–36). Fulkerson is also critical of how the term *post-process* shifts so radically among the collection's contributors and argues that this should remind us that a no more cohesive post-process "movement" exists now than ever did for process. Speaking to the differences between process and post-process, Kevin Porter describes a position to which many, I suspect, are sympathetic. He speculates "that if you blunt the extreme rigidity of the charges leveled against process theory (as well as some of the more extreme claims made by early advocates of it)" and argue, rather, that process theory represents attempts to better understand writing and to translate those understandings into effective pedagogies, "then these charges [made by post-process advocates] lose most of their excitement" (712).

Last, Susan Miller clearly does not "celebrate the post-process movement now said to theorize composition anew" ("Why" 55). To Gary Olson's critique that the attempt of process to achieve a generalizable explanation of writing has been "misguided" because such explanations elide the local, she offers this rebuttal: "Certainly, many generalized explanations may be misguided, as I think this one is. That is, without a stake in a general theory of how composing and texts work, there is no justification—as some already suspect—for hiring composition specialists who claim more interest in generalized explanations of reading than in general theories of writing" ("Why" 55–56). What a post-process model would portend for the field, according to Miller, is bleak. "Its administration will be in the hands of those with no general idea about writing and no disciplinary mandate to develop them"; "we will also be without all power but that to read, not write, our own, ended, history" (56). Miller responds to what the logical conclusion of post-process would indicate for rhetoric and composition as a discipline.

Process: A Rebuttal

It seems only fair at this moment that process should have an opportunity to address critiques that it engenders a myopic focus on the individual student, that its goal was/is universality, and that it constitutes, or tried to constitute, writing as a codified system. Of these three, overdetermined individuality receives the greatest emphasis in critiques made by post-process, a charge, I would note, undoubtedly more easily made if process is deemed to have no part in the social/cultural turn.

Process scholarship, plentiful and vast, offers the only genuine rebuttal to the critiques of post-process. The following, then, constitutes a brief profile of process scholarship through the early social/cultural turn that contributed to the substantiation of writing process as a domain of knowledge, or a unity of discourse, in our field. Such statements have traditionally focused on (1) the intersection of process with the disciplinarity of rhetoric and composition; (2) the nature of what writing is; (3) the nature of the process that we teach as well as how we teach it; and (4) the actual process students engage to produce writing.

Because post-process has been especially critical of the focus on individuality in process theories, I attempt in this brief process profile to bring some attention to notions of the student-subject, even when these notions are only tacit. We should again be reminded that process theories constituted a response to current-traditional theory that had virtually elided any consideration of the individual. Nevertheless, my primary purpose is to (re)acclimate our sensibility to the historical richness of writing process discourse and to bring into relief those aspects of process against which post-process situates itself.

Process Profile

Among the first to research and advocate the importance of writing in the educational curriculum was Janet Emig. In "Inquiry Paradigms and Writing," Emig recommends an agenda to which the research of writing should adhere: "inquiries into writing, into composition, probably need to be informed by at least four kinds of theories: 1) a theory of meaning; 2) and if this is different, a theory of language; 3) a theory of learning; and 4) a theory of research," all of which, she added, "should be consonant or congenial" (165). Certainly, the tacit presence of the student-subject inheres in this excerpt, for it is in relation to the student-subject that meaning, language, and learning matter. It was and is the student-subject, quite as much as the contribution to the constitution of a scholarly field, that renders these questions worthy of inquiry.

In the keynote address given at the Conference on College Composition and Communication Convention in San Francisco in March 1982, Emig offers a blueprint of what she imagines writing pedagogy should accomplish (and tacitly of what it ought to prepare students to be). Arguing that notions of literacy need to change to include writing, her blueprint provides criteria for what any literacy "worth teaching" ought to accomplish. It should provide access, sponsor learning, unleash literal power, and "activate the greatest power of all—the imagination" ("Literacy" 177–78). Emig's ideal pedagogy would direct what student-subjects might experience. Emig's 1964 article, "The Uses of the Unconscious in Composing," which argues that writing is not often accomplished by a rational, conscious, coherent method, also foregrounds the student-subject. Because it involves the unconscious, writing, Emig insists, is messy, and she further advocates that teachers change their curriculum not just to allow this messiness but to encourage it. Situated at the site of the student-subject, then, the unconscious that Emig recommends for consideration constitutes a fuller conception of the student-subject.

In her discussion of qualifying paper for the Harvard Graduate School of Education in 1963, Emig reveals an even more explicit consideration of the student-subject. She reports that she chose to focus on the inconsistencies in 19th century authors' texts regarding the acts that led to writing because she believes that "the teaching of writing was [as] deformed in the past as it is in the present by concentrating on what the teacher does, not on what the student writer is experiencing" ("The Relation" 1). Her starting point for a consideration of what leads to writing is the student, not pedagogy. In "The Origins of Rhetoric: A Developmental View," Emig adds that she wanted to look at "the origins of rhetoric in the life of an individual rather than in the life of a culture" (55). While we would now contend that the life of an individual is inseparable from the life of a culture, Emig's stated goal attests to an intention to examine the individual student-subject who learns to write. Of course, there are Emig's seminal works, *The Composing Process of Twelfth-Graders,* which focuses on the writing processes of real subjects, real students, and "Writing as a Mode of Learning," which advocates writing not just as one of many modes of learning but as a unique mode of learning. Significantly, writing as learning is described as "active, engaged, personal—more specifically, self-rhythmed—in nature" (124). This statement also attests to her belief in the primacy the student-subject ought to occupy in any notion of learning and in any notion of writing.

Other scholars call for a synthesis of approaches to writing and for broader conceptions of writing. Janice Lauer speaks to pedagogical issues, James Kinneavy to the nature of writing process, and Sondra Perl to the nature of writing itself. In "Instructional Practices: Toward an Integration," Lauer argues that the two major pedagogical directions of composition teaching—art and as nurturing natural process—should be integrated, along with the pedagogies of imitation and practice. This integrated approach, she writes, "offers a more stimulating and supportive context in which students can learn to write and write to learn" (3). Lauer argues for a both/and perspective rather than an either/or, a syntheses of approaches that expand the pedagogical horizon. In "The Process of Writing: A Philosophical Base in Hermeneutics," Kinneavy voices a concern that writing process was often too narrowly conceived, and he calls for a more comprehensive notion of process. He provides theoretical and pedagogical depth by applying Martin Heidegger's notion of hermeneutics to the notion of writing process. Such a perspective, he suggests, provides a more flexible, recursive, exploratory, and, especially, pluralistic perspective than the "almost monolithic notion floating in the journals that there is a single process underlying all invention, prewriting, writing, and editing stages" (8). Speaking to the complexity of writing and the need for deeper understandings of its process, Perl discusses teachers' insights into their own composing processes and products, noting one teacher's conclusion "that at any given moment the process is more complex than anything we are aware of" ("Understanding" 369). Perl maintains that these sorts of insights "show us the fallacy of reducing the composing process to a simple linear scheme and they leave us with the potential for creating even more powerful ways of understanding composing" (369). This call for an examination of actual writers' insights into their own writing situates the starting point of inquiry with the student-subject, the writer.

Lester Faigley contends that a disciplinarily shared definition of process is needed if a discipline of writing is to ever achieve legitimacy. If writing process were to continue influencing the teaching of writing, he argues, "it must take a broader conception of writing, one that understands writing processes are historically dynamic—not psychic states, cognitive routines, or neutral social relationships" ("Competing" 537). From the expressive perspective, he says, we should study the possibilities that technological changes engender for personal expression. From the cognitive focus on problems, we should study the imbrication of writing process and power; and from the social perspective, we should study how texts serve power as well as the power relations that shut down certain discourses. Faigley's broad characterization of what writing process ought to be implies a complex notion of the student-subject.

Richard Gebhardt and Charles Kostelnick also discuss the need for broader perspectives, suggesting that early theories to date did not yet approximate the complexity of writing process. Gebhardt notes that "the processes of writing are sufficiently complex, and sufficiently variable from writer to writer, that they cannot be reduced to a pat formula but demand models of great breadth and flexibility" (294). Kostelnick, on the other hand, says that writing process parallels design process. He further argues that a comparison of the two underscores the importance of building models that would account for the full spectrum of the writing taught and researched. Both scholars, however, attest to the complexity of writing process and articulate a broader spectrum of possibility that suggests student heterogeneity.

Both D. Gordon Rohman and Erika Lindemann also implicitly reject a homogeneous notion of the subject. They speak to the need for writing process theory to include notions of situatedness as well as flexibility. Rohman, for example, says that writing is usefully conceptualized as a process, "something which shows continuous change in time like growth in organic nature" (106). The analogy of writing process to organic nature suggests that the student-subject is the logical antecedent to process. Just as notions of writing should not be static, he argues, neither should notions of the student-subject for which those notions are formulated. Lindemann is even more specific in her support for a heterogeneously conceived notion of writing process: "writing involves not just one process but several. [. . .] Also, the processes change depending on our age, our experiences as writers, and the kind of writing we do. Indeed, they seem as complex and varied as the people who use them" (21). Lindemann therefore describes a highly rhetorical conception of writing process, as heterogeneous as those who use it.

Still other scholars offer new conceptualizations of writing process, or they discuss those they believe to have been overemphasized or neglected in the past. Lee Odell, for example, recommends that we could best help students by identifying the intellectual processes reflected in their writing. Linda Flower and John Hayes provide the ground for further research on the thinking processes involved in writing. Barry Kroll recommends a "cognitive-developmental" theoretical approach to composing, which draws upon the psychology of Jean Piaget and the educational psychology of John Dewey. He argues for an emphasis on writing as process because, he says, it could provide students with strategies to manage their writing that would not oversimplify their process.

Although George Jensen and John DiTiberio argue that C. G. Jung's system of identifying different personality types would benefit both composition instruction and composition research, they also acknowledge that different people use different processes. This observation suggests that what was most needed was a better understanding of how people differ and how these differences affect writing process. Personality, then, was the element they believe had been neglected. C. H. Knoblauch takes issue with a perceived overemphasis on the textual aspects of writing choices, and he insists that behavioral aspects are worthy of teaching scholarship. We should, he argues, ask questions about the correlation of writing choices to both the kind of task attempted and to the competence of a specific writer. When these questions are answered we better understand how to develop advantageous behaviors in the classroom.

Jack Selzer, however, believes composing habits do differ among writers, but he does not believe these differences inhered within a writer. Carol Berkenkotter maintains that changes in aim, an element she contends is overlooked, also changes the composing habits of experienced writers. Sondra Perl, however, argues that parts of the writing process cause changes not only from writer to writer but also from topic to topic ("Composing Processes"). It is an overemphasis on the rationalization of composing that Richard Young maintains was the "great danger of a technical theory of art—of art as grammar" (201).

Patricia Conners argues that our research ought to focus on intuition and intuition ought then to inform our teaching practice. "A persistence in viewing *intuition* and the whole problem-solving process of writing as inexplicable and mysterious," she says, "is a little like insisting the world is flat—no true wonder is lost in a more accurate understanding" (77). Alice Brand identifies affective elements as the overlooked element in what she contended was a concentration of scholarship on the cognitive aspects of writing. "Understanding the collaboration of emotion and cognition in writing," she maintains, "is both fundamental and far-reaching. It is in cognition that ideas make sense. But it is in emotion that this sense finds value" (442). Finally, Susan McLeod justified the need for scholarship of the affective: "we can help with strategic self-management in the affective as well as in the cognitive domain" (433).

This profile of process recognizes a wide array of scholarship: the recommendation to study intellectual processes; the critique of an overemphasis on cognition and rationality; the call for a theory of the affective; the recognition of the role of intuition, the argument that we should study behavior; the nomination of Jungian psychology to ascertain personality types; and the cognitive-developmental theory drawn from Piaget and Dewey. In addition, process theorists have suggested that aim changes the composing habits of experienced writers, that topic changes the composing process of the writer, and that composing habits differ among writers but not within a writer. While this sampling of scholarly opinions is broad, it represents only a scant portion of the total scholarship that speaks in some way to writing process. Nevertheless, it helps to capture a panoramic view of writing process as both discourse and practice

Process, Post-Process: A Point of *Stasis*

Regarding the nature of academic debates, Ralph Cintron writes that they "are to a significant degree performances. Differences—and they do exist—push themselves forward by creating caricatures of each other. Although it may seem paradoxical, differences are deeply relational: To denounce the other's position is to announce one's own" (376). We know that process caricatured current-traditional rhetoric to create a space for itself and we also understand something of the costs of that move. Post-process appears now to harbor a similar impulse. Indeed, Paul Kei Matsuda writes that

> while Kent is careful to note the divergence of perspectives among proponents of post-process theory, the term 'post-process' seems to be used in his volume as a way of solidifying disparate critiques of so-called expressive and cognitive theories and pedagogies. That is, post-process [. . .] seems to be on its way to constructing its own narrative of transformation with process as the necessary caricature. (74)

As Lad Tobin writes in the 1994 collection *Taking Stock: The Writing Process Movement in the '90s,* "recent reports of the death of the writing process movement have been greatly exaggerated" (9). Paradigm *hope* may thrive, but we know only too well from our own history, and our understanding of what Paul Feyerabend has to say on the utopian yearning for paradigms and paradigm shifts, that no such possibility exists. A shift may, indeed, be occurring, but is it a relational one.[10] There is every reason to assume, then, that a point of *stasis,* representing some shared value, can be articulated and can lead to a productive and mutually enriching dialogue.

The process profile reveals a panoply of perspectives, each of which can be viewed as enlarging the knowledge domain of the discursive formation that writing process was and is. Some statements speak to institutionalization, some to the nature of writing, some to aspects of writing process, some to how writing process should be taught, and some to the process an individual student-subject uses to produce writing. It is important to recall that these discussions were stimulated by frustrations with the current-traditional approach that hardly considered the individual student-subject.[11] Thus, the individual student-subject began to receive attention in the context of the questioning of the nature of writing and the best pedagogy for writing. Admittedly, some who rejected the current-traditional approach made the individual student paramount even going so far to evoke the image of a lone genius. This position, along with that of current-traditional, established the ends of a continuum in which the discourse of writing became situated. The composite constitutes the unity of a discursive formation that would lead to its institutionalization. Writing process, or simply "process," has functioned as a disciplinary metaphor for this discursive formation.

"Process," as a disciplinary metaphor, became strained, however, with the advent of social/cultural scholarship in the 1980s, when writing process was submitted not only to further (re)formulations but also to the more stringent critiques associated with these reformulations (see Berlin, Bizzell, and Faigley). The social/cultural turn did constitute a significant shift in rhetoric and composition's disciplinary discursive formation. However, not only was there no break with process during this period, there was also never a serious suggestion that there ought to be. No such suggestion was seriously made until the 1990s, when the scholarly discourse coalesced around the metaphor *post-process,* a time at which, significantly, many post-process advocates began to claim the 1980s social/cultural scholarship as their own. To date, only a few in the post-process camp have situated themselves in radical opposition to process by disavowing the 1980s social/cultural scholarship altogether. The movement from early process to radical post-process is depicted along the following continuum, plotted thusly as Figure 1:

Figure 1. Early Process/Post-Process/Radical Post-Process Continuum.

This continuum suggests a point of *stasis* between process and post-process at the point where each incorporates the scholarship of the social/cultural into their theories and practices. This is not to say that process and post-process are in alignment at this point; rather, it is to say that this is a point at which both share a common value, the scholarship of the social/cultural turn that theorized the factors that impinge upon the act(or) of writing.

Writing Process/Post-Process Unbound: Networked Process

As indicated, the profile of post-process includes well-rehearsed critiques of the overdetermined individual, though the profile of writing process reveals that this charge is debatable. Less evident, perhaps, is that not even radical post-process is immune to this critique.

For example, Kent's theory of paralogic hermeneutics centers around Donald Davidson's notion of triangulation. To examine the individuality inherent in this notion, I will use just one example, which I take from Kent's published interview with Davidson. This example also illustrates that his appropriation of Davidson's theory is mediated by his own specific notion of paralogy. Kent asks Davidson to explain triangulation, and Davidson responds that it is part reality, part metaphor. The reality factor of triangulation, as Davidson explains it, revolves around the notion of objectivity, a concept that exists, he argues, only because of interpersonal relations. Alone in the world, we would have no use for the concept of truth, since we would have no cause to question the correspondence of what we think to what is. But precisely because we do not exist alone, our source of objectivity is intersubjectivity, which Davidson conceives as a triangle constituted by two communicants and the world.

The metaphorical equation of triangulation can be illustrated through a thought experiment. Suppose, Davidson says, that you were alone in the world; things would impinge upon you. For example, perhaps the pleasant taste of a peach impinged upon you; to what would you attribute the pleasant taste? You could not say the peach itself since there would be no shared, interpretive ground with another person to determine that it was in fact the peach that pleased "rather than the taste of the peach, or the stimulation of the taste buds, or, for that matter, something that happened a thousand years ago" (10). In this metaphorical situation, you would be, at best, in a state of infinite regress, since there could be no answer without the foundational, intersubjective ground for formulating a mutually agreed-upon objective answer. Indeed, there could be no answer, since, without a fellow interpretive communicant, you could not ask the question anyway. The point of triangulation is that the triangle is completed when I react to the peach and you react to the peach and we then react to each other's reaction to the peach. Only then can we locate a *common* stimulus. It cannot be located in my mouth only, in your mouth only, or in some event located thousands of years ago. Rather, "it locates it just at the distance of the shared stimulus which, in turn, causes each of the two creatures to react to each other's reactions. It's a way of saying why it is that communication is essential to the concept of an objective world" (11).

If this resonates with a notion of social-epistemic rhetoric, it differs in Kent's appropriation in its radical extreme, which issues from his particular formulation of paralogy. If you were to subscribe to a notion of social-epistemic rhetoric, you might surmise the previously described instance of triangulation to have occurred multiple times across a group of people who, let's say, share the same peach orchard. In this situation, there might eventually be some malleable but fairly stable, generally agreed-upon "knowledge" regarding people's interactions with peaches. Kent would criticize this assumption, however, on the basis that each instance of triangulation is not just different but is so radically unique and different as to defy the possibility of a gist of repeatability (intertextuality) and its transference across a range of socially shared responses. To so think would, according to Kent, suggest that some codified procedure, system, or process (logico-systemic process) functioned foundationally as mediation between communicants. Kent's appropriation of triangulation, according to his own theory of paralogy overdetermines the reality factor of Davidson's notion of intersubjectivity. It conceives of intersubjectivity so radically as to at least insinuate the privileging of the individual, radical indivisibility of each instance of triangulation. This privileging is proportionate to an overdetermined notion of triangulation and therefore to an overdetermined notion of individuality.

Some strands of early process and radical post-process ironically share a privileging of the individual, even though the manner in which they do so differs. Significantly, however, it is the grappling with writing's possibility, the person who writes, that is indicated across the entire range of the process/post-process continuum seen in Figure 1. Thus, whether tacit or explicit, all theories of writing and the theories of rhetoric that inform them make certain assumptions regarding writing's condition of possibility: the person who would write. This holds true for expressivist, cognitivist, social constructionist, social-epistemic, feminist, Marxist, cultural studies, postmodern, post-process, and/or radical post-process informed theories of rhetoric/writing.

The point of *stasis* indicated in the middle of the continuum by the acknowledgement of *some* strands of process and of post-process for the value of social/cultural scholarship is telling, since this scholarship effectively moved us off overdetermined notions of the individual and toward theorizing (1) the complex networks with(in) which writers are imbricated by merely *being* and (2) the complex networks that influence and pressure the act(or) of writing. The point of *stasis* between process and post-process—with their mutual suspicion of the overdetermined, individual and their mutual appreciation of the complex social/political/cultural networks that pressure writers/writing differently—marks the place of *stasis* and creates a new space for productive dialogue between the two positions. As the point of *stasis* for process and post-process, this material and conceptual space of writer/writing/network needs a name that exceeds the limitations of process and post-process. *Networked process* is such a name.

The space of networked process, then, would require not only that we conceptualize theories of rhetoric/writing according to some notion of a material writing subject who exists within complex social, political, and cultural networks, it would also require that we articulate this notion. Networked process would also enable us to re-envision the field's identity and, more importantly, its *possibility*.

The person who writes has long been too thinly treated in disciplinary theories of rhetoric/writing.[12] Such thinness has alternately led, for example, to a number of conflicting positions: privileged notions of individual autonomy; universal assumptions of the individual; formulations of the social nature of subjects; articulation of differences that pressure subjects differently; a sometimes myopic focus on various elements with which the subject is a tacitly assumed presence; and avoidance of an agentless subject altogether. For much of our history, this thinness is explainable through our limited knowledge and scholarly preoccupations. But, structuralism, post-structuralism, and postmodernism, have foregrounded the subject thoroughly. That we have failed to adequately respond may be due to our fear of accusations of capitulating to grand narratives. But, given the pragmatic aspect of our disciplinary mission—the effective teaching of and student engagement with writing—we can ill afford such timidity, for it serves only to undermine our potential to intervene in the everyday practices of the various lives and contexts we would affect. Networked process addresses this deficiency by articulating a theory of the subject who writes (and is written) within and among complex social, political, and cultural networks.

2 Exploring Networked Process in James Berlin's Cognitive Maps

> A critique of any theoretical system is not [merely] an examination of its flaws or imperfections. It is not a set of criticisms designed to make the system better. It is an analysis that focuses on the grounds of that system's possibility. The critique reads backwards from what seems natural, obvious, self-evident, or universal, in order to show that these things have their history, their reasons for being the way they are, their effects on what follows from them, and that the starting point is not a (natural) given but a (cultural) construct, usually blind to itself. [. . .] Every theory starts somewhere; every critique exposes what that starting point conceals. [. . .] The critique does not ask "what does this statement *mean?*" but "where is it being made from? What does it presuppose?
>
> —Barbara Johnson[1]

In the 1980s, James Berlin was, luckily for us, pre-occupied with the connection between rhetoric(s) and writing process(es). I say "luckily" not because he necessarily got it right and certainly not because everyone agrees that he got it right, but because his classifications provide us such a rich vein of scholarship to mine. In other words, Berlin's classifications had and continue to have "effects on what follows from them."

The grounds of Berlin's work in the 1980s are various theoretical formulations of rhetoric and writing. Hindsight indicates a trajectory

---

1. "Introduction" to Jacques Derrida's *Dissemination* (xv).

in these theories that brought about both the advent of post-process in the 1990s and the notion of networked process. In each of these theoretical formulations, Berlin provides different "cognitive maps." The maps are offered in keeping with Fredric Jameson's conclusion that the political component of theory ought to provide cognitive maps so that we may "begin to grasp our positioning as individual and collective subjects and [thus] regain a capacity to act and struggle which is at present neutralized by our spatial as well as our social confusion" (*Postmodernism* 54).[13] A reading of Berlin's maps, as well as a reading across these maps, can help to chart the landscape that gave rise to networked process. Moreover, to critique his maps is to begin to (re)draw the landscape yet again.[14]

Because the map does necessarily precede the inquiry, the map will in large part determine the nature of the inquiry and its findings. It cannot be otherwise.[15] The map of this critique, then, pre-occupied as it is with Berlin's cartography and yielded landscapes, seeks to illuminate the nature, function, and relationship of the following networked process sites: the subject who writes (students and teachers), rhetoric(s), writing processes (curriculum and pedagogy), composition classrooms, the disciplinarity of rhetoric and composition, and the broader culture. The developing map of networked process, which this critique constitutes, can be reasonably expected to "find" knowledge regarding the subject who writes and the webbed relations within which it is implicated.

Berlin's Cognitive Maps

The following works, which were published across an eight-year span during the 1980s, are particularly salient for a fuller conceptualization of a networked process map. They attest to Berlin's attempts to understand the relationship among writing processes, rhetorics, teachers, students, disciplinarity, and culture:

1. "Current-Traditional Rhetoric: Paradigm and Practice" (co-authored with Robert P. Inkster), 1980 (referred to as "Current-Traditional" throughout this chapter);

2. "Contemporary Composition: The Major Pedagogical Theories," 1982 (referred to as "Major Theories" throughout this chapter);

3. *Writing Instruction in Nineteenth-Century American Colleges,* 1984 (referred to as *Writing Instruction* throughout this chapter);

4. *Rhetoric and Reality: Writing Instruction in American Colleges 1900–1985,* 1987 (referred to as *Rhetoric and Reality* throughout this chapter); and

5. "Rhetoric and Ideology in the Writing Class," 1988 (referred to as "Rhetoric and Ideology" throughout this chapter).

Throughout these works, Berlin insists that teachers become more reflexive about the ramification of their classroom practice for themselves, their students, their institutions, and the larger culture. The following challenge, one among many, is perhaps most representative of the "felt" dissonance that compelled him to this scholarship.[16]

> The numerous recommendations of the "process"-centered approaches to writing instruction as superior to the "product"-centered approaches are not very useful. Everyone teaches the process of writing, but everyone does not teach the *same* process. The test of one's competence as a composition instructor, it seems to me, resides in being able to recognize and justify the version of the process being taught, complete with all of its significance for the student. ("Contemporary Composition: The Major Pedagogical Theories" 247)

Throughout these works, Berlin calls teachers to raise the stakes. His article, co-authored with Robert Inkster in 1980 ("Current-Traditional Rhetoric: Paradigm and Practice"), addresses the issue that would capture his intellectual and emotional energies for years to come: "we need to scrutinize carefully the epistemology implied by our practice in the teaching of composition" (14). More urgent, as illustrated in the above quoted passage from "Contemporary Composition: The Major Pedagogical Theories," Berlin ties the need to scrutinize the epistemology of practice directly to teachers' competence, while in *Writing Instruction in Nineteenth-Century in American Colleges,* his appeal expands to invoke a professional, teacher *ethos* and to foreground teaching as an ethical obligation. "One of the purposes of this study," he writes, "has been to convince writing teachers of their importance.

[. . .] Most students [. . .] learn what we teach them. For this reason, it is important to be aware of what we are teaching, in all its implications. [. . .] We owe it to our students and ourselves to make certain that we are providing the best advice that we can offer" (91–92). By 1987's *Rhetoric and Reality: Writing Instruction in American Colleges, 1900–1985*, however, Berlin asks teachers to consider the implications of teaching beyond students' personal welfare: "Our decision, then, about the kind of rhetoric we are to call upon in teaching writing," he says, "has important implications for the behavior of our students—behavior that includes the personal, social, and political" (7). In "Rhetoric and Ideology in the Writing Class," Berlin's agenda is even more emphatically articulated as he writes: "It should now be apparent that a way of teaching is never innocent. [. . .] A rhetoric cannot escape the ideological question, and to ignore this is to fail our responsibilities as teachers and as citizens" (492–93). An abiding issue for Berlin, then, involves the responsibilities and obligations that teachers of writing can fulfill only by appreciating distinctions among rhetorics and their attendant writing processes.[17]

Berlin makes the connection between rhetoric and writing process explicit in yet another call for teachers of writing to understand the implications of their practices, as explained in his 1984 monograph, *Writing Instruction in Nineteenth-Century American Colleges*. Rhetorics are, he writes, multiple, varied, and changeable, characterized as "the codification of the unspeakable as well as the speakable. No rhetoric [. . .] is permanent, is embraced by all people, or even by some one person or group, at all times. A rhetoric changes" (1). The connection between rhetorics and writing processes, he says, has to do with the underlying assumptions of a specific rhetoric, for these determine

> how the composing process is conceived and taught in the classroom. What goes into the process—the way in which invention, arrangement, and style are undertaken, or not undertaken, as is sometimes the case—is determined by the assumptions made, and often unexamined, about reality, writer/speaker, audience, and language. Each rhetoric, therefore, indicates the behavior appropriate to the composing situation. Beyond that, it directs the behavior of teacher and student in the classroom, making certain kinds of activity inevitable and other kinds impossible. (2)

There exists, then, at all times multiple rhetorics. In teaching writing, any sort of writing, we must inevitably use some process to teach the student, although notions of what constitute this process vary and emanate from both formal theory (institutionally legitimized) and informal theory (lore). Rhetorics have historically been concerned with notions of rhetorical situation/reality, speaker/writer, listener/reader, and language/discourse, while theories of writing process have variously addressed how the elements that constitute a writing process correlate with the elements of a particular theory of rhetoric. It is the relationship between rhetorics and processes that prescribes, or, according to Berlin, ought to prescribe, teaching and learning. Writing processes, then, represent material instantiations of theory and practice.

"Current-Traditional Rhetoric: Paradigm and Practice"

It is interesting to note the pastiche quality of James Berlin and Robert Inkster's definition of rhetoric. Initially, they borrow Richard Young's characterization of *paradigm*, a term that functions to allow/disallow what comes into the discipline, what is taught/not taught, what problems are deemed worthy/unworthy of inquiry, and what research is/is not valued for development. On the authority of "Abrams, Kinneavy, and other scholars," Berlin and Inkster add the elements of the communication triangle—reality, writer, audience, and discourse—all of which must be reasonably justified for an "adequate conception of rhetoric" (2). Commenting on the recent emergence of alternative conceptions of rhetoric, they suggest that all these conceptions share a common feature: "the way in which the writer, the reader, and their relationship are imagined" (14).

But while the external components of current-traditional rhetoric are known, Berlin and Inkster write, the philosophical assumptions that underlie it are not so obvious. Their goal, then, is to explore current-traditional rhetoric, particularly its philosophical assumptions. The most important of these is epistemology, which, they say, involves "concepts of the mind, reality, and the relation between the two" (1). They then trace the epistemological assumptions of the current-traditional paradigm to assess its contribution to an adequate conception of "the rhetorical process," which, they maintain, must account for the elements of the communication triangle: reality, writer, audience, discourse. "An adequate method of instruction in writing," they write, "must give a prospective writer a conceptual framework that encourages exploration of each of the elements in the communication triangle in the attempt to bring forth discourse" (2). Changes in the way these elements of the communication triangle are imagined occasion further changes to "the way meaning is seen to occur and to be shared," changes that are epistemological and thus carry profound ethical, social, and political ramifications (14).

Their method begins with an examination of the current-traditional paradigm's historical origins, which, they say, will "provide a useful background" (1). They then proceed to examine four contemporary textbooks, using a cognitive map that entails reading the epistemological concepts of mind, reality, and the relation between the two across the communication triangle: reality, writer, audience, and discourse. They employ in this methodology a heuristic, which they explain is one of three available processes by which to work through any sort of cognitive or creative act. Placed along a continuum—algorithmic/heuristic/aleatory—the three available processes range procedurally from the algorithmic process, a strictly rule-governed process that produces predictable outcomes, to the aleatory process, which is completely random and produces unpredictable outcomes. The heuristic method, which is not a compromise between the poles but occupies "a wide middle ground of activities that are neither wholly rule-governed nor wholly random," entails "a systematic way of moving toward satisfactory control of an ambiguous or problematic situation, but not to a single correct solution" (3). While Berlin and Inkster's methodological benchmark draws upon the heuristic perspective, they incorporate the continuum itself into their interpretive matrix. This then becomes the underlying field by which they interpret the relation of reality and writer that constitutes the epistemology of the current-traditional paradigm.

They apply the heuristic continuum to assess the ongoing argument in English departments regarding what can and cannot be taught in the composition class. Those who take the position that "stylistic correctness or facility" is the proper classroom content assume the algorithmic position on the continuum, while those who would teach composition as an act of genius occupy the aleatory (13). The paradox, according to Berlin and Inkster, is that both poles of this binary share "epistemologies [that] are wholly consistent with one another" (13). I make a point of this because Berlin alters this interpretation in his 1982 article, "Contemporary Composition: The Major Pedagogical Theories." In claiming that the underlying epistemologies of those who equate composition with stylistic correctness and those who equate it with genius are consistent, Berlin and Inkster's assessment is based, quite naturally, on the terms by which they define epistemology: the mind, reality, and the relation between the two. From the perspective of "the mind," then, the two poles are consistent, in that both the algorithmic and the aleatory assume that knowledge is located "outside" of the individual mind. In the algorithmic view, knowledge is constructed to the point of reification, while in the aleatory, knowledge is "found." What this continuum elides and what Berlin later attempts to correct with a more social orientation, is the emphasis on the individual mind, autonomous and unconstrained by outside forces.

Also related to their claim of algorithmic/aleatory epistemological consistency within the current-traditional paradigm is Berlin and Inkster's purpose to not only "dissect the paradigm, but to evaluate it, to make some statement about its adequacy for shaping a contemporary rhetoric" (1). The value of freshman composition had been and continued to be contested not only within the English department but also in the academy and beyond. Berlin and Inkster place responsibility for this crisis directly on a faulty rhetorical paradigm and, indirectly, upon those who remain intellectually entrenched within it. There is, then, a concern for reshaping notions of writing process and effecting change in the classroom. This article indicts the current-traditional paradigm as dangerous "to teachers, students, the wider purposes of our educational enterprise, and even our social and human fabric" (14). This goal—remapping notions of writing process and effecting change in the classroom in order to secure the space of the freshman composition course in the academy—permeates Berlin's work.

"Contemporary Composition: The Major Pedagogical Theories"

In response to recent articles attempting to distinguish various approaches to teaching composition, Berlin in this article contrasts his theoretical approach with that of accepted wisdom that says since the elements of the composing process—writer, reality, reader, language—are uncontested, differences in composing processes must issue from the degree of emphasis given the elements. Berlin says this is a contention with which he "strongly disagree[s]," for "from this point of view, the composing process is always and everywhere the same because writer, reality, reader, and language are always and everywhere the same" (765). It is quite clear to Berlin that since it is common "to speak of the composing process as a recursive activity involving prewriting, writing, and rewriting, it is not difficult to see the writer-reality-audience-language relationship as underlying, at a deeper structural level, each of these three stages" and thus determining the sort of instruction that is or is not prescribed for each activity (765). "Pedagogical theories in writing courses," he maintains, "are grounded in rhetorical theories, and rhetorical theories do not differ in the simple undue emphasis of writer or audience or reality or language or some combination of these" (765). They differ, he says, in the way writer, reality, audience, and language "are conceived—both as separate units and in the way the units relate to each other" (766). Perhaps I overlook some subtlety, but I do not believe that a change in the emphasis on any specific element precludes a difference in how it is conceived, unless Berlin is claiming that the difference is legitimate only if it is explicit.[18] I believe that the elements do, indeed, make a difference, and that, in fact, Berlin's methodological practice throughout these works depends upon that difference.

While Berlin maintains that composing processes are grounded in rhetorical theories of writer, reality, audience, and language, he contends that the differences between composing processes are explainable by "diverging definitions of the composing process, itself," specifically in the way each element is characterized (765). The focus should be each composite definition, which presents "a different world with different rules about what can be known, how it can be known, and how it can be communicated" (766). To achieve his goal of explaining how and why teaching approaches differ, Berlin situates the "writer, reality, audience, language relationship" (765) as underlying each element in the activity of composing: prewriting/writing/rewriting. Together, this matrix represents an "epistemic complex" that determines the pedagogy prescribed for each composing process activity: invention/arrangement/style (766). He then organizes and analyzes each of the four dominant pedagogical groups—Neo-Aristotelians/Classicists; Positivists/Current-Traditionalists; Neo-Platonists/Expressionists; New Rhetoricians/Social-Epistemic—according to this "epistemic complex."

There are subtle but significant differences between Berlin's descriptions of underlying assumptions in this article and that in "Current-Traditional." In "Current-Traditional," Berlin makes epistemology an explicit element in his coding, characterizing it as involving "concepts of the mind, reality, and the relation between the two" (2). This conception of epistemology is thus firmly grounded in the cognitive. Because he describes epistemology in terms of one mind and one reality and their relation, he suggests tacit individuality. In "Major Theories," however, epistemology enters the coding matrix through his notion of "epistemic complex," which represents the composite of the "writer-reality-audience-language relationship" (765) underlying and influencing each element of the composing process (prewriting/writing/rewriting). All of these, he writes, present "a different world with different rules about what can be known, how it can be known, and how it can be communicated" (766). Another related difference between the two articles is the way in which reality itself is evaluated. Epistemology in "Current-Traditional" foregrounds the mind; in this article, it appears that Berlin distances himself from a cognitive emphasis and its tacit individuality and folds epistemology into ideology by placing greater emphasis on reality.

In "Current-Traditional," characterizations of reality were analyzed according to an epistemic continuum said to represent "the processes one may follow in working through any kind of cognitive or creative act" and which range across algorithmic, heuristic, and aleatory positions (3). Berlin equates the assumptions of the binary fields, algorithmic and aleatory, as having consistent, but erroneous, epistemological assumptions, and he recommends the heuristic process as providing the best rhetoric. But what is significant to the present discussion is that Berlin's continuum foregrounds the writer, so that, again, his entree into the epistemological equation comes by way of the individual. In "Major Theories," Berlin, although ostensibly continuing to champion a notion of the "heuristic" perspective, displaces this continuum in his view with an analogy to Richard Rorty's difference between hermeneutic and epistemological philosophy:

> For the hermeneuticist truth is never fixed finally on unshakable grounds. Instead it emerges only after false starts and failures, and it can only represent a tentative point of rest in a continuing conversation. Whatever truth is arrived at, moreover, is always the

product of individuals calling on the full range of their humanity, with esthetic and moral considerations given at least as much importance as any others. For Current-Traditional Rhetoric truth is empirically based and can only be achieved through subverting a part of the human response to experience. Truth then stands forever, a tribute to its method, triumphant over what most of us consider important in life, successful through subserving writer, audience, and language to the myth of an objective reality. (777)

The "heuristic" position of the continuum has thus previously been depicted as the process of choice for an individual involved in "any kind of cognitive or creative act." The "hermeneutical" position that Berlin now describes, where truth is located in "the product of individuals calling on the full range of their humanity, with esthetic and moral considerations given at least as much importance as any others," allows Berlin to make an explicit social and political overture, a sign, if you will, of positions yet to come.[19] For the time being, however, Berlin justifies the compromise of "truth" and thus "the mind/cognition" and, tacitly, the "individual" as the basis for changing his notion of epistemology toward a greater social and political orientation.

WRITING INSTRUCTION IN NINETEENTH-CENTURY AMERICAN COLLEGES

As Donald Stewart notes in the foreword, Berlin urges us to ask why we think what we think, why we teach what we teach, and why we think that what we teach is important. That we are unable to answer these questions is due to never having asked the questions of ourselves. Even if we have asked them, he argues, we lack the historical knowledge necessary to inform a significant reply. Berlin continues to argue for rhetoric's consequences for human behavior, but he now contends that it is in the composition or communication class where students are "indoctrinated in a basic epistemology, usually the one held by society's dominant class, the group with the most power" (2). Teachers in these courses thus have a great responsibility, which he says explains why throughout history, rhetoric enjoyed a central role in students' education. Why now, since the late nineteenth century, Berlin questions, is the value of rhetoric courses so contested, despite their often being one of the few required courses in the curriculum? He proposes to answer this through an examination of both the noetic fields informing the rhetorics taught and their place in the larger culture. It is also his intention, to study how noetic fields determine how a composing process is conceived and taught.

To get a sense of how *noetic field* figures in his cognitive map, it is important to understand how he now describes rhetoric: "A rhetoric is a social invention [. . .] the codification of the unspeakable, as well as the speakable. [. . .] In any social context, furthermore, there are usually a number of rhetorics competing for allegiance" (1). Relative to rhetoric's propensity for change and conflict, Berlin explains that

> [r]hetoric has traditionally been seen as based on four elements interacting with each other: reality, writer or speaker, audience, and language. Rhetorical schemes differ from each other, I am convinced, not in emphasizing one of these elements over another. Rhetorical schemes differ in the way each element is defined, as well as in the conception of the relation of the elements to each other. Every rhetoric, as a result, has as its base a conception of reality, of human nature, and of language. In other terms, it is grounded in a noetic field: a closed system defining what can, and cannot, be known; the nature of the knower; the nature of the relationship between the knower, the known, and the audience; and the nature of language. Rhetoric is thus ultimately implicated in all a society attempts. It is at the center of a culture's activities. (2–3)

This notion of rhetoric is considerably enlarged from previous conceptions, where in "Current Traditional," rhetoric provides a framework for instruction designed to encourage "exploration of each of the elements of the communication triangle in the attempt to bring forth discourse (2), and in "Major Theories," a rhetoric is determined by the conception of its units (writer, reality, audience, and language) "both as separate units and in the way the units relate to each other" (766). Now Berlin's conception of rhetoric subsumes these characterizations and expands to assume its place at the very center of culture. It is a bold claim. Berlin justifies it through the adoption of the notion of *noetic field*.

Berlin borrows the term noetic field from Walter Ong's *Orality and Literacy*, pages 317–334. It is meaningful, I think, that the heading at the top of page 317 reads "Crisis in the Humanities," since part of Berlin's goal is to argue the legitimacy of the composition course. I extrapolate from this passage in Ong the notions that apparently influence Berlin to embrace noetic field as appropriate to his burgeoning enterprise.

Ong writes that noetic structures "have held together man's [*sic*] life world," so that it is through the changes of these structures that he attempts to explain changes in the humanities that may have been, he says, previously obscured "or guarded and not always advantageous" (318). Further, the failure to grasp these changes may be due to our inability to adequately discern the interrelatedness of the study of humanities and other human responses to actuality. The principal agents of change in the humanities, those altering noetic and psychological structures, are attributable to the growth of knowledge in four areas. The first has to do with the atrophy of traditional puberty rites, where paradoxically, the importance of the rite was assumed, even though that importance could not be described prior to experiencing it. Relevance could be apprehended only after the rite was experienced. If, Ong asks, "the humanities function as an initiation rite, an induction, an entrance into some area, what area are we to choose?" (322). Learning proceeds from the known to the unknown, so the student must be placed in a space described as "one where the lore of the culture is centered" (322). Berlin would appear to answer Ong that the composition course can provide students this rite of passage, but to so argue, Berlin must situate rhetoric, indeed, place it "at the center of a culture's activities" (*Writing Instruction* 2–3).

The second area of knowledge growth involves the romantic cultivation of the unknown, which, Ong writes, is the consequence of "an overload of organized knowledge" (324). The result is that "consciousness of the unconscious is [now] a permanent part of our thinking" (325). The remote, the formless, the "vaguely limned areas of human consciousness" are now part of our noetic field and are as reflectively organized as the rational knowledge that preceded it. Recall that now part of Berlin's description of rhetoric is that it is "the codification of the unspeakable, as well as the speakable" (1).

The synchronic present is the third area, the place where "knowledge of the past thus bears in on us to define the here and now, where all ages meet" (326). Due to the overload of knowledge and a demand for relevance, the past has been diminished as the present assumes greater distinction, a "stampede," Ong writes, that "may prove self-annihilating if it crowds out first hand knowledge of the past by neglecting the linguistic and other tools that make such knowledge possible" (327). From this, Berlin justifies his approach to historiography and its particular relevance to the field as an aid in legitimizing its claims in the academy and in the culture.

The fourth area, the anthropologizing of knowledge, however, might have been particularly significant to Berlin. Referencing Pierre Teilhard de Chardin's work, Ong says that de Chardin's purpose was to anthropologize actuality through an interpretation of the world through the interpretive lens of the phenomenon of man [sic]. It is the business of the writer, Ong concludes, "to take hold of the maximum in the tradition and transform it as completely as possible" (332). This transformation "entails anthropologizing because it centers history not in the movement of material and the redefining of political boundaries, but in the human consciousness and in the patterned shifts in personality structures which in great part determine the externals of cultures and of history and at the same time are determined by these externals" (334).

This is the crux, then, of what Berlin wanted to accomplish with the use of noetic field: the relationship between rhetoric, reality, human consciousness, and culture or that which, as Ong says, has "held together man's [sic] life world" (318), a relationship that renders rhetoric far more fundamental than Berlin has thus far ever claimed. While he insists that noetic fields should be viewed relative to their position in larger social structures, it is likely that Berlin stopped using the term after this publication because it is too imbricated in humanism and its concomitant focus on individuality, autonomy, and transcendence to serve his ideological purpose.

RHETORIC AND REALITY: WRITING INSTRUCTION IN AMERICAN COLLEGES, 1900–1985

Although Berlin's purposes in writing this monograph are multiple and broadly conceived, I contain my discussion to his cognitive mapping of rhetorics and writing processes. This work represents a significant departure for Berlin, as his cognitive map is now drawn in a distinctly different manner. He has abandoned the use of *noetic field* and resumed the use of *epistemology*. Significantly, he has also now explicitly included ideology and added literacy as factors in his interpretive matrix. Apparently at a point of transition in his conceptualization, Berlin becomes more difficult to interpret, in part because there is a dissonance between his composite conceptualization and his need to produce a system of classification.

Part of Berlin's purpose in this monograph is to counter monolithic notions of rhetorical theory that continue to prevail in English departments, which have been indifferent to innovation. To this end, he states: "In considering the rhetorical theories of the period, I have chosen epistemology rather than ideology as the basis for my taxonomy, doing so because it allows for a closer focus on the rhetorical properties—as distinct from the economic, social, or political properties—of the systems considered" (6). Electing to use ideology as the primary coding would have required using a strategy of deduction, which would not, therefore, have produced the taxonomy that Berlin wished to accomplish. Interestingly, Berlin comments more than usual on his taxonomy, noting that the three categories—objective, subjective, and transactional—are not monolithic, as "each offers a diversity of rhetorical theories" (6). Further, he provides the caveat that "this taxonomy is not meant to be exhaustive of the entire field of rhetoric, but is simply an attempt to make manageable the discussion of the major rhetorics I have encountered in examining this period" (6). Perhaps Berlin is experiencing some ambivalence about a taxonomy in light of his more complex cognitive map.

Nevertheless, while the rhetorical properties continue to consist of "the nature of the real, the interlocutor, the audience, and the function of language" (7), Berlin now variously interprets rhetoric as "the production of spoken and written texts," as part of "the indispensable foundation of schooling" (1), and as "a diverse discipline that historically has included a variety of incompatible systems" (3). Rhetoric's goal, literacy, is defined as "a particular variety of rhetoric—a way of speaking and writing within the confines of specific social sanctions" (3–4), while it functions as an intermediary "between the writing course and larger social developments" (5).

As in *Writing Instruction,* Berlin argues that rhetorics are multiple and changeable, their differences having to do not with "a matter of the superficial emphasis of one or another feature of the rhetorical act" but rather with the differences that issue from epistemology, "with assumptions about the very nature of the known, the knower, and the discourse community involved in considering the known" (3). But "transformations" in rhetorics, Berlin writes, are also related to larger social and political factors, the consideration of which places us in the area of ideology, a term he insists that he uses in its "most descriptive and neutral sense" (4).

> Ideology will simply refer to the pluralistic conceptions of social and political arrangements that are present in a society at any given time. These conceptions are based on discursive (verbal) and non-discursive (nonverbal) formations designating the shape of social and political structures, the nature and role of the individual within these structures, and the distributions of power in society. It is not difficult to see the close relationship between these elements and the elements of the rhetorical context—the individual interlocutor, material reality, the audience, and language. The plurality of competing rhetorics is always related to the plurality of competing ideologies. (4–5)

Rhetoric and ideology seem now to be in competition in this interpretive matrix. In order to evaluate this contest, however, it is necessary to view how Berlin is situating epistemology relative to ideology. Berlin has said that epistemology—used in the context of rhetoric defined as "a diverse discipline that historically has included a variety of incompatible systems" (3)—explains differences in rhetorics and that it is ideology, used in the context of rhetoric as "related to larger social and political developments" (4), that explains transformations of rhetorics. Again, literacy functions as the intermediary "between the writing course and larger social developments" (5). To recap, epistemologies are tied to discourse communities and effect *differences in rhetorics,* ideologies are tied to larger social and political developments and effect *transformations in rhetorics,* and literacy involves a particular variety of rhetoric that functions as *intermediary* between the two.

Ideology, which is based on both discursive and non-discursive formations that determine social and political structures, the nature and role of the individual, and the distribution of power in a society, subsumes rhetoric. Rhetoric as "the production of spoken and written texts" is part of "the indispensable foundation of schooling" (1). Rhetoric thus produces literacy, so that we might think of literacy as the text of rhetoric. Epistemology, now characterized as "assumptions about the very nature of the known, the knower, and the discourse community involved in considering the known" (3) is now qualified in a new way, with the addition of discourse community, which also serves to indirectly qualify rhetoric and, of course, to reconstitute a notion of the social lost with the previous use of *noetic field*. Before, Berlin has acknowledged competing and multiple rhetorics, but the tacit suggestion has been that they are traceable to larger social events in a culture, for example, faculty psychology, Freud, the Heisenberg uncertainty principle, etc., which thereby restricts their competitive number at any specific time. However, given the notion that rhetorics are as numerous and variable as the discourse communities in which they operate, Berlin's system of classification must discern how to account for these variations. He offsets this difficulty to some extent with the use of ideology, as he has characterized it relative to literacy. Through his definition of literacy as "a way of speaking and writing within the confines of specific social sanctions," we are to infer that he contextualizes the "confines of specific social sanctions" to classrooms. Once he has established that classrooms sanction discourse, Berlin can extrapolate classifications as usual. Classifications, as literacy texts, then, feed into larger ideological social and political structures.

It also is possible to equate Berlin's characterization of ideology with his earlier conclusion that to promote a rhetoric and composing process is to determine the character and worldview of a student. To interpret Berlin in this way, however, requires that we assume he believes that ideology subsumes rhetoric, rather than viewing rhetoric as either prior to or totally imbricated with ideology. Ideology, characterized as conceptions of social and political arrangements, is based on both discursive and non-discursive formations. The characterizations of epistemology and ideology that Berlin provides could also be interpreted to mean that epistemology provides "assumptions" about reality, while ideology "constitutes" reality. The elements that now capture Berlin's interest are thus articulated, but their relationship remains nebulous. But the ambivalence that Berlin apparently experiences in the formation of his cognitive map used in this study is resolved, in part, in his next article, "Rhetoric and Ideology in the Writing Class."

"RHETORIC AND IDEOLOGY IN THE WRITING CLASS"

Berlin's cognitive map is simplified, problematically, in this study. Here, the interpretive matrix consists of reading a particular rhetoric (mind, audience, language, reality) across economic, social, and political arrangements. His notion of ideology, however, is far more developed than of that used in "Rhetoric and Reality," and he now explicitly articulates rhetoric's envelopment within it. From the perspective of rhetoric, he says, "ideology provides the language to define the subject (the self), other subjects, the material world, and the relation of all of these to each other" (479), rendering rhetoric "as always already ideological" (477). Berlin also indirectly comments upon his own method as he writes: "A rhetoric then considers competing claims in these three realms [economic, social, political] from an ideological perspective made possible both by its constitution and by its application—the dialectical interaction between the rhetoric as text and the interpretive practices brought to it" (477). He then applies this interpretive practice, a consideration of the competing claims that issue from the economic, social, and political to "the three rhetorics that have emerged as most conspicuous in classroom practices today" (477). Having made this application, he recommends social-epistemic rhetoric.

But it is in the heuristics embedded within the notion of ideology that a fuller characterization of the term *ideology* is found. Drawing exclusively upon Goran Therborn's use of the term in *The Ideology of Power and the Power of Ideology*, Berlin writes that

> no position can lay claim to absolute, timeless truth because finally all formulations are historically specific, arising out of the material conditions of a particular time and place. Choices in the economic, social, political, and cultural are thus always based on discursive practices that are interpretations, not mere transcriptions of some external, verifiable certainty. [. . .] Therborn calls upon Foucault's "micropolitics of power" without placing subjects within a seamless web of inescapable, wholly determinative power re-

lations. For Therborn, power can be identified and
resisted in a meaningful way. (478)

This conception of ideology that informs the economic, social, and political coding that Berlin now uses leaves space for rhetoric by conceding a degree of agency to the subject through an ability to interpret and to practice resistance. The heuristics imbricated in ideology consist of three questions: What exists?; What is good?; and What is Possible?—all of which are appropriated from Therborn and represent different modes of interpellation. The first question, involving ideology, addresses, "What exists?" and deals, according to Berlin, with epistemology, which "interpolates the subject in a manner that determines what is real and what is illusory, and, most important, what is experienced and what remains outside the field of phenomenological experience, regardless of its actual material existence" (479). The second question, "What is good?," deals with the aesthetic, the structuring and normalizing of desire. The third, "What is possible?," establishes the boundaries of expectation, of what can and cannot be done. This last mode is closely related to power relationships in a culture, that is, who has it and who decides to what ends it will be applied. Power is thus intrinsic to ideology and is thus inscribed in all discursive practices. Furthermore, power appears natural because it is socially endorsed; nevertheless, ideologies do compete for power "and a given individual reflect(s) one or another permutation of these conflicts," Berlin says, "although the overall effect of these permutations tends to support the hegemony of the dominant class" (479).

In Berlin's formulation, changes in rhetorics are no longer caused by different epistemologies and/or different literacies, as rhetoric, its underlying epistemological structure, and its productive texts of literacy are subsumed within ideology. As a result, categorizing discourses is at once complicated and simplified. On the one hand, many competing ideologies complicate classification, while on the other hand, classification essentially collapses into a binary: hegemonic/resistant. The problem here is that Berlin begins with a classification of rhetorics—cognitive psychology, expressionism, and social-epistemic—and then discusses representative theorists within each category, interpreting each with the cognitive map previously discussed. Significantly, Berlin does not produce a system of classification, yet he continues to practice his interpretation in the spirit of classification. Ideology, however, proves perhaps to be too conceptually comprehensive for evaluating specific writing process theories. The danger is that such an interpretation too easily leads to gross overgeneralization. Indeed, some writing process theorists Berlin examined took issue with his assessment in a response article: "Three Comments on 'Rhetoric and Ideology in the Writing Class' and 'Problem Solving Reconsidered,'" which appeared two months following the publication of Berlin's "Rhetoric and Ideology."

The three respondents, Karen Scriven, Linda Flower, and John Schilb, take Berlin to task on various points of his methodology and interpretation. Karen Scriven, for example, writes that for Berlin "to misrepresent by simplification [. . .] those fields such as cognitive psychology with empirical insights potentially vital to inquiry in writing is, even if unintentionally, false to the spirit of open inquiry marking humanistic endeavors" (765). Similarly, Linda Flower questions: "Does this aspect of a research-based ideology—the desire to test one's theories with observation and the constant focus on a need to know (rather than assert imperatives)—fit comfortably in the package Berlin has created? I am not sure it does, and I wonder what happens when (with care and good faith) we package the ideology of others in order to make a comparison and a case for our own?" (766). John Schilb, also troubled by Berlin's method, writes:

> For me, he [Berlin] lapses here into connected assumptions all too common in English studies nowadays: that a wide range of theorists can be yoked under the aegis of one particular worldview, and that the political correctness of said worldview can then be decisively gauged by zeroing in on particular institutions or movements who've shared it. My fear is that if we adopt such an approach, we'll blur significant differences between theorists in our taxonomic zeal, and we'll avoid the rigorous task of charting the whole variety of ways that a worldview can be appropriated or purveyed. (770)

Berlin makes a significant stride in his own conceptualization through this work, but it comes at great cost, mainly, a leveling of much of the theoretical richness with which he had for so long been preoccupied.

The Platform That Berlin Built

The cognitive maps used by Berlin attest to his efforts to negotiate pertinent issues of the field's scholarship in this historical period. Throughout his inquiry, he successfully argued for the viability of rhetoric/composition as a field within the academy, the appropriateness of first-year composition in the curriculum, and the responsibilities that teachers of writing bear toward themselves, their students, their institutions, and to the larger culture. He also significantly expanded a general domain by which an individual relates to the world, as he moved from promoting a position of cognitive individuality to consider aesthetic, moral, personality, and discursive and non-discursive factors. However, Berlin's ultimate goal, the justification of social-epistemic rhetoric as the premier rhetoric of choice, became a terministic screen that eventually strained the maps he employed.

Moreover, the classification systems of writing process he developed to assist teachers of writing did not effectively serve as a tool to make the changes for which he called, due to an unresolved tension between the characterization of the nature of the subject (student/writer/teacher) and the subject's relation to the world. Berlin's classification systems, then, in some degree offered an imaginary resolution of real contradictions.

A recapitulation of this scholarship illustrates that the tensions which characterize earlier publications continue to appear even though they are not necessarily explicitly theorized by Berlin, whose preoccupations varied with each publication. These tensions are cumulative, though, because in each publication, Berlin examines the individual subject and its relation to the world, and in so doing, attempts to supersede the inadequacies of previous cognitive maps. Therefore, while Berlin grappled with the issue of the nature of the individual subject and its relation to the world, he also never adequately theorized this.

In "Current-Traditional Rhetoric: Paradigm and Practice," the cognitive map consists of mind, reality, and the relation between the two across the communication triangle—reality/writer/audience/discourse. The algorithmic/heuristic/aleatory continuum acts as an interpretive benchmark for situating different rhetorics/writing processes. The characterization of epistemology as involving "concepts of the mind, reality, and the relation between the two" (1) emphasizes the individual, as does the notion that a good method of teaching writing begins with the writer. What this instruction of writing must do,

Berlin and Inkster say, is provide the writer the means to explore each of the elements of the communication triangle. The writer, then, is seemingly situated in this cognitive map at the starting place for all of Berlin and Inkster's subsequent considerations of rhetorics, writing processes, epistemologies, and pedagogies.

Regardless of this emphasis on the individual, this cognitive map reveals a tension over the nature of the individual/agency and its relation to the world. This tension impacts how teachers, students, and the curriculum are theorized. Ostensibly, Berlin and Inkster argue that different rhetorics/writing processes/pedagogies assume and impose differing worldviews on students, and this argument suggests that students are fully interpellated by whatever rhetoric/writing process/pedagogy the teacher promotes. But, if a student is fully interpellated by the teacher's pedagogy, what of the student's agency? Are we to assume that the student becomes sensitive to discourse only upon arrival to the writing classroom, never having before experienced the interpellative aspect of discourse? Or, are we to assume that a student walks into the classroom and then unproblematically adopts, of her/his own free will, the pedagogy her/his teacher has chosen for her/him? Any response to these questions is further complicated when we consider that the classroom is comprised of multiple students, who are presumed by this cognitive map to share a common epistemology.

As for teachers, Berlin and Inkster declare for themselves and other teachers that "we need to scrutinize carefully the epistemology implied by our practice in the teaching of composition" (14). This, along with the article's goal to persuade teachers to reconsider the rhetoric/writing process/pedagogy they use, strongly implies that Berlin and Inkster assume autonomy for teachers. This cognitive map suggests that teachers are capable of appropriating any rhetorical/writing process position on the algorithmic/heuristic/aleatory continuum and are capable of enacting its associated pedagogy unproblematically. This assumption points to another troublesome insinuation regarding curriculum, that the discourse of a specific rhetoric/writing process/pedagogy is "pure" and can be "purely" enacted by teachers in the classroom. I use the word *pure* here to suggest that an assumption inheres that language is an unproblematic representation. But, certainly, there is no allowance that discourse is characterized by conflict and that rhetorics/writing processes/pedagogies can be and perhaps are, unavoidably, conflated in practice. Teachers, then, are tacitly theorized to enjoy full autonomy, as they can not only choose and enact a specific rhetoric/writing process/pedagogy, but also are implied to have full control of the discourse of that specific rhetoric/writing process/pedagogy.

Other issues, such as the epistemological aspects of "truth" and "knowledge" also produce theoretical tension. Where is truth, who can get it, and how is it to be had? Where is knowledge, who can get it, and how does it come to be what it is? If truth or knowledge is universal, then neither rhetoric nor the student can do anything but attempt to represent it, and rhetoric and agency are both severely constrained. If, however, the student is able, through rhetoric, to make knowledge and truth, then a rather broad notion of agency as well as rhetoric inheres. But the notion that the student can make knowledge raises another issue. Is it knowledge merely because the student says it is, or must others agree that it is knowledge before it assumes that status? What is the role of the social in attributing knowledge its status? These are issues not directly addressed in this article but are ones that must have preoccupied Berlin, since he does attempt to address them in his next article.

In "Current-Traditional Rhetoric: Paradigm and Practice," tensions exist regarding the nature of the individual/agency and its relation to the issue of reality and the social, tensions that appear in the cognitive map. So, even though Berlin and Inkster have ostensibly foregrounded the individual/writer, both the nature of this individual and its relationship to the world remain problematic.

But, in the cognitive map that Berlin draws in "Contemporary Composition: The Major Pedagogical Theories," there is a much broader notion of epistemology that is folded into ideology through a greater emphasis on reality. Epistemology becomes epistemic complex. That is, rhetorics differ, according to Berlin, in the way writer, reality, audience, and language are conceived both separately and in relation. Writing processes thus differ due to the notion of rhetorical relationship that underlies, "at a deeper structural level" (765), each of the three composing stages, all of which represent the composite of epistemic complex. Each epistemic complex, moreover, prescribes rules regarding what can be known, how it can be known, and how it can be communicated. This cognitive map thus complicates the issues of reality and truth in a way they were not in "Current-Traditional Rhetoric: Paradigm and Practice."

In turning to a theory of the social, Berlin also distances himself from the mind/cognition individuality he used in "Current-Traditional Rhetoric: Paradigm and Practice." The "heuristic" position of the continuum that was previously depicted as the process of choice for an individual involved in "any kind of cognitive or creative act" is now displaced with the "hermeneutical" position that Berlin takes from Richard Rorty, where truth is located in "the product of individuals calling on the full range of their humanity, with esthetic and moral considerations given at least as much importance as any others" (777). "Truth," Berlin writes, "then stands forever a tribute to its method" (777). Note that truth is aligned with method and not to an individual nor even to a group of individuals.

Thus, although Berlin has now introduced a notion of the social into his cognitive map, the relationship of the individual (student/writer/teacher) to the social remains obscure. No less unresolved, then, are the tensions regarding both the nature of the individual and its relation to the world that were identified in "Current-Traditional Rhetoric: Paradigm and Practice."

Writing Instruction in Nineteenth-Century American Colleges sees a change in cognitive maps from those in "Contemporary Composition: The Major Pedagogical Theories." Whereas the former prescribed rules regarding what could be known, how it could be known, and how it could be communicated the latter grounds rhetoric in a noetic field: "a closed system defining what can, and cannot, be known; the nature of the knower; the nature of the relationship between the knower, the known, and the audience; and the nature of language" (2–3). So, whereas in "Contemporary Composition: The Major Pedagogical Theories" rhetoric prescribed ideology, rhetoric now is grounded in ideology, a move which enlarges the scope of rhetoric considerably but which also places rhetoric as hierarchically subsequent to ideology. This new relation between rhetoric and ideology may well have issued from one of Berlin's goals in this article, to argue for the centrality of rhetoric to a culture and the composition course as the medium, or rite of passage, from the known to the unknown.

This enlargement of the scope of rhetoric and the securing of composition's place in the curriculum, however, exacts a price. In "Contemporary Composition: The Major Pedagogical Theories," Berlin explicitly theorizes a notion of the social and, in the process, distances himself from the individual. In appropriating the notion of noetic field for this cognitive map, Berlin borrows from Ong, and through Ong, Pierre Teihard de Chardin, in order to make his arguments for the place of rhetoric and the composition course. Although Berlin may have wished to continue to distance himself from the notion of individual used in the cognitive map of "Current-Traditional Rhetoric: Paradigm and Practice," his argument for the centrality of rhetoric and the composition course is problematically and ironically accomplished by his subscription to a very humanist interpretation, one that privileges individuality, autonomy, and the possibility of transcendence.

Curiously, then, Berlin's turn to the social and its strong reliance on the role of ideology incorporates a tacit notion of the individual, to which is accorded a near god-like autonomy and totalizing degree of agency. With the cognitive map used here, therefore, we are no closer to a resolution of the tensions regarding both the nature of the individual and its relation to the world than when these were alluded in "Current-Traditional Rhetoric: Paradigm and Practice."

In *Rhetoric and Reality: Writing Instruction in American Colleges 1900–1985,* Berlin abandons the use of *noetic field* in his cognitive map and replaces it with *epistemology*. He chooses epistemology, rather than ideology, he says, because he wants to focus on the rhetorical properties, as distinct from the economic, social, or political properties, of the systems he considers. Moreover, he maintains that differences in rhetorics issue from differences in epistemology. Epistemology is characterized, however, differently than before. Now it encompasses assumptions about the very nature of the known, the knower, and the discourse community involved in considering the known. The addition of discourse community to this matrix thus allows Berlin to reconstitute a notion of the social that was compromised by his appropriation of *noetic field* in *Writing Instruction in Nineteenth-Century American Colleges.*

Now he explicitly incorporates ideology, which he insists is used merely as a descriptive and neutral notion, while literacy represents a wholly new addition to Berlin's cognitive maps. It is, however, arguable, as to whether Berlin is enveloping rhetoric into ideology or whether rhetoric and ideology are in competition. In any event, this ambiguity is resolved in Berlin's next article, as ideology does dominate there. But, here, Berlin writes that transformations of rhetorics are related to ideology or to larger social and political factors. In this matrix, epistemology explains differences in rhetorics in the discourse communities of classrooms; ideology explains transformations of rhetorics, which are tied to larger social and political developments; and literacy functions as intermediary between epistemology and ideology. Epistemology, it could be said, thus provides "assumptions" about reality, while ideology "constitutes" reality. Of individuals/students/writers, Berlin simply says that ideology designates the nature and role of individuals within the social and political structures of ideology. This does nothing to illuminate the problems located and previously discussed in "Current-Traditional Rhetoric: Paradigm and Practice," regarding the tensions between the nature of the individual and its relation to the world.

In "Rhetoric and Ideology in the Writing Class," Berlin's cognitive map is used to read particular rhetorics across economic, social, and political arrangements. No longer are changes in rhetorics caused by different epistemologies and/or different literacies, as rhetoric, its underlying epistemological structure, and its productive texts of literacy are subsumed within ideology. "Ideology," he writes, "provides the language to define the subject (the self), other subjects, the material world, and the relation of all of these to each other" (479). This, then, indirectly speaks to the issue of agency raised in the critique of "Current-Traditional Rhetoric: Paradigm and Practice" (1980), that is, to the tension between the power of ideology to interpellate and a subject's degree of agency: Is the power of ideology to interpellate total? If not, when is this the case and, more importantly, how is it the case? Based on Berlin's statement here regarding the function of ideology, we might well infer that subjects are fully, and without remainder, interpellated. Such a reading, however, again conflicts with Berlin's source of appropriation of the notion of ideology, which is taken from Therborn's usage. Of Therborn, Berlin writes that he maintains that subjects are, indeed, interpellated, but that they are not without access to resistance. Therborn calls upon Foucault's "micropolitics of power" without placing subjects within a seamless web of inescapable, wholly determinative power relations. Therborn, then, maintains that power can be identified and resisted in a meaningful way (478).

Nevertheless, even though Berlin nods to a notion of possible resistance through his appropriation of Therborn, a tension regarding the issue of agency, for example, that "ideology provides the language to define the subject" (479), continues to inhere in his cognitive map. One wonders if Berlin does not really harbor a closer ideological affinity to Althusser than to Therborn but perhaps elects to use Therborn to gain access to a notion of power as intrinsic to ideology, without having to access the fullness of Foucault's notion of knowledge/power relations. Suffice to say that the subject or individual is treated most directly in this cognitive map since Berlin's first cognitive mapping in "Current-Traditional Rhetoric: Paradigm and Practice." Nevertheless, the tensions that surround the nature of the individual subject and its relation to the world continue as unabated here as they were there and thus present a curiously circuitous route back to the thorn that abides in all of Berlin's cognitive maps: an unresolved notion of the individual subject and its relation to the world.

The analysis of this specific portion of Berlin's work regarding classification systems of writing process has yielded a rich array of notions imbricated in any notion of writing process: writer, reader, reality, language, discourse, epistemology, ideology, literacy, and their relationship, along with the social and political implications that inherently accrue. While it is interesting to speculate about the motivation that drove Berlin's various permutations of cognitive maps, I have focused specifically on how each functioned. I have identified tensions, which apparently contributed to the momentum that drove Berlin to reformulate his theories but which also were not resolved in this body of work.

Primary among these are the tensions dealing with the individual, the social, agency, and ideology. These tensions have repercussions for Berlin's original challenge to teachers: what degree of agency do students possess if they merely act as sponges of our chosen discourse? Conversely, if we assume that students can and will choose to adopt our pedagogical discourse of choice, what sort of agency are we to attribute to this possibility? What *is* the nature of the individual subject and its relation to the world? Given Berlin's impassioned calls that teachers be able to identify the writing process they use in the classroom, responses to these questions assume great urgency for teachers.

The tool Berlin offered teachers as a means by which to meet his calls—varied classification systems of writing process—represent notions of particular writing processes, as contained "wholes." This suggests a forced unity that is not without cost. Much of the richness and complexity of varied writing process theories must be forfeited to derive the categories by which such unities are achieved. Another cost of unity, alluded to earlier, is the assumption that teachers can unproblematically enact said unity in the classroom, that there can be no conflation of differing and competing writing process discourses in the classroom, and that students will be compelled to adopt the advocated discourse of choice. Putting aside the important question of the individual subject and its relation to the world, it would not be desirable to replicate any of the unities imposed by a writing process. Such a wholesale appropriation would preclude ethical consideration of a teacher's particular context.

Moreover, is a "good" teacher merely synonymous with a "good" pedagogical discourse? I do not think so, but an assumption in Berlin's work is that if teachers of writing will only utilize a particular classification category of writing process consciously—and I use "consciously" here rather than "reflexively" to differentiate degrees of critical awareness and thus different degrees of agency—then they will have progressed toward, if not achieved, his call for them to "recognize" the version of writing process they use, along with all of its broader implications. But mere recognition, even if a viable option, is not sufficient, for in addition to Berlin's call, we ought to also call for teachers to reflexively and evaluatively formulate a writing process(es) that most effectively suits the context in which their acts of teaching writing occurs, along with all of its ramifications. In reflexively and evaluatively *formulating* versus mere *recognizing*, teachers obtain greater degrees of professional and ethical agency that assumes their instantiated writing process(es) are formulated contextually. Teachers are thus not situated in a bind as to where or to whom they might look for the most enlightened version of pedagogy, the one, presumably, that they ought to intuit as the one worthy of "recognition." Instead, they presume a degree of agency that translates into the assumption of professional and ethical responsibility for their curricular decisions, along with the far-reaching social and political effects that accrue to those choices.

Admittedly, these tensions and issues in Berlin's work represent very real and material consequences for not only teachers and students but also for the larger culture. Nevertheless, the maps of these classification systems do provide a platform from which to articulate networked process, a platform comprised of the individual subject, the realm of the social/political, constructedness/agency, epistemology, ideology, the teaching of writing, the state of the discipline, and the ramifications of all of this for the larger culture. So, while Berlin's work in this period does not resolve the tensions among these issues, it does successfully explore a landscape that continues to compel us to complicate our notions of not only rhetorics and writing processes, but also how their constituent factors and sites co-exist. This networked relationship is meaningful, however, only in relation to individual subjects, which is the ground of possibility for the complex and dynamic relation of networked process to which we now turn our attention.[21]

3 Networked Subjectivity

Networked subjectivity functions similarly to Fredric Jameson's appropriation of Kevin Lynch's notion of cognitive mapping as a mitigation of contemporary alienation. Lynch, in his book *The Image of the City*, used the term *cognitive mapping* to describe a literal sort of mapping of a city's layout, based on his experiment of having people draw a mental or cognitive map of their urban environment on paper. His conclusion was that the more easily this was done, the less alienated people felt living in the city they mapped. As Jameson says, "Lynch suggests that urban alienation is directly proportional to the mental unmapability of local cityscapes" (415). Indeed, "the incapacity to map spatially," Jameson contends, "is as crippling to political experience as the analogous incapacity to map spatially is for urban experience" (416). People apparently feel themselves more grounded and less alienated when they are able to imagine their own location within the rest of the city. Similarly, as scholars and teachers, we too can be more effectively and more ethically grounded—we can exercise more rigorous evaluation and more thoughtful reflexivity of our curricular and pedagogical goals and objectives—when we are able to map ourselves (and perhaps our students) within our situated, partial, and contingent positions within networked process. Networked subjectivity offers this heuristic map.

Teaching writing involves teaching *a* writing process that, as the analysis of Berlin's cognitive mappings illustrates, is imbricated with many networked process sites, all of which exist relationally. Berlin insisted that an emphasis on any specific rhetorical element is trivial, but I argue that given the pragmatic nature of our educational enterprise, we are compelled to emphasize the rhetorical site of a thoroughly networked subject. This more complex articulation of subjectivity is important for us because students of any educational enterprise come to us not *tabula rasa* but as subjects whom we attempt to effect relative to specific purposes and goals, the end-goal of which is an ideal of some way we believe the student ought to be in the world.[22] Subjectivity is equally important to the entire range of networked process, specifically for notions of writing, writing processes, and the teaching of writing. All pedagogical manifestations instantiate a networked process by which we attempt to transform students into what we would have them be. Failure to include a theorized subjectivity of our students in our disciplinary and pedagogical maps promotes an alienation that threatens our ability to map ourselves relative to our own praxis.

Because any theory of writing is, at the least, tacitly concerned with the individual who writes, it is not particularly difficult to indict such theories for their privileging of the individual. It is far more difficult to ascertain how different theories of individuality or subjectivity are constructed and weighted relative within their network of relations. In this chapter, I offer a theory of the subject who writes, with a caveat: while the theory of networked subjectivity necessarily foregrounds individual subjectivity, this foregrounding should not be construed as a hierarchical privileging, but rather as a point of entry into the description of the complex networked process that is made by writing.

Subjectivity: Entering the Network

Subjectivity is tacitly implicated in all theorizing, but it is philosophers who have historically focused on the nature of the individual as an object of study. While this remains the case, the nature of the individual has also captured the attention of other disciplines, which have contributed their own notions in accord with their disciplines. These notions can serve as a generalized backdrop, while a look to rhetoric and composition scholarship can help to gauge and assess our own treatment of subjectivity.

In the period of the Enlightenment, the individual or subject was constructed as rational, self-determined, unified, and autonomous. Language was considered subsequent to consciousness, so individuals were conceived to be in control of discourse and themselves. Agency was thus total: "Modern theory—ranging from the philosophical project of Descartes, through the Enlightenment, to the social theory of Comte, Marx, Weber and others—is criticized for its search for a foundation of knowledge, for its universalizing and totalizing claims, for its hubris to supply apodictic truth, and for its allegedly fallacious rationalism" (Best and Kellner 4). But structuralists rejected humanism, and in their approach the subject "was dismissed, or radically decentered, as merely an effect of language, culture, or the unconscious, and [was] denied causal or creative efficacy" (19). The mind was believed to have an innate, universal structure and it was upon this that many structuralists focused.

Poststructuralists, however, claimed the subject to be a historical construction that has varied in different historical periods, and so they stressed the historical, political, and everyday (20). According to Steven Best and Douglas Kellner, "both structuralists and post-structuralists abandon the subject," but with post-structuralists, there is an interest in how individuals are constituted as subjects (24). Lacan, for example, "argues that subjectivity emerged in the entrance of the individual into the symbolic of language, while Althusser theorized the 'interpellation' of individuals in ideology, whereby they were called to identify with certain subject positions" (24).

Postmodernists reject totalizing theory as Enlightenment rationality and characterize it as reductive; they argue that it obscures the nature of the social and politically suppresses plurality, diversity, and individuality "in favour of conformity and homogeneity" (Best and Kellner 38). Postmodernists, Best and Kellner write, "valorize incommensurability, difference, and fragmentation as the antidotes to repressive modern modes of theory and rationality" (38). Theorists of postmodernity, such as Baudrillard, Lyotard, and Harvey claim that cultural processes involving new technology, new knowledges, and altered social and economic conditions create new modes of subjectivity (3).

As most would agree, Derrida, Baudrillard, and Lyotard have posited notions to undermine universal theories and have also been criticized for lacking a political component by disallowing the subject a degree of resistance. While this might be conceded for the case of Baudrillard, who writes, "everywhere, in whatever political, biological, psychological, media domain, where the distinction between poles can no longer be maintained, one enters into simulation, and hence into absolute manipulation—no passivity but the *non-distinction of active and passive*" (366). But neither Derrida, whom I discuss directly, nor Lyotard precludes agency altogether. Lyotard, for example, writes: "a *self* does not amount to much, but no self is an island; each exists in a fabric of relations that is now more complex and mobile than ever before" (15). Moreover, he views subjects as located at "nodal points," or at posts through which all sorts of messages pass. But no one, he says, "not even the least privileged among us, is ever entirely powerless over the messages that traverse and position him [sic] at the post of sender, addressee, or referent" (15).

Foucault explores how humans are made into subjects in our culture. Techniques of power, he says, are felt in the everydayness of life, "which categorizes the individual, marks him [sic] by his own individuality, attaches him to his own identity, imposes a law of truth on him which he must recognize and which others have to recognize in him" ("The Subject" 781). Still, he says, "it would not be possible for power relations to exist without points of insubordination which, by definition, are means of escape" (794).[23]

Althusser contends individuals are hailed into existence by various "ideological state apparatuses" and are thus interpellated into the economic system based on the values and beliefs of the ruling class (158). Ideology functions to recruit subjects, transforming individuals into subjects through an operation, he says, "I have called *interpellation* or *hailing*" (174). Ideology is eternal, he writes, saying that "I must now suppress the temporal form in which I have presented the functioning of ideology, and say: ideology has always-already interpellated individuals as subjects [. . . so that] *individuals are always-already subjects*" (175–76). Therefore, while the degree of agency that Althusser concedes is arguable, the window that does exist for it in his theory is narrow.

Jameson argues, according to Dominic LaCapra, that due to the diminished quality of historicity in our culture, it is difficult for us to locate ourselves in a meaningful way, thus we lose a sense of both personal and community history. This leaves us isolated in the moment, which Jameson, borrowing from Lacan, characterizes with his notion of the schizophrenic. Isolated in the moment without a means for making meaning, or decentered, individualism is thus impossible since no continuous individual identity can be named. Jameson, however, does concede there are multiple ways for being in the world, but his notion of the schizophrenic renders subjectivity a relatively moot issue.

Feminists are wary of a wholesale appropriation of postmodernism, since it mitigates notions of resistance. Nevertheless, feminists, too, are divided in their perspectives of what postmodern theory can offer, especially in the area of subjectivity and agency. Teresa Ebert, for example, maintains that while postmodern theories have the potential to usurp, they cannot sustain resistance; thus, she resists an incorporation of postmodern theory into feminist theory. Seyla Benhabib, however, advocates a more accepting yet cautious approach, as she criticizes the strong version of postmodernism for announcing the death of man, history, and metaphysics in one fell swoop, undermining as it does "concepts of selfhood, agency, and autonomy" that emancipatory ideals require. But Benhabib is also wary of essentialized subjectivity, since it elides notions of difference and is imperious to criticism. Therefore, she says that although postmodernist positions regarding the subject, "thought through to their conclusions," might threaten feminist theory and challenge the emancipatory ideals of women's movements, there are, nevertheless, "points of convergence" (231). Benhabib thus proposes a weak version of postmodernism for feminist theory. Rather than a position that would constitute the "dissolution of the subject into yet another position in language" where intentionality, accountability, self-reflexivity and autonomy disappear, she situates the subject "in the context of various social, linguistic and discursive practices" (214).

In feminist theory, issues of subjectivity often do revolve around notions of essentialism, which are voiced in critiques of identity. bell hooks addresses this, writing that because it is as subject one achieves voice, it might seem that a critique of identity threatens to silence those who have been subjected to colonization and domination. "It never surprises me," she writes, "when black folks respond to the critique of essentialism, especially when it denies the validity of identity politics by saying, 'Yeah, it's easy to give up identity, when you got one'" ("Postmodern" 515). She asks: "Should we not be suspicious of postmodern critiques of the 'subject' when they surface at a historical moment when many subjugated people feel themselves coming to voice for the first time?" (515). But such a comeback, she maintains, while apt and even often appropriate, nevertheless fails to engage the discourse in a way that can alter or transform it. Thus, hooks views the critique of identity as an opportunity for African-Americans to reformulate outmoded notions of identity imposed from both outside and inside reductive notions of blackness. The postmodern critique of identity, which challenges a universal, static, and overdetermined identity, she says, "can open up new possibilities for the construction of self and the assertion of agency" (515). Regarding the fear that a critique of identity forfeits African-American history and experience, as well as the culture and sensibility that issue from this experience, hooks responds by saying that such a critique can be conducted while emphasizing the significance of "the authority of experience" (516). "There is a radical difference," she writes, "between a repudiation of the idea that there is a black 'essence' and [a] recognition of the way black identity has been specifically constituted in the experience of exile and struggle" (516). hooks, then, avidly defends agency and believes postmodern notions of subjectivity create spaces for resistance and for producing new racial and gendered meanings.

Teresa de Lauretis, too, embraces theory that would provide new readings of women subjects. She argues that to define women subjects, we must look to specific, situated contexts, as well as to the contradictions that obtain in the social arena. Woman subjects cannot be understood, she says, with the narrative of "femininity as a privileged nearness to nature, the body, or the unconscious," nor in a conception of the feminine as private and marginalized, nor even in "the chinks and cracks of masculinity, the fissures of male identity" (*Feminist* 256). We must, instead, practice self-reflexivity regarding the relations of the subject in the social and historical sphere, informed by a notion of the political and theoretical (256). Like hooks, she rejects an essentialist approach and looks beyond the boundaries of feminist theory to re-imagine the possibilities of subjectivity for women.

Two feminists, Helene Cixous and Donna Haraway, transform how women might resist the subjectivities they presently inhabit. Their arguments suggest ways marginalized individuals reformulate subjectivity. Cixous makes writing synonymous with the body, so that in order to claim their bodies, women must write themselves into the text. While this end is local, there is also a universal element, as Cixous believes that writing the individual body contributes to the constitution of a "universal woman subject," whose purpose is to "bring women to their sense and to their meaning in history." Cixous advocates women be the "sowers of disorder" relative to the power of the "symbolic," that women do not have to buy into lack, into the "religion of the father," into the negative. It is time, she says, to "explode" and "dislocate" the "within" in the discourse of man (1240). While Cixous's notion of the female subject can be critiqued as being overdetermined, the imagination of the practice, as well as the subject position it would enable, is nevertheless intriguing.

A more radical practice and subject position is posited by Donna Haraway, who believes the notion of the cyborg offers women a way to resist traditional Western binaries through a celebration of fragmentation. The cyborg, in this vision, is the ontology that provides its own politics: it disregards distinctions between the private and the public; it has no stake in the community; it has no origin; it has no investment in reunification. Multiple perspectives of this world yield different scenarios. From one perspective, it represents "the final abstraction," or "the final appropriation of women's bodies," while from another, it represents an altered social and bodily reality, as people put their fear of a conflation of animal and machine aside and embrace partial identities and contradictory positions (154). Haraway's proposal is equally as vulnerable to critique as Cixous's, but it, too, is valuable in its disavowal of essentialism and its enthusiasm for the potential of resistance through an appropriation of multiple and contradictory subject positions.

Relative to education, Paulo Freire advocates a specific goal for subject formation in radical pedagogy: "*integration* with one's context, as distinguished from *adaptation*" (*Education* 4). Integration, he says, entails the capacity "to adapt oneself to reality *plus* the critical capacity to make choices and to transform that reality," which is a "distinctively human activity" (4). Freire's notion of the subject is in some degree constructed, yet it retains the necessary agency to participate in making meaning.

Adopting Freire's notion of subject formation, Diana George and Diana Shoos nominate it as a way to radically reformulate relationships between teachers and students and thus create a dialogic framework for the classroom, where it becomes "the site of exchange and reciprocity" (296). As teachers, they say, we are advised to view subjectivity as fluid, not static, with the value of this notion for the composition classroom being that it revises the poststructuralist notion of subjectivity as fully constructed to one that allows the subject to actively intervene in meaning-making. Peter McLaren, too, advocates adapting Freire's notion of the subject, writing that "even though human subjectivity is not an irreducible nexus of action, desire, belief, and intention, individuals can still act as 'contrary antagonists' to the education system and its role as a cultural medium for acceptance, passivity, and accommodation" (11). George, Shoos, and McLaren thus adopt a notion of subjectivity that not only recognizes but encourages the agency necessary for both resistance and the production of new meaning.

Others in rhetoric and composition are critical of a notion of the subject often posited for students. Marilyn Cooper and Linda Brodkey, for example, are critical of a view of the writer as lone artist, while Reed Way Dasenbrock calls for situating the subject socially and historically. He argues that "we need to broaden our interdisciplinary conversation to include new, less reductive concepts of the self and its relation to society and tradition" ("The Myths" 30–31). The issue of the subject has thus long been recognized as an underexplored notion in our field. While some in rhetoric and composition have suggested notions of the subject, many maintain that there is still a void in our theorizing.

James Berlin has suggested a notion of the subject reminiscent of Althusser's notion of interpellation. Writing that the subject serves as "a point of conjuncture for a plethora of discourses inscribed in the personal of the individual" ("Composition Studies" 2), Berlin says these discourses, which pre-exist us, also interpellate us, providing "scripts" regarding behavior and conduct and address such categories as race, class, and gender. While material conditions also contribute to our shaping, he says these, too, are mediated by discourse. Berlin's position, however, as discussed previously, is problematic because of the conflict between the degree of agency he concedes to a universal notion of the subject on the one hand and the situated composition student on the other.

Marshall Alcorn contributes to a critique of Berlin's theory and addresses the void he believes continues to exist in our field regarding subjectivity. Although he largely agrees with the postmodernist composition program Berlin advocates, he also believes it is "important to argue that the human subject is more complex than Berlin and others theorize" (331). Current notions of the subject, he maintains, are "insufficiently complex for understanding relationships among language, subjectivity, and ideology" (332). Robert Yagelski similarly argues that the key to reconciling process with postmodern thinking is a reconceptualization of the self. We must, he maintains, reconcile our notions of writing process with a new understanding of discourse as a social and cultural activity. Both Alcorn and Yagelski thus call for a transformation in the field's conceptualizations of the subject, but

Yagelski, significantly, addresses this need specifically for notions of writing process.

Curiously, perhaps, at least a partial re-imagining of the notion of the subject can be found in Barry Brummett's 1976 discussion of subjectivity in terms of reality and meaning. He argues that because reality is not objective, things cannot be defined objectively; they can be defined only by their contexts. But because contexts consist of different elements which draw upon the context for their meaning, everything in the context both defines and is defined by all others. This has relevance to each person: "I can define those things that in turn define me" (29). Therefore, Brummett says, "if contexts give meaning, then the meaning of a person or thing or idea is constantly changing" (29). People are engaged in various contexts, all of which are defined differently, so the contexts by which one is defined are always changing. He calls this view of reality "process." In this instantiated act of intertextuality, Brummett's notions indirectly anticipate and support the notion of multiple subjectivity, the subject as subjected and subjecting, and a degree of agency for the subject. Nevertheless, while Brummett's work speaks to the justification for a reformulation of the notion of subject, more recent rhetoric and composition research continues to not only press this as an issue but to also elevate it as a priority that our field ought to address.

Lester Faigley articulates what is perhaps the most forceful and urgent call for a reformulation of the subject in his book *Fragments of Rationality*. Faigley maintains it is the question of the subject that fuels many of our conflicts within composition studies (225), arguing that "one of the chief sites, if not the primary site, for scholarly debates is the subjectivity of the student writer" (16). Pervading our everyday teaching practices, he says, is the belief in a rational, unified subject, in a modern Cartesian notion of the self as an autonomous individual, free to choose and thus totally responsible for its outcomes. "Many of the fault lines in composition studies," he concludes, "are disagreements over the subjectivities that teachers of writing want students to occupy" (17). Faigley thus situates the issue of subjectivity as primary to our disciplinarity and to our teaching practices.

But it is the research of Marguerite Helmers that speaks most movingly of the ramifications that accrue to pedagogy, classrooms, teachers, and, especially, to students as a result of our inability to strike upon a transformative notion of the student-subject. She writes that her research of student representations in published teacher-research indicates that students "are named with first names, but their characters are not necessary to the development of the plot" (37). She argues we need to envision new ways to represent students.

> While varying epistemological outlooks informed the terms by which students were described in testimonials, pervasive modes of representation that characterize them as those who lack, are deviant, or suffer from excess remain stable enough to suggest that power relationships between students and teachers can be reversed neither by a change in epistemology [. . .] nor by an alteration of ethos (authoritarian to student-centered). In the final analysis, it would appear that composition must negotiate its own academic troubles before its discourse may reflect a change in attitude toward students. (149)

Inadequate representations of students, Helmers suggests, reverberate throughout the field and are thus manifest in many other issues (networked process sites) with which we are concerned.

Postmodernist discourse has put into question the very notion of the subject, which has fueled rhetoric and composition's historical concern for the student-writer in productive ways. However, the field has yet to adequately address a notion of student-subjectivity that places the student in a relation to itself, others, and the world. A new set of statements for networked process is needed, a set that can transform our notion of the individual student and the webbed relations with which and in which it exists.

Articulating Networked Process: Mapping Networked Subjectivity

Figure 2 is a visual depiction of networked subjectivity, meant to indicate that the subject exists in an imbricated relationship with discourse, others, and the world.[24] To explain this mapping, I combine specific features and discuss them separately from the rest, for example, space/time/history. This will be visually represented in the form of an overlay, and by the conclusion of the discussion, the map of networked subjectivity will be intact. Note that while I focus discus-

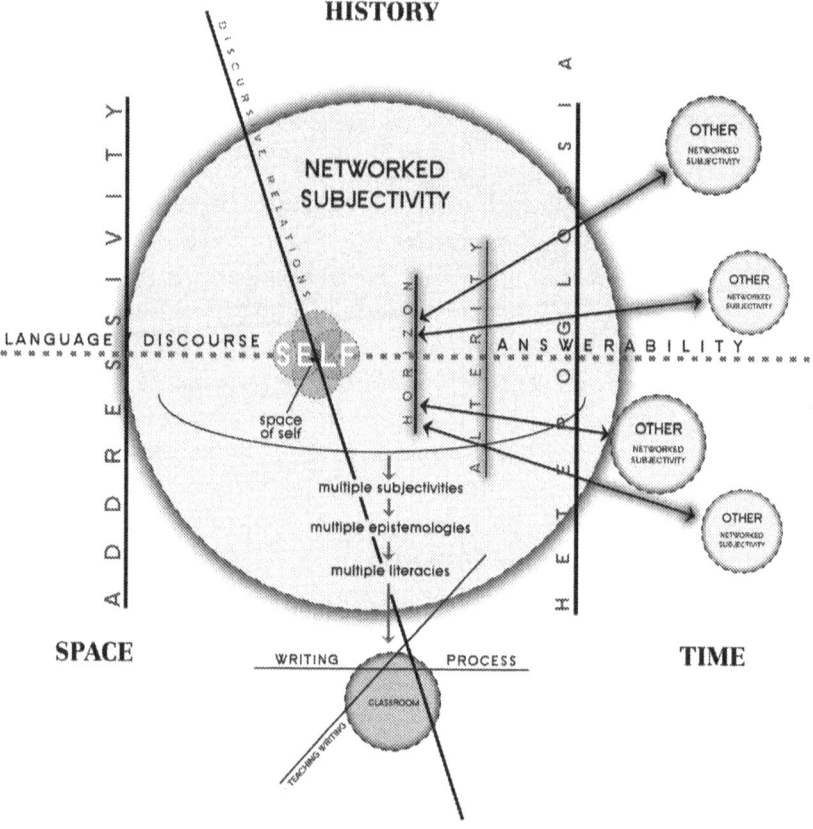

Figure 2. Networked Subjectivity.

sion on the specific features being addressed, content will necessarily overlap. Because these features are mutually dependent, this overlap is unavoidable.

The philosophy of language used for this mapping is appropriated from Mikhail Bakhtin, whose work is problematic for reasons that fall beyond the scope of this project.[25] Bakhtin, however, was an eclectic thinker and the author of a large body of work whose ideas were in a constant state of dialogue. As a result, his ideas underwent various transformations.[26] My own interpretation of Bakhtin is informed by Don Bialostosky's comment that judgments about Bakhtin's work "depend at least as much on how their authors understand 'rhetoric' as on how they understand Bakhtin" (65). Because networked subjectivity is discussed piece-meal, Bakhtin's full philosophy of language will not be realized in the discussion of any specific element in the model. Rather, this fuller notion of Bakhtin appears only in the complete discussion of networked subjectivity.

Space/Time/History

As depicted in Figure 3, I have not visually bound subjectivity by a world context beyond that of space, time, and history, as these are phenomena common to every subject. Thus, this discussion of networked subjectivity begins with a description of the subject's relation to time, space, and history, as a ground. That is, I seek to physically place the subject in the world and then account for the subject's relation to time. To do so, I borrow from Bakhtin the same *a priori* upon which his work depends: a law of physical placement and a conclusion

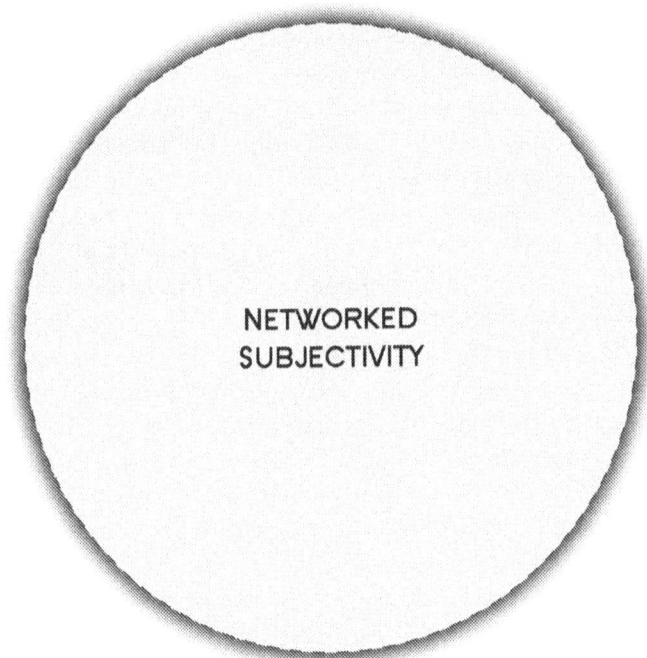

Figure 3. Space/Time/History.

from Einstein's thought experiments in relativity, that the perception of time is relative to the system to which it refers. We may, for example, register the passage of time according to a clock, or to a context of mutually shared events, or we may register it according to a calendar. In any event, the registration of a passage of time is relative, or conceptual and pragmatic, rather than absolute. What remains absolute, however, is the impossibility that any two physical bodies can simultaneously share the same space. This, then, is the *a priori* of networked subjectivity that I hereby propose: a subject occupies an absolute and unique space/place in the world but organizes passages of time according to socially conventional constructs.

Language/Discourse

To suggest a model of subjectivity, one that is rhetorically networked, one that positions the subject in a context and suggests its nature and relationship to itself and to the world, as well as the mode by which this is realized, it is fruitful to begin with a focus on language itself. To talk about language is to talk about how things mean. To talk about the subject is to talk about how the subject means: how it means to itself, how it means to the world, and, ultimately, how our disciplinary sites of interest can be situated in this relation of meaning.

This investigation thus begins with a look at various theories of language. This is not to say that these theories exist in a causal relationship to the development of rhetoric and composition, but, rather, that since linguists and philosophers share with us a concern for language and its relationship to meaning, these theories exist as a discourse with which rhetoric and composition has been and continues to be in dialogue. These notions of language are thus chosen to illustrate the range of ideas that variously circulate.

Relative to rhetoric and composition, an enduring notion of language that has informed writing instruction in this country is current-traditional rhetoric, the heritage and history of which is complex and debated. Nevertheless, its institutionalization into the academy has privileged reason and reduced composing to an unproblematic, linear process. Discourse is posited as natural. As Sharon Crowley notes, a writer's thought process, assumed to be natural to all normal people, would insure that any "right-thinking" person could get it down right the first time (*The Methodical* 157). Thus, there is faith that knowledge, suitably packaged, can eliminate disagreements among rational, right-thinking persons (157). This packaging favors the discourse of exposition, which Crowley says effectively eliminates differences of opinion. Writing in this theoretical approach is viewed neither as a mode of learning nor as action, as language is assumed to unproblematically represent the writer's thinking and intention.

Semiology, an influential linguistic theory of language formulated by Ferdinand de Saussure, posits that language is comprised of a closed system of signs whose meaning is arbitrary. A sign, comprised of a signifier (specific mark and sound) and a signified (specific concept), derives its meaning through its difference from other signs within the system. A sign accrues meaning relative to what it is not, or, as Saussure writes, "In language, there are only differences *without positive terms*" (120). The relationship between signifier and signified is arbitrary, then, because meaning can only be found within the context of the semiotic system itself. Such a conception of language, however, mitigates notions of rhetoric. Indeed, Louise Rosenblatt writes that Saussure's theory represents a Nietzschean view of "the prison-house of language," where "both author and reader are seen as simply conduits for arbitrary codes, conventions, and genres" (381). Within the parameters of Saussure's configuration, she says, the efforts of process and reader-response theorists, alike, "to do justice to the individual or personal" were and are frustrated. So, while Saussure's theory is beneficial to the extent that it negates a reductive correspondence notion between signifier and signified, the sign is nevertheless arhetorical, as it bears no relation to the cultural context in which it is used and thus carries no social or historical trace.

Speech-act theories, such as that proposed by J. L. Austin, attempt to take a broader view of language, with a focus on everyday language and its function within specific contexts. Speech-act theory, however, is criticized for not having a full notion of writing, since its focus is the spoken utterance, and writing, some maintain, requires a different theoretical model. Derrida, for example, is especially critical of Austin's notion of the performative, which among other things, he says, assumes "a context to be exhaustively determinable," since the speaker's "conscious intention would at the very least have to be totally present and immediately transparent to itself and to others, since it is a determining center of context" ("Signature Event Context" 192). Nevertheless, as Reed Way Dasenbrock says, Austin's work bears upon the concerns of our field, as he suggested that words do things in addition to merely referring to them (54). The importance of Austin's work, then, is his rhetorical view of language as constituting a mode of acting in the world, as well as a mode for merely reflecting upon it.

But it is the philosophical work of Charles Sanders Peirce that ushers into the conversation a more nuanced rhetorical conception of how language functions to mean in a culture. Peirce describes the sign as "something which stands to somebody in some respect or capacity. It addresses somebody, that is, it creates in the mind of that person an equivalent sign or perhaps a more developed sign" (5). Peirce's conception of the sign is thus triadic, consisting of the sign, its referent, and the "interpretant," where "interpretant" is not equated with a literal, physical interpreter but represents a new sign created by the interpreter in the process of understanding, of making meaning. This notion stands in contradistinction to Saussure's notion that meaning is derived only in relation to the system in which the sign is part. Instead, Peirce's notion insists rather that meaning derives from how the sign characterizes its referent along with the human action that subsequently transpires. Teresa de Lauretis describes it this way: For Peirce, she says, "the 'outer world' enters into semiosis at both ends of the signifying process: first through the object, more specifically the 'dynamic object,' and second through the final interpretant" (39).

In Peirce's system, then, signs bear an arbitrary relation to their referent, and, most importantly, are conditioned by the context in which they are used. Sign systems can never be stable, as signs carry traces of multiple interpretations, all of which are conditioned by the context of interpretation or by differing cultural conventions. This relationship between cultural contexts, the sign, and interpretation indicates that meaning, likewise, is not stable and it is this constant engendering of signs/contexts/interpretations that contributes to the changes that we read as history. But while Peirce's theory does much to advance a more complex rhetorical conception of discourse, it only indirectly addresses the relationship of language to the subject.

Because the student has too long been tacitly conceived as a monolith construct, Mikhail Bakhtin's philosophy of language is useful to how we might conceive the nature of the student and his/her relationship to the world, as well as to how the various sites of networked process are implied into this relation. Bakhtin's theory of language, of the utterance, provides a means by which to dialogize our way into a thoroughly rhetorical, networked notion of subjectivity, to understand the subject's rhetorical nature and relationship to the world. Because our disciplinary sites of concern are rhetorical, as Berlin has surely demonstrated, such an understanding can help us to conceive how these sites integrate with this relation.

Bakhtin is not interested in what he calls an abstract approach to language, which is the view for which he criticizes linguistics. His interest lies with the utterance, which he equates to an event, a deed, an action, and which is produced through a sort of language that we would now characterize as discourse. Bakhtin distinguishes the language of the linguist, which he compares to words in a dictionary, from situated language use, that is, the language a person appropriates and directs toward another person in a specific context. Bakhtin focuses on language used in discourse to produce an utterance.

Fundamental to his notion of language or discourse is his theory of dialogism, which posits that language is characterized by degrees of sameness and difference. The pole of sameness is monologic, which functions as a centripetal force within discourse and which Bakhtin says represents the discourse of religion, the state, or the parent. Dogmatic thought, he writes, is "like a fish in an aquarium, [that] knocks against the bottom and the sides and cannot swim farther or deeper" (*Speech* 162). "The monologue," he says, "is accomplished and deaf to the other's response; it does not await it and does not grant it any *decisive* force" (qtd. in Todorov 107). Monologue, then, ignores the other, pretending to be "the *last word*," which is why "to some extent it objectivizes all reality" (qtd. in Todorov 107). It is important to note, however, that the monologic tendency in discourse can never be fully realized.

In contradistinction to monologism's centripetal impulse is the centrifugal force of heteroglossia:

> Language is not an abstract system of normative forms but rather a concrete heteroglot conception of the world. All words have the "taste" of a profession, a genre, a tendency, a party, a particular work, a particular person, a generation, an age group, the day and hour. Each word tastes of the context and contexts in which it has lived its socially charged life; all words and forms are populated by intentions. Contextual overtones (generic, tendentious, individualistic) are inevitable in the word. (*Dialogic* 293)

This heteroglot notion of language is visually represented in Figure 4, which situates language/discourse as (1) that which comes to the subject from the world, (2) that with which the subject must grapple to make meaning, and (3) that which then the subject struggles to approximate to its own intentions, as it speaks to the world and, in the process, makes its own contribution to the rich heteroglot nature of discourse. Heteroglossia thus insures two things. The first is that discourse is unique in each instance of utterance, that is, "as an utterance or part of an utterance, no one sentence, even if it has only one word, can ever be repeated: it is always a new utterance (even if it is a quotation)" (*Speech* 108). The second is that discourse is both thoroughly social and political, a situation that obtains through the notion of dialogism.

Bakhtin conceives of dialogism as a relational triad, composed of (1) the utterance, (2) the centripetal and centrifugal forces that obtain in language and that exist in relation, along a sort of continuum, and (3)

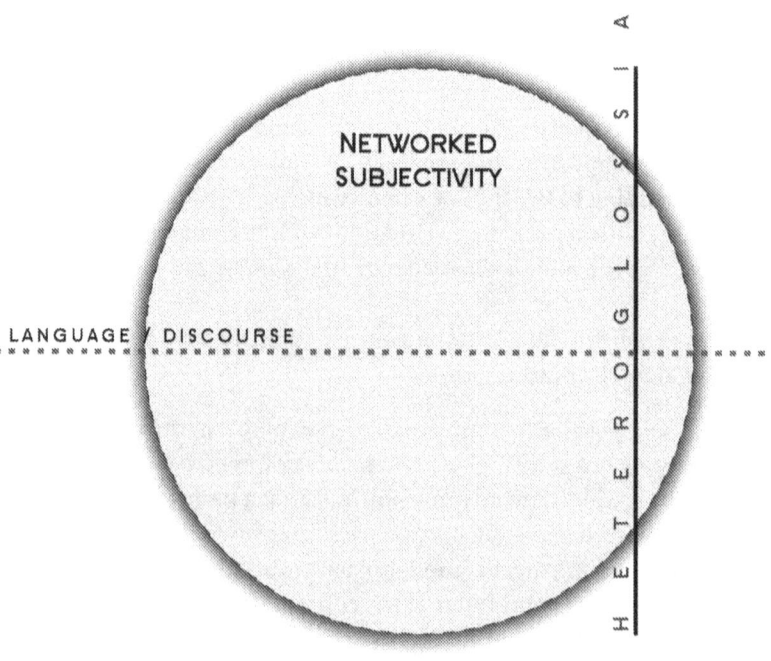

Figure 4. Language/Discourse.

the heteroglot mediation of these two forces, whose relationship fluctuates ceaselessly. The only absolute in this triad, Bakhtin maintains, is the fluctuation itself. How this mediation occurs will be addressed subsequently. Suffice to say now that the social and political effects of heteroglossia are achieved not merely because dialogized language partakes of the opposing wills of two subjects and their ideologies, but also because the opposition is itself reconceptualized through social heteroglossia. Bakhtin concludes that dialogized heteroglossia can thus never be fully "exhausted" (*Dialogic* 326). Discourse is characterized by a sort of power relation in which centrifugal and centripetal forces compete endlessly in dynamic relation; the ratio that fluctuates between them renders the relation thoroughly dialogic. Last, a strong ethic also inheres in Bakhtin's theory, as human subjects are compelled to impose order and form on their lives, an architectonic act that can be accomplished only through dialogic mediation.[27]

Therefore, while both Peirce and Bakhtin focus on the relationship of language and meaning, the ground of Peirce's theory remains the sign, while for Bakhtin, the ground is the relationship itself. As Bakhtin writes: "No natural phenomenon has 'meaning,' only signs (including words) have meaning. Therefore, any study of signs, regardless of the direction in which it may subsequently proceed, necessarily begins with understanding" (*Speech* 113) and "the relation to *meaning* is always dialogic. Even understanding itself is dialogic" (121). Meaning, then, may be studied with a focus on the sign, but understanding must begin with a focus on the language user, the subject.

The last theorist of discourse I discuss is Jacques Derrida. I do so because I wish to draw attention not to "samenesses" between Bakhtin and Derrida, but to point to some resonance between the theories of both, specifically, with Derrida's notion of *différance*. Writing in *Positions*, Derrida defines *différance* thusly:

> First, *différance* refers to the (active and passive) movement that consists in deferring by means of delay, delegation, reprieve, referral, detour, postponement, reserving. [. . .] Second, the movement of *différance* as that which produces different things, that which differentiates, is the common root of all the oppositional concepts that mark our language. (8–9)

So, *différance*, conceived as a noun, envelops a sense of deferring, "the action of putting off until later," and the sense of differing, "to be not identical to the other" (*Margins* 8), while as a verb, it is characterized as "the name we might give to the 'active,' moving discord of different forces, and of differences of forces" (*Writing* 18). This quality of language is not totally unlike what Bakhtin envisions the function of heteroglossia as serving, that is, he says heteroglossia mediates between opposing forces in language, this mediation constitutes an act, it can never be fully exhausted, and it works to constantly reconceptualize the word, which Bakhtin says can never be repeated. There is, then, a strong sense of opposition and deferral in Bakhtin's notion of dialogism.

A significant difference between the two theorists, however, is the philosophy each brings to these theories. Derrida's purpose is to critique Western foundational meaning, or what he refers to as "the metaphysics of presence." His notion of *différance* acts to destabilize interpretation and thus meaning through the position that these are culturally context dependent. His interest, however, is not with the cultural context, itself, but rather with the methodology *différance* inspires. Conversely, while Bakhtin's theory is heavily informed by difference, as will soon become even more apparent, this difference is celebrated precisely because it enables interpretation, even though he says that interpretation is never stable.

Additionally, Derrida's theory is criticized for its apolitical quality, which is arguable. Nevertheless, Bakhtin's approach is thoroughly social, political, and ethical, again, precisely because he dares, happily and joyously, to dangerously inhabit the boundary of Derrida's "metaphysics of presence" abyss. Bakhtin, in other words, dares to theorize the user of language, which is not at all the same as saying that the subject is the ground of language. But language as used by subjects in culturally constructed contexts is marked by struggle, which contributes to lend a rich social and political aspect to Bakhtin's philosophy of language, and by extrapolation, to us, to students, and to networked process. Writing about Bakhtin's theory in "The Violence of Rhetoric," Teresa de Lauretis says his "conception of the sign as open and porous both to its object and to the other sign systems that surround it provides us with a semiotic model of representation that is at once fully historicized and politically inflected" (36).

The role and function of discourse, then, is a pivotal, constituent component in how individual and cultural meaning obtains. As such, it must be factored in any notion of the relationship of the subject to writing and to the world. These concerns are inherent to the rhetorical positions we assume, and they carry real consequences for our notions of subjects and our various, disciplinary sites. For example, constructivist notions of rhetoric view rhetoric as more than just the communication of thought, a perspective that leads to a more complex theory of writing. For when language is viewed as constructing reality in addition to communicating it, writing must be viewed as action as well as a skill with which to mediate that action. Social constructivist notions of rhetoric theorize the relationship of the writer to language, suggesting that individuals are effects of context-dependent cultural discourse groups and that knowledge is a function of the conventions within these groups. Social-epistemic notions extend the function of rhetoric even further, articulating a pivotal epistemological role for rhetoric. Not only does rhetoric construct the reality and the subject, but it also constructs the relations among subjects, relations that nominate the conventions that constitute and legitimize systems of knowledge. Cultural studies marshals the social and political ramifications of these approaches to rhetoric in order to examine representation in the everydayness of individuals' lives. Each of these approaches assumes something a little different about the role and function of language. As such, each recommends varying notions of writing. Thus, it is only through a complex notion of language, the language user, and the context in which that language is enacted that we can hope to fully gauge what our notions of networked process really constitute.

Self

Of utmost importance to any notion of rhetoric and writing is this: If the subject's networked subjectivity is the effect of a process, that is, of being written by language, rather than an inherent characteristic, how then does the subject achieve agency? How can we posit that writing is action without allowing some degree of agency to the writer? Although subjects are constituted in large part by language, thereby creating a condition of "sameness," there is also an element of self that renders each subject "different," the mediation of which suggests agency and thus partakes of an ethic. The question of agency depends on the capacity to impose and deduce meaning.

Note in the map, Figure 5, four interlocking circles, which create a center margin of shared space. This shared space, the "space of the self," represents a notion of the self's agency. Both the size and the location of this representation are arbitrary, as I make no case for the degree of agency that obtains to subjects, since the degree of their agency depends upon the degree of mediation each subject is able to accomplish within the historical, cultural contexts of their physical lives. Significantly, a variety of scholars have spoken to some notion of the self, but it is the concept of dialogism that is most influential to my notion of self and agency.

As discussed by Western philosophy, and according to Professor E. J. Lowe in *The Oxford Companion to Philosophy*, the word "self" is used interchangeably with the word "person" and emphasizes the inner or psychological dimension of personality. The self, he says, "is conceived

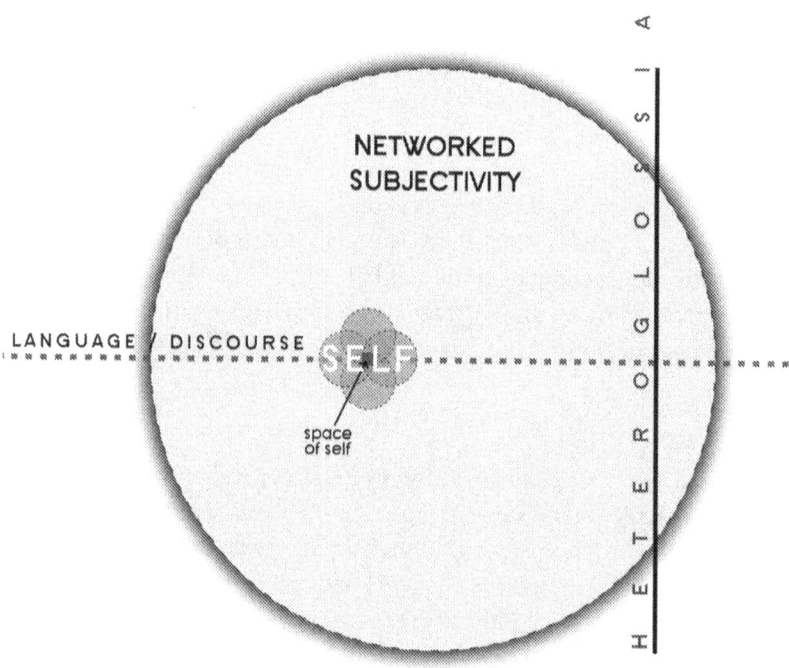

Figure 5. Self.

to be a subject of consciousness, as being capable of thought and experience and able to engage in deliberative action" (816). The self, then, has a capacity for self-consciousness, which is indicative of a capacity for first-person thought and first-person knowledge.

Professor Owen Flannagan of Duke University, however, contends that "there is heated debate over what exactly consciousness is, whether, or if so how, it can be studied; what if anything its causal role is; and whether, despite the fact that it is so far always realized in biological systems, it must be so realized" (152). Flannagan, therefore, recommends thinking of consciousness as conscious mental states rather than as some unified entity. Consciousness, he reminds us, because it involves experience and awareness, indicates that "mental life has a phenomenal side, a subjective side" (152). In any discussion of the self, then, it must be conceded that the self does have a subjective side, which must necessarily render anyone's discussion of the self subjective as well. This is unavoidable.

And, of course, any discussion of the self is vulnerable to Derrida's critique of metaphysics. Dobrin argues that Derrida sees consciousness as constituted through language; thus, the privileging of the mind is a function of language and thus a construct. This circularity renders metaphysics or consciousness a myth, just one more mere construct of language (34). But even Derrida, who has shown the space where meaning is made to be metaphysical, nevertheless concedes this metaphysical space is a necessary condition for the use of language. Derrida avoids susceptibility to this charge as far as possible, while Bakhtin actively engages and negotiates the boundaries of the metaphysical.

Bakhtin also maintains that existence precedes consciousness, that we are physically present before we are self-consciously so. He writes:

> All that touches me comes to my consciousness—beginning with my name—from the outside world, passing through the mouths of others (from the mother, etc.), with their intonation, their affective tonality, and their values. At first I am conscious of myself only through others: they give me the words, the forms, and the tonality that constitute my first image of myself. . . . Just as the body is initially formed in the womb of the mother (in her body), so human consciousness awakens surrounded by the consciousness of others. (qtd. in Todorov 96)

Bakhtin does concede, therefore, that consciousness is constituted through language. Moreover, while there is certainly metaphysical yearning in Bakhtin's notions, he, like Derrida, recognizes this impulse as utopian.[28] Still, it is implied in the very notion of dialogism, whose mediating ratio fluctuates constantly. But this ratio circumscribes the possibility of realizing an absolute state, a unification, a totality. Because it cannot be measured, we are, indeed, squarely back in the realm of the subjective.

Bakhtin also maintains that just as language is bestowed, it must also be appropriated in order to mediate the gap between subjects. That is, the gap emerges because subjects cannot simultaneously inhabit the same space, cannot experience time uniformly, and cannot eradicate the gap between inner and outer self. Existence, according to Bakhtin, is not a given or a privilege. Because this appropriation is marked by struggle, and because language precedes and constitutes consciousness, consciousness is itself thoroughly dialogic.

Two problems arise, however, in the subject's appropriation of language. One is that no subject can control all the social and political contexts that surround language, that is, heteroglossia. Thus, it is difficult, in Bakhtin's terminology, to make the word serve the deed or event, which he equates to an utterance. A second difficulty ensues, he says, due to the pronominal "I," which unlike other words, has no specific referent. "I" refers to anyone who appropriates it, thus Bakhtin characterizes this appropriation as the subject's attempt to establish consciousness. The subject must struggle to attempt to define itself within the limitations of its own contexts, that is, to attempt a unified totality. It is an attempt that can never be fully realized, Bakhtin says, because my idea of "I" is always in the form of an image, "a concept of an experience, a sensation, and so forth" (*Speech* 146). My "I" cannot encompass all of me precisely because it is a changeable phenomenon according to the shaping events that constitute my life. Paradoxically, then, while the "I" is the subject's only alternative to assume totality, it is also inherently marked by limitation, which insures that the self can never completely coincide with itself.

To illustrate this non-coincidence, Bakhtin uses the analogy of a person looking into a mirror: I do not coincide with the mirror image because I recognize and intuit that I am not fully represented in the mirror, that something larger is not contained in the image (*Speech* 146). "The mirror," he says, "is incapable of capturing all of me," so

"I am both in front of the mirror and not in front of it" (*Art* 32). Nevertheless, although the gap between inner and outer self can never be closed, it can be mediated to move this relation to a more positive ratio of totality.

Refusal of the self to appropriate the "I," to assume its responsibility to itself, precludes its assumption of responsibility to the world, to an assumption of its ethical position relative to the world (this will be covered in greater detail in the section on addressivity and answerability). "The *I* hides in the other and in others," Bakhtin says, and "wants to be only an other for others [. . .] to cast from itself the burden of being the only *I* in the world" (*Speech* 147). When this happens, the self can have a dialogic relation neither with itself nor with another subject. The self's refusal to assume the "I" thus results in limitation, a closing in of consciousness, which is equivalent to a monologic relationship with one's self.[29]

The means to mediate the gaps between inner and outer self, as well as between subjects, is language and perception. Words, Bakhtin says, although they receive the categorical distinction of being either one subject's or another's, live on the boundary between subjects. This boundary, due to dialogic struggle, is constantly in flux (142), because language is "not a neutral medium that passes freely and easily into the private property of the speaker's intentions [because] it is populated—overpopulated—with the intentions of others" (*Dialogic* 294). Moreover, each utterance constitutes a language system with two poles, the first of which represents all that is repeatable and reproducible or all that conforms to the language system (*Speech* 105), while the second pole represents all that is unique and unrepeatable or all that which renders the utterance its significance, its plan and purpose (105). The first pole, Bakhtin says, is, therefore, only a "means to an end," while the second pole he compares to the "semantic (signifying) unrepeatability of the fingerprint" (106). "The text (as distinct from the language as a system of means)," can thus, he says, "never be completely translated, for there is no potential single text of texts" (106). "Expropriating it [language], forcing it to submit to one's own intentions and accents, is," Bakhtin says, "a difficult and complicated process" (*Dialogic* 294), a process of dialogic struggle enacted on the boundary between subjects, but one which makes participation a necessity.

Another requirement of mediation between inner and outer self and between subjects is what Bakhtin calls responsive understanding, which is prefaced by shallow understanding. Defined as "an exact and passive reflexion, of a redoubling of the other's experience within me," shallow understanding serves as a bridge to active, responsive understanding, which, Bakhtin says, is "a matter of translating the experience into an altogether different axiological perspective, into new categories of evaluation and formulation" (qtd. in Todorov 22). "Responsive understanding is a fundamental force," he says, "one that discourse senses as resistance or support enriching the discourse" (*Art* 280–81). Because active, responsive understanding also requires evaluation, Bakhtin considers understanding and evaluation as constituting "a unified integral act" (*Speech* 142). Active understanding, then, promotes dialogism in that it reveals the "multiplicity of [. . . the utterance's] meaning" and acts as a supplement that "continues creativity" (142). "The object [consciousness] is [thus] created in the process of creativity" (120), which explains the necessity of the self's participation in dialogic struggle.

The notion of process also refers to Bakhtin's belief that self-consciousness is perpetually active and allows nothing to escape it. "It renews the life of those experiences which tend to fall away and become consummated," he says, and "that is what constitutes my responsibility, my fidelity to myself with respect to my own future" (*Art* 125). Experience, then, is remembered not only for its literal content but also for its yet-to-be-achieved meaning. Axiological remembering, Bakhtin says, enables me to "renew the still-to-be-achieved character of every-one of my experiences" (126). Unified totality, therefore, always lies in the yet-to-be achieved, so all that is positive in this unity represents a task and all that is negative is the literal and static given (126).

It is the hope for meaning, Bakhtin says, that keeps life in motion, as "the center of gravity in this world is located in the future, in what is desired, in what ought to be, and *not* in the self-sufficient givenness of an object" (*Art* 98). The organizing principle of consciousness, Bakhtin says, is the self-consciousness that relative to what is of most importance, the self does not yet exist, that is, "I cannot count and add up all myself, saying: this is *all* of me—there is *nothing more* anywhere else or in anything else; I already exist *in full*" (127). According to Bakhtin, then, even though ultimate meaning is constantly deferred, we nevertheless strive toward it, with the knowledge that it is unattainable. This represents a task or a process, an ethical process, and one with which we have no choice but to engage. As Bakhtin writes, "Life is dialogical by its very nature. To live means to engage in dialogue, to question, to listen, to answer, to agree, etc." (qtd. in Todorov 97), and "for the word (and, consequently, for a human being) there is nothing more terrible than a *lack of response*" (*Speech* 127).

I call your attention again to the space of the self, which is represented as the nexus of four interlocking open circles in Figure 6.

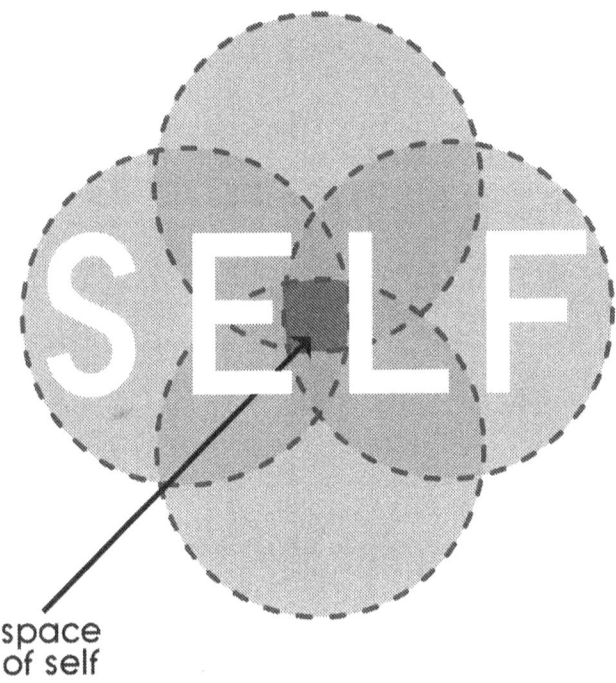

Figure 6. Space of the Self.

These circles, as well as their number, too, are arbitrary, as what they suggest is that forces combine to render a unique aspect to each subject, which is not transcendental, nor unified, nor autonomous. Rather, it could be equated similarly to Bakhtin: more as a space of becoming, where meaning is, ideally, continually acted upon and enlarged. Generally speaking, these four open circles represent the cognitive, affective, biological, and psychological. But these are arbitrary designations, which should figure into any configuration of the self, but which are not the only factors that could or should be included. Others speak to an awareness of the self and to factors that comprise it, factors that can increase the understanding of how the self might be conceived.

For example, Kathleen Kirby offers a cautionary perspective, preferring to leave the psychological space of the subject open, because, she says, "I suspect that it is inside in the dark matter of the unconscious, or in its better-lit annex, consciousness, that we begin untying and reweaving the threads of cultural logic, manipulating them to suit our own purposes so that we can then project our patterns back on reality" (34–35). She thus considers it necessary to conceptualize subjectivity as "a place where we live, a space we are, on the one hand, compelled to occupy, and, on the other hand, as a space whose interiority affords a place for reaction and response" (34–35). While Kirby is reluctant to explain exactly what might constitute the self, she nevertheless views it as a unique space that functions as a mode of mediation, as a reciprocity between public and private meaning making.

Evelyn Ashton-Jones and Dene Kay Thomas positively endorse the contributions of Piaget and Vygotsky. They attest to the benefits of exploring both the idiosyncratic and the social involved in the constitution of the self. Piaget, they argue, believed the development of morality requires only the presence of peers, a position that "pitted himself against the received view, often looking at the forms of the child's knowledge that were idiosyncratic to the child" (291). Original thought, then, and not shared thought, was one aspect of his focus, which, they say, helped many to "break out of the received view" (291). Conversely, Vygotsky promoted a deeper understanding of the social nature of language and thought, as he explored "the role of language and community in the development of thought and how language operates both internally and externally" (291). Jones and Thomas appreciate the dialogue that increases the breadth and depth of understanding regarding the nature and functioning of language and thought, for here the realm of the idiosyncratic, the social, and internal/external factors are conceded to contribute to a fuller understanding of what a self might be.

A more specific factor contributing to the constitution of the self is bell hooks's contrast of "authority of experience" with "passion of experience." According to Diana Fuss, hooks believes we discount the "passion of experience," which is mainly about suffering and which Fuss describes as "a way of knowing that is often expressed through the body, what it knows, what has been deeply inscribed on it through experience" (91). Fuss recommends that pain, physical and emotional and psychic, be registered as components that contribute to constitute a self.

Karl Mannheim, however, takes a broader survey of the self. In *Ideology and Utopia,* he writes that

> all these three factors, the nature and structure of the process of dealing with life-situations, the subjects' own make-up (in his [sic] biological as well as historical-social aspects), and the peculiarity of the conditions of life, especially the place and position of the thinker—all these influence the results of thought. But they also condition the ideal of truth which this living being is able to construct from the products of though. (298)

Mannheim's perspective does not explore mode, but it does offer suggestions of what influences the constitution of the self and, more importantly, it suggests a reciprocity of conditioning between public and private. Here, then, is a notion of the self as situated, partial, and contingent.

Another interesting area for inclusion into the fabric of the self is the senses, specifically, sight. Long an obsession of Western philosophy and a major motif in contemporary feminist issues, the role of sight complicates the self in productive ways. Martin Jay, for example, concedes that antiocularcentric discourse has argued successfully regarding the status of visuality in the dominant cultural traditions of the West. This critique, he believes, has been beneficial since it has accomplished the following:

> It has weakened any residual belief in the claim that thought can be disentangled entirely from the sensual mediations through which it passes, or that language can be shorn entirely of its sensual metaphoricality. It has shown the cost of assuming the eye, however it is understood, is a privileged medium of knowledge or an innocent instrument in human interaction. It has also highlighted the ways in which the concomitant

> denigration of other senses brings with it certain cultural losses that warrant redress. Finally, it has posed the vital question, how open is our sensual interaction with the world to radical change? (589–90)

Jay, too, thus offers a cautionary tale, this one regarding a premature dismissal of the visual and its relationship to the other senses, to language, and to the body. "When 'the' story of the eye is understood as a polyphonic—or rather, polyscopic—narrative," he says, "we are in less danger of being trapped in an evil empire of the gaze, fixated in a single mirror stage of development, or frozen by the medusan, ontologizing look of the other. Permanently 'downcast eyes' are no solution to these and other dangers of visual experience" (592). Cognition and the senses are thus complexly and reciprocally cast by Jay as factors that should enter a notion of the self. In describing the complexities of visuality and thus visual experience itself Jay also complicates the self in productive ways.

Jonathan Crary also complicates the visual by adding a political element to the individual and social elements associated with visuality and visual experience with his historical investigation of the reorganization of vision in the first half of the nineteenth century. The effect of this reorganization, he says, was that a new sort of observer was produced. Crary argues that "problems of vision then, as now, were fundamentally questions about the body and the operation of social power" (3). Certainly, these individual, social, and political concerns regarding visuality, as well as its relationship to the other senses and to language, have great potential for adding richness to notions of the self.

Finally, Malcolm Budd provides a more traditional philosophical investigation of sight in "Wittgenstein on Seeing Aspects" by calling on Wittgenstein to argue that the phenomenon of seeing is polymorphous in nature due to "its irreducibility either to a purely sensory or to a purely intellectual paradigm" (17). Wittgenstein's concept of "noticing an aspect" has to do with the way our "seeing" of an aspect of a thing sometimes changes, even though the thing itself is no different than it was (1). "The philosophical importance of noticing an aspect," Budd says, "is crucial to a conception of the mind—a point from which radiates in all directions across the psychological field of phenomena" (2). The question is the kind and degree of relation between the sensory and the intellectual. Wittgenstein, he says, wrestled with the "noticing an aspect" issue, as he questioned if the transition from one "seeing experience" to another was the result in "a change *in the experience itself*" and, if so, if such a change would "exemplify a difference in *seeing* rather than a difference merely in *interpretation*" (10). But the question of whether seeing an aspect is seeing or interpreting, Budd says, "is not as all-embracing as the question of whether it is seeing or thinking" (11). I would maintain that Budd's theorizing, from our current vantage point, could benefit from a complex notion of rhetoric, along with Jay's and McCrary's work, and Heisenberg's work in quantum physics (Zukav). Nevertheless, it remains important for the questions it poses to the issue of the self and how it derives meaning and organizes itself relative to itself, to others, and to the world.

A notion of the self is not definitive. At most, we can suggest possibilities that might accrue to contribute to some portion of a self's unique nature. Maintaining some degree of the unique for the self is not tantamount to claiming for it transcendence, unification, or autonomy. It is, however, to claim for it a space for agency, for acting with and upon the world. It is to claim for the student-subject a space to engage in a productive act of writing. Although a reciprocity necessarily obtains between the inner/outer self, there can never be complete coincidence of the two, a situation that thus precludes transcendence, unification, or autonomy. But the mediation of the gap between the inner/outer self, which is imbricated in the gap between self/other and which is addressed in Bakhtin's discussion of alterity, provides further support to the argument that some measure of the self is unique, constituting a portion of the space from which agency obtains.

Alterity/Other/Horizon

Sydney Shoemaker, writing in *Identity, Cause, and Mind*, says that while some believe self-consciousness is consciousness of a particular kind of object, the self, another perspective is that just as the eye cannot see itself, the self (where self is understood as a subject of awareness) cannot be aware of itself as an object. For Schopenhauer, he says, the idea that the self can be an object unto itself is a contradiction. Shoemaker says a more cautious argument, however, is that "the core of the intuitive notion of self-consciousness is what might be called *introspective* self-awareness, and that one cannot be introspectively aware of oneself as an object" (qtd. in Cassam 817). That is, when one is conscious of oneself as an object (such as when you see yourself in a mirror), one must identify the presented object as oneself. But identification, he says, carries with it the possibility of misidentification, so that first-person statements based on this type of awareness are not immune to error relative to the pronominal "I." The paradox, Shoemaker says, is that it seems to be a requirement of introspective self-awareness that it must be able to ground first-person statements, thus providing immunity to this kind of error.

Shoemaker, then, addresses necessity indirectly in his description of this paradox. In response to this problem, Bakhtin recommends dialogism as a mode for mediation of the gap between inner and outer self and between the subject and other, both of which gaps are inevitably and permanently entangled in the same web of necessity. As Bakhtin writes, "I cannot do without the other; I cannot become myself without the other; I must find myself in the other, finding the other in me (in mutual reflection and perception)" (qtd. in Todorov 96).

The subject thus finds itself, as well as others, through the dialogic quality of language. Initially, it is the language of others that provides the subject with consciousness, while subsequent to consciousness, it is necessary for the subject to continually struggle to appropriate language from the other, as it is this action that insures mediation between both inner/outer self and subject/other. This process is necessary in that language is no more a given than is existence: "The word (or in general any sign)," Bakhtin says, "is [always] interindividual" (*Speech* 121), so that "no utterance in general can be attributed to the speaker exclusively; it is the *product of the interaction of the interlocutors*" (qtd. in Todorov 30). The dialogic nature of language inheres through (1) the subject's initial requirement that language be supplied by the other, and (2) the struggle that ensues as the subject struggles to appropriate and shape language to its intentions. Bakhtin expresses it thusly:

> Language, for the individual consciousness, lies on the borderline between oneself and the other. The word in language is half someone else's. It becomes "one's own" only when the speaker populates it with his own intention, his own accent, when he appropriates the word, adapting it to his own semantic and expressive intention. Prior to this moment of appropriation, the word does not exist in a neutral and impersonal language (it is not, after all, out of a dictionary that the speaker gets his words!), but rather it exists

> in other people's mouths, in other people's contexts, serving other people's intentions: it is from there that one must take the word and make it one's own. (*Dialogic* 293–94)

The subject's struggle to appropriate from others' language, saturated in heteroglossia, so as to issue an utterance, then, is a profoundly social and political experience. But this constitutes necessity because language is not a given, not a privilege, and it is language that provides the subject with the means to attempt to impose order on its existence.

But yet another tandem appropriation from the other is necessary to a subject's efforts to order its existence. This involves the appropriation of vision, which simultaneously mediates the gaps of inner/outer self and subject/other. Appropriation of vision is a necessity because the gap between inner and outer self inheres, Bakhtin says, due to the subject's space and time constraints, along with the limitation of one's self-perception that obtains in these constraints. That is, because the subject's existence is ordered by time and space, which precludes a complete coincidence of these categories with any other subject, subjects have no alternative but to order existence differently from other subjects. Thus a unique perspective to each subject within a shared context is ensured, a situation Bakhtin calls the law of placement, a term that says what we see and perceive is contingent upon our physical place within a situation. I, for example, can see aspects of a context that you cannot, while you can see aspects of it that I cannot, a situation Bakhtin refers to as a surplus of seeing.

Each subject requires this surplus of seeing due to the non-coincidence between inner and outer self. A subject's vision, limited by the physical and conceptual reality that each subject constitutes the center of his/her own universe, requires that the subject must order its existence differently from all others. Thus the subject distinguishes reality according to the center, that is, its own consciousness, and all that is not the center, that is, the realm in which all others exist as objects. To achieve total coincidence with one's self, a subject would have to fully conceptualize her/himself as an object, which is a physical and thus conceptual impossibility. All the subject can do is to appropriate the surplus vision of others in order to strive toward a full approximation of itself as an object. I must attempt to alter my position, conceptually in order to construe what it is you see that I do not, and you, likewise, must do the same. This represents the process, the ideal situation, by which the subject attempts, through appropriated discourse and vision, to perceive itself as an object.

Each subject, therefore, structures both the setting of the world and the position of others–what Bakhtin calls environment—according to the situation of their unique position in it, so that the place of perception shapes the meaning of that perception. The place of perception Bakhtin calls horizon, which constitutes the context from which the subject authors her/his utterances and which is visually represented in Figure 7. Horizon thus encompasses conceptual as well as physical aspects of a context, which Voloshinov calls the "extraverbal context of the utterance" (qtd. in Todorov 42). He says this context is composed of three aspects: "(1) the spatial *horizon common* to the interlocutors (the unity of the visible: the room, the window, etc.); (2) *knowledge and understanding of the situation,* also *common* to both; [and] (3) their *common evaluation* of the situation" (qtd. in Todorov

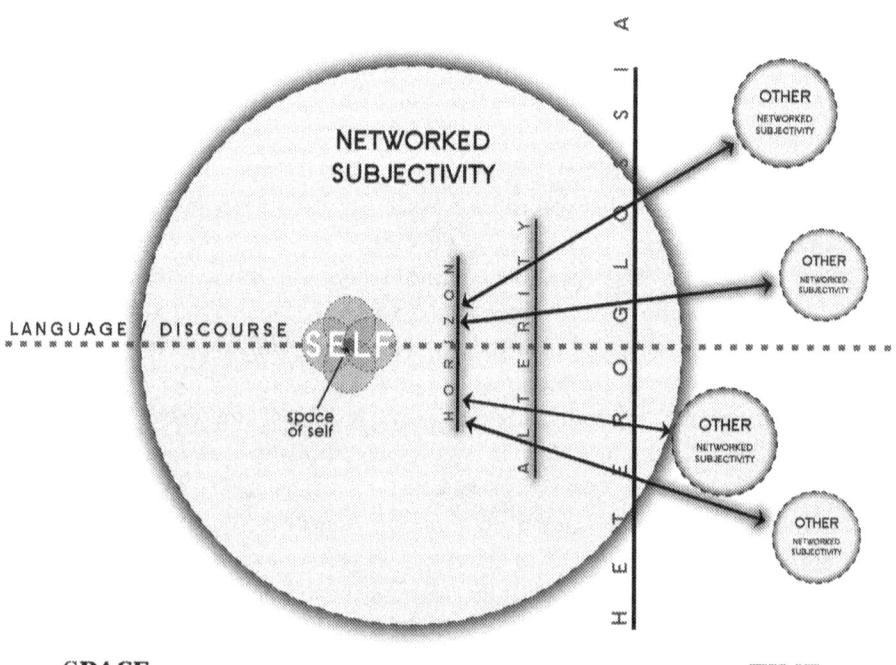

Figure 7. Alterity/Other/Horizon.

42). Horizon is thus profoundly characterized by reciprocity, or alterity, which Bakhtin maintains is the only source of enrichment:

> If there are two of us, what matters from the point of view of the actual productivity of the event is not that alongside of me there is *yet one more* man, essentially *similar* to me (*two men*) but that he is, for me, an *other* man. In this way, his simple sympathy for my life is not tantamount to our fusing into a single being and it does not constitute a numerical duplication of any life, but an essential enrichment of the event. Because the other co-experiences my life in a new form, as the life of an other man, perceived and valorized otherwise, and justified in a way other than his life. The productivity of the event does not lie in the fusion of all into one, but in the tension of my extopy and my nonfusion, in the reliance upon the privilege afforded me by my unique position, outside other men. (qtd. in Todorov 108)

A subject's utterances, then, are thoroughly social, as "no utterance in general," Bakhtin says, "can be attributed to the speaker exclusively; it is the *product of the interaction of the interlocutors*, and broadly speaking, the product of the whole complex *social situation* in which it has occurred" (qtd. in Todorov 30). Horizon thus comprises the fullness of context from which each subject forms an utterance, which is what Bakhtin says we do at every moment: "we appraise ourselves from the point of view of others, we attempt to understand the transgredient moments of our very consciousness and to take them into account through the other . . . ; in a word, constantly and intensely, we oversee and apprehend the reflection of our life in the plane of consciousness of other men" (qtd. in Todorov 94). Utterances issue from a subject located within a unique horizon but also inevitably partake of the imbrication of each interlocutor's horizon. This is the process of alterity, which is visually represented in Figure 7 through the interactive arrows, indicating the relationship between "horizon" and "other." All of this interaction emanates from language/discourse and which thus intersects heteroglossia.

Due to its fundamental dialogic nature, the subject in existence is never whole and unified, and therefore its coexistence with the environment and others is a necessity. "I achieve self-consciousness, I become myself only by revealing myself to another, through another and with another's help," so that "the most important acts, constitutive of self-consciousness," Bakhtin says, "are determined by their relation to another consciousness" (qtd. in Todorov 96). I need your alterity; you need mine. Without it, we cannot realize self-consciousness; we cannot exist as subjects.

Addressivity/Answerability

Dialogism is a fundamental feature of existence and is thus inherently political due to the struggle of this relation. It is social as well, in that nothing exists only for itself. The political struggle—suggested by terms like event, deed, action, and response—emphasizes that existence can never be passive either. Likewise, dialogism's social aspect cannot be passive, and Bakhtin's term for this social aspect is addressivity. Each of us, he says, is addressed by the world, and the subject, responsible for its unique position in space, has no recourse but to answer. This necessity is visually represented in Figure 8, which situates addressivity in the world, outside the subject, but which is depicted as compelling the subject, through language/discourse, to an act of answerability ultimately directed back to the world.

Addressivity, Bakhtin says, is thus an essential quality of the response, of the utterance itself:

> This addressee can be an immediate participant-interlocutor in an everyday dialogue, a differentiated collective of specialists in some particular area of cultural communication, a more or less differentiated public, ethnic group, contemporaries, like-minded people, opponents and enemies, a subordinate, a superior, someone who is lower, higher, familiar, foreign, and so forth. And it can also be an indefinite, unconcretized *other* [. . .]. All these varieties and conceptions of the addressee are determined by that area of human activity and everyday life to which the given utterance is related. Both the composition and, particularly, the style of the utterance depend on those to whom the utterance is addressed, how the speaker (or writer) senses and imagines his addressees, and the force of their effect on the utterance. (*Speech* 95)

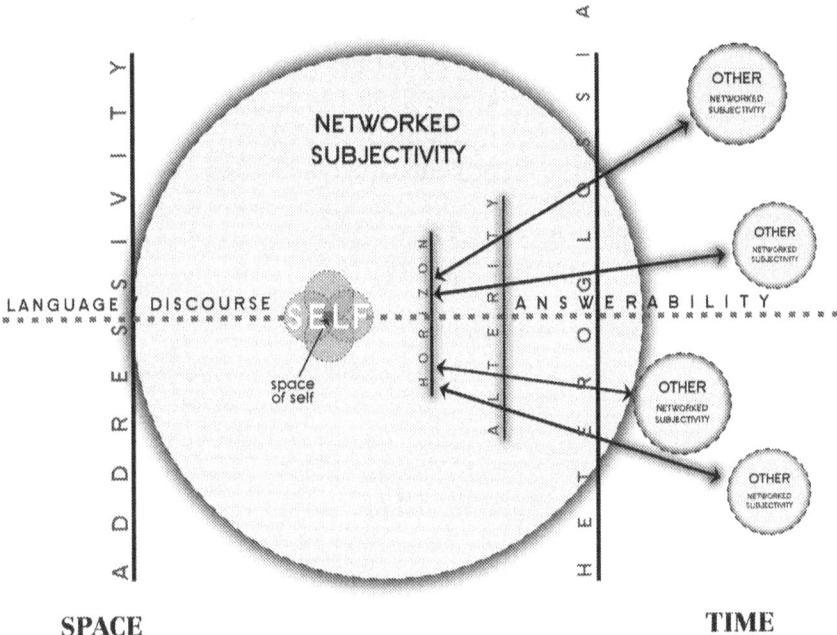

Figure 8. Addressivity/Answerability.

Addressees, then, are the equivalent of the world, and the response or answer to which Bakhtin refers is called "authoring," so that each subject is addressed and thus compelled to author its unique position in space, in the world. No subject can answer for another nor can any subject abdicate, for a refusal to answer nevertheless constitutes an answer. Bakhtin refers to this necessity of the subject to author its position as having no alibi in existence.

Bakhtin equates answerability to a performance, that is, to the action of authoring, which is constituted by a subject's struggle to impose form upon its own time and space. Meaning is accomplished in tandem with the act of answerability, and values accrue as patterns of meanings accrue. Moreover, authoring for Bakhtin constitutes an architectonic as well as an aesthetic, as both are concerned with the relation of parts to whole. Bakhtin offers this situation to characterize the architectonic of answerability:

> If I tell (orally or in writing) an event that I have just lived, insofar as I "*am telling*" this event, I find myself already outside of the time-space where the event occurred. To identify oneself absolutely with oneself, to identify one's "I" with the "I" that I tell [is] as impossible as to lift oneself up by one's hair. The represented universe can never be chronotopically identical with the real universe where the representation occurs, and where the author-creator of this representation is to be found. (qtd. in Todorov 52)

Therefore, according to Bakhtin, "pure everyday life is a fiction, a product of the intellect [so that] human life is always shaped" (*Speech* 154). Of course, the other is always imbricated in this shaping of the life, as text, for as Bakhtin writes, "the event of the life of the text always develops *on the boundary between two consciousnesses, two subjects*" (*Speech* 106). Through the architectonic of answerability, then, the subject takes responsibility for itself in existence and, in this act, acquires and constructs meaning and value to its life.

Answerability is thus social and political, as well as ethical, since it envelops the meaning and value we impose on our existence. We cannot exist outside of this necessity, Voloshinov says, for, as he writes:

> There is no such thing as abstract biological personality [. . .]. *Human personality becomes historically real and culturally productive only insofar as it is part of a social whole, in its class and through its class.* To enter into history, it is not enough to be born physically—that is the way of animals, yet they do not enter history. A second birth, *social* this time, is necessary as it were. A human being is not born in the guise of an abstract biological organism, but as a landowner or a peasant, a bourgeois or a proletarian, and that is of the essence. Then, he is born Russian or French, and finally he is born in 1800 or in 1900. Only such a social and historical localization makes man real, and determines the content of his personal and cultural creation. (qtd. in Todorov 30–31)

Answerability, then, speaks to not only the shaping of the subject's personality and its social and political imbrication in the whole culture, it also speaks to the ethic of situating that shaping from a partial and contingent position. Indeed, as Bakhtin says, "a human act is a potential text and can be understood [. . .] only in the dialogic context of its time" (*Speech* 107).

Answerability as authoring or as utterance constitutes an event or an act that is also ethical in nature, since it is the process and not the product that constitutes the ethic. None of these actions is discrete, as each is a necessity of the other, so it is advantageous to think of them as comprising a relational network. Existence is neither a given nor a privilege but a responsibility of the subject to author itself both for itself and for the world. Existence, then, is dialogic, in that answerability represents the mediation between the gap of subject and the world.

Networked Process: Networked Subjectivity and Writing Process(es)

Some notion of the self, of agency, is necessary to any conception of rhetoric that views writing as learning and as action. In this mapping, I have speculated as to some of the factors that may coalesce in some degree of individuality beyond the biological. Due to our unique place in the world, each of us is privy to a unique world context, or horizon. This situatedness colors our reading of reality, which then colors the meaning, value, and order we attempt to impose on our lives. This sort of notion of the self is necessary to our conception of the student-writer, if indeed we view writing as a mode of learning and as action.

Straddling the notion of "writer," however, is the notion of alterity, with which a conception of "other," or reader/audience is also imbricated. We cannot achieve consciousness without an "other," and the language or discourse that we appropriate in order to impose form on our lives issues from "others," so that the value we elicit for ourselves is also dependent on "others." And Bakhtin maintains that even when our language/discourse has no tangible audience, that is, when, for example, we write in a private diary or journal, we nevertheless tacitly imagine what he calls a superaddressee and we direct our writing toward this conceptual audience. A superaddressee is anyone/thing with perfect understanding and thus that with which we imagine to seamlessly communicate. It is a concept of the "perfect" reader, whom, perhaps, we imagine understands us better than we do ourselves. But important to note in the notion of alterity is the doubling operation inherent in its function. One cannot do/be without one's "other"; likewise, that other cannot do/be without an "other." Writing, then, is never a wholly individual act. Some notion of an "other" or an audience is always a prerequisite.

Without language and discourse, no subject could achieve consciousness and without consciousness there would be no mode by which to recognize, much less "read," the unique rhetorical situation in which each subject finds itself in the world. Also, the language by which consciousness is constituted is rife with conflict, with centripetal and centrifugal impulses that function to render discourse more or less monologic or dialogic, the ratio of which is constantly in flux. Language is, therefore, the building-block of consciousness and thus of reality. Language is not static; as Kenneth Burke reminds us, no one can legislate it.

The nature of language also supports the notion that some aspect of the self is unique, because language, according to Bakhtin, is rendered unique in each and every instance of use because of its intrinsic heteroglot composition. Language is arbitrary, and the subject must struggle to make the word serve the writing deed, understanding that a perfect correspondence between intention and word is impossible. The struggle immanent in the act of writing, therefore, speaks to some notion of agency. It also portends ramifications for networked process(es), as the will to struggle to communicate with an other, to make meaning, is very much at issue in notions of writing process.

Equally at issue with both networked subjectivity and networked process is the ethic of authoring. We are addressed by the world and we are responsible for answering or authoring the space of the physical place we occupy in it. We must assist others to achieve consciousness and make meaning for themselves, in order to have those same things accrue to ourselves. We can do so only through the reciprocity intrinsic to alterity and thus to authoring as well. Our authoring literally constitutes the meaning that has aggregated to our lived lives, meaning constantly in flux because to live is to be embroiled in a process of meaning-making. Addressivity, then, acts as a sort of exigency, which authoring both contributes to constitute and answer.

Relative to networked process, the notions of addressivity and answerability resonate in the concepts of *kairos* and *stasis*. James Kinneavy describes *kairos* as "the appropriateness of the discourse to the particular circumstances of the time, place, speaker, and audience involved" ("*Kairos*" 84) and contains, within it, according to John Poulakos, the time and situation in which the rhetorical act occurs, as well as the generative impetus, that is, the tension or dissonance, for discourse. *Kairos* acts to break up opposing elements, Kinneavy says, and enables rhetors to convince themselves and others of differences between right and wrong. *Stasis,* moreover, partakes of *kairos,* as it implies a stopping point so that rhetoric may begin and it functions, according to Hermogenes, as a practical method "based on the established laws and customs of any given people" for disputing issues. *Stasis* is thus a strategy by which the point at issue is identified. More generally, it is, as Janice Lauer writes, "the inventional art of beginning well" ("Issues" 127). As addressivity and answerability are imbricated, so, too are the notions of *kairos* and *stasis,* as both generally represent the need for the right word issued at the right time. Drawing upon Lauer's characterization of *stasis,* it can be said that the notions of *stasis* and answerability have in common the prerequisite of interruption. Although meaning-making never ends, the subject must, after reflection, impose a moment of *stasis* upon itself to compose the meaning s/he has garnered at that (opportune) moment and then s/he must author that meaning for the world, recognizing the act of authoring as constituting only a temporary and on-going understanding and knowledge-making action. Intrinsic to this act of authoring is always the struggle to make meaning and to make ourselves understood.

As symbiotic concepts, *kairos* and *stasis,* similar to addressivity and answerability, are germane to the nature of the rhetorical situation. Regarding the determinacy of the rhetorical situation, Lloyd Bitzer writes "it is the situation which calls the discourse into existence" (2) and each situation inherently presumes some imperative, an "exigence," rendering, he says, situation "so controlling [. . .] that we should consider it the very ground of rhetorical activity" (5). Richard Vatz, in contradistinction to Bitzer, theorizes that "situations are rhetorical [. . . that] utterance strongly invites exigence [. . .] the rhetoric controls the situational response [. . . and] situations obtain their character from the rhetoric which surrounds them or creates them" (159). In Bitzer's view, situation reflects reality, and meaning is intrinsic to the situation, whereas in Vatz's perspective, situation constitutes reality, and meaning is created by the rhetor. Scott Consigny criticizes Bitzer for an overdetermined notion of situation and Vatz for an overdetermined notion of the rhetor. He argues "that the antinomy of rhetor and situation can be resolved by the notion of rhetoric as art" (67), for which he nominates an art of topics. Consigny concludes that the most pressing issue for rhetoric revolves around the extent in any situation "to which the rhetor can discover and control indeterminate matter, using his [sic] art of topics to make sense of what would otherwise remain simply absurd" (67). Consigny's view, therefore, more accurately represents the imbrication of addressivity and answerability that Bakhtin envisioned. As subjects we have agency, but the degree varies from situation to situation.

The networked subjectivity map drawn and described herein provides a way to conceptualize the rhetorical nature of the subject and its way of being in the world, which is fundamentally a process of authoring, that is, a thoroughly social, political, and ethical act. The rhetorical building-blocks of subjectivity—language/discourse, self, other, situation/reality—are fundamental to the subject's very existence, while authoring is imbricated socially, politically, and ethically in not only the fundamental nature of the subject's existence but also in the *quality* of that existence. We ought to view our students as no less complex than this generalized model of networked subjectivity.

Networked subjectivity can serve teachers as a general tool by which to practice reflexivity and evaluation relative to the writing process they choose for their students, for the authoring of writing in the classroom is not substantially different from the authoring of a life in the world. This notion of dialogic, networked process thus resonates for specific formulations of writing process, especially when we argue that writing is both a complex mode of learning and a moment of *stasis* in a subject's movement toward understanding and meaning. We speak of the student's need to commit to a thesis, while acknowledging that *stasis* is a necessity of the writing process itself, and in no way represents a final statement of understanding. Tacit in the notion of *stasis* are multiple interpretations and the action of commitment, all of which constitute an ethic, the engagement of which tangibly enhances the self of the writing subject as well as its relationship with others and the world. If our goal is to engage the whole student in our pedagogies, we must choose/design notions of process(es) that accomplish this engagement.

While this mapping of networked subjectivity is a useful construct, it is, nevertheless, a generalized construct. What must now be addressed is a way to think about how the student-subject in a specific teacher's classroom can be more particularized, thus enabling us to understand the forces that impose themselves upon the very possibilities for authorship and agency and which thus mark subjects differently according to their situatedness in the world.

4 Situating Networked Subjectivity

A rudimentary relation of the subject to itself, to others, and to the world has been addressed in the previous discussion of self, alterity, addressivity and answerability. But, as a generalized (and idealized) heuristic, networked subjectivity requires some theory by which it can serve at the local level, for we must have the capacity to conceptualize networked process forces that impose themselves upon the very possibilities of subjectivity and agency and therefore upon authorship. Thus, the present discussion attempts greater specificity by placing the subject in relation to a cultural network, where culture is understood to be comprised of complex social and political processes, characterized by power relations.

The theory that would begin to imagine the local potential of networked subjectivity is based upon Michel Foucault's conceptualization of *discursive relations*. Foucault's discursive relations can bring to our disciplinary and pedagogical decisions a more positive negotiation of our social, political, and ethical obligations. Conceptually, discursive relations relies on an understanding of discourse as the myriad

> ways of constituting knowledge, together with the social practices, forms of subjectivity and power relations which inhere in such knowledges and relations between them. Discourses [then] are more than ways of thinking and producing meaning. They constitute the "nature" of the body, unconscious and conscious mind and emotional life of the subjects they seek to govern. (Weedon 108)

This conceptualization of discourse and discursive relations represents Foucault's attempt to understand the relationship among subjectivity, language, social institutions, and power, a relationship with which we are likewise ethically obligated to struggle. All networked process sites, writing process(es) included, represent discursive formations that function as instruments of disciplinary power, not only for the discipline of rhetoric and composition but also for the disciplines of the larger cultural network. Therefore, an appropriation of Foucault's theory for a theory of localized networked subjectivity is in order.

The site of focus with which all networked process sites are imbricated is, again, no less than the networked subjectivity of students, whose nature it is our intention to educate. If we are to critically evaluate our pedagogical choices, we must examine how whatever networked process sites we tap function to enact this education, as well as the goals that education serve.

The following navigation through a discursive field of relations traces the vestiges of notions that inform my particular theory of the term *discursive relations* while also establishing the importance of these issues for a more complex theory of networked subjectivity. As in the previous chapter, I provide a map (see Figure 9) to depict specific el-

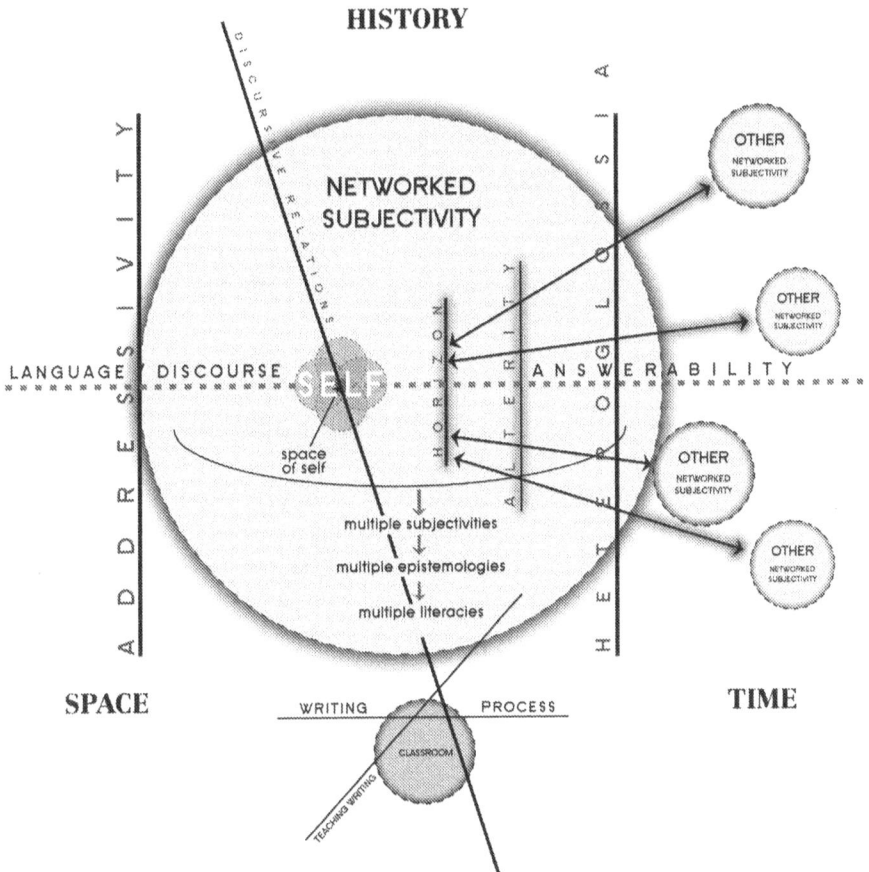

Figure 9. Networked Subjectivity.

ements—discursive relations, multiple subjectivities, multiple epistemologies, multiple literacies—that I will articulate. The map attempts to indicate that multiple subjectivities, epistemologies, and literacies are part and parcel of networked subjectivity; the subject and its relation to the networked world, including the classroom and the practice of teaching writing, is shot through and through with discursive relations. As I discuss the map's articulation, I will again visually represent each element in the form of an overlay, so that by the conclusion of the discussion, the map of networked subjectivity will, again, be intact but will have also expanded to encompass a greater degree of networked process complexity.

Discursive Relations

For some, an alternative term for discursive relations is ideology, a term that, though not synonymous with the notion of discursive relations, is imbricated in the network that constitutes them. Certainly, ideology has a long and complex history, which Raymond Williams traces, beginning with its use in the 1700s, as a way to distinguish ideology, or the science of ideas, from ancient metaphysics. In the 19th century, in large part due to Napoleon's use of it, he says, ideology was associated with "abstract, impractical or fanatical theory," a usage that pervaded epistemology and linguistic theory throughout the 19th century, as well as the discourse of conservative social policy criticism, characterized as the conscious derivation of some specific social theory (154). Williams says that the pejorative sense of ideology as used by conservative thinkers was also popularized by Marx and Engels, so that the term came to represent "abstract and false thought," or to be characterized as "illusion, false consciousness, unreality, [and/or] upside-down reality" (155–56). However, another view was also put forth by Marx, which had ideology, in addition to constituting the expression of the economic conditions of production, also representing the forms in which people became conscious of changes in the economic conditions of production. The latter characterization, Williams says, has enjoyed popular use in the 20th century, where it is broadly conceived to encompass "the set of ideas which arise from a given set of material interests or [. . .] from a definite class or group" (156). But these two senses of the term have, he says, been used "confusingly" within Marxist tradition, so that the characterization of ideology as superfluous social thought and its juxtaposition to science continues to be controversial (156). In current popular argument, though, ideology continues to be used in Napoleon's sense as a term of abuse: "sensible people rely on EXPERIENCE (q.v.), or have a *philosophy;* silly people rely on ideology" (Williams 157).

Tracing the term as it emerged from Marxist discussions into composition studies, Patricia Harkin writes that three different emphases of ideology obtain: as false consciousness, as hegemony and critical consciousness, and as practice. In the emphasis on ideology and false consciousness, two strands are prevalent, one characterized by Ira Shor as "'manipulated action and reflection which lead people to support their own repression'" and the other, characterized by Patricia Bizzell, as a term "to demonstrate that no person has access to unfiltered reality. . . . [an adherence] more to Louis Althusser's notion of ideology as an interpretation that constitutes reality" (qtd. in Harkin, "Ideology" 120). The emphasis on hegemony and critical consciousness questions the possibility and potential for awareness and thus resistance. Some in composition believe, for example, that ideology is invisible and thus insinuates itself as natural. It is thought that we then accept this ideology without reflection, which "might usefully be considered," Harkin says, "in the context of what Antonio Gramsci calls hegemony" (121). Others, however, conceive of ideology as a set of beliefs about which a subject is consciously aware but, nevertheless, chooses to adhere. The third emphasis, ideology as practice, Harkin says, questions whether ideology is best strictly conceived as a system of beliefs or, rather, as a political force that is best mediated through resistant strategies. The tendency in composition studies, Harkin says, "is overwhelmingly toward the latter construction" (121). So it is to a conception of ideology as a political force, one about which a subject can be consciously aware and about which a subject obtains some space for conscious compliance or resistance that I look to articulate the function of discursive relations in networked subjectivity.

I look to this notion, precisely because, as Lester Faigley says, "attention to the politics of writing has led to examinations of what systems of power are implicated in particular discursive practices and what exclusions are necessary to maintain these practices and meanings" (*Fragments* 22). No less attention must be paid to the politics of curriculum. If we adopt a notion of ideology that has the subject so thoroughly written and imbricated in a system of ideas as to be unconscious, without remainder, of the situation, then there is no potential for critical awareness, much less resistance. If, however, some measure of individuality is possible—as in the networked subjectivity heuristic field of relations I have thus far discussed—then a space for both critical awareness and resistance is possible. While a subject comes to consciousness through language, which is at first bestowed by others and later appropriated from others, and while this language is thoroughly saturated with heteroglossia, the dialogic mediation necessary for the subject to relate to itself, to others, and to the world nevertheless includes some measure of space unique to the subject. The approach we take to ideology thus appears dependent upon whether we subscribe to a notion of ideology as a privileged and foundational epistemological claim to knowledge or whether we adopt a notion of ideology as dialogic. I adopt the latter position, which is why I prefer the term discursive relations.

The term ideology as dialogic rests upon the notion of ideology as semiotic. Nevertheless, it is a preferable term for the same reasons offered in the discussion of discourse for a preference of Bakhtin's notions over that of Saussure in chapter three, namely that the sign, language, is placed in relation to a language user and the world. The relation between the sign and the way a subject understands it is arbitrary, not motivated, Keith Moxey says, so that the relation between the world and the sign is not a relation of cause and effect (45). This, too, is my understanding. To construct a notion of ideology as dialogic, I look, first, to Bakhtin's notion of language and heteroglossia:

> Thus at any given moment of its historical existence, language is heteroglot from top to bottom: it represents the co-existence of socio-ideological contradictions between the present and the past, between differing epochs of the past, between different socio-ideological groups in the present, between tendencies, schools, circles and so forth, all given a bodily form. These "languages" of heteroglossia intersect each other in a variety of ways, forming new social typifying "languages." [. . . Indeed] all languages of heteroglossia [. . .] are specific points of view on the world, forms for conceptualizing the world in words, specific world views, each characterized by its own objects, meanings and values. As such they may all be juxtaposed to one another, mutually supplement one

another, contradict one another and be interrelated dialogically. (*Dialogic* 291–92)

Just as the language of the individual is thoroughly heteroglot, so, too, Bakhtin says, are the many languages of ideology. This characterization thus establishes that multiple ideologies obtain and that they function similarly to language. However, Bakhtin also situates the subject in relationship to ideology:

> Consciousness finds itself inevitably facing the necessity of *having to choose a language*. With each [. . .] performance, consciousness must actively orient itself amidst heteroglossia, it must move in and occupy a position for itself within it, it chooses, in other words, a "language." Only by remaining in a closed environment, one without writing or thought, completely off the maps of socio-ideological becoming, could a man fail to sense this activity of selecting a language and rest assured in the inviolability of his own language, the conviction that his language is predetermined. (*Dialogic* 295)

According to Bakhtin, then, each subject must choose a language, an ideology, which is itself imbricated in a morass of other languages/ideologies. It might seem, then, that Bakhtin has the subject written by ideology, unable to situate itself outside an ideological construct. Indeed, I believe this is the situation. But Bakhtin nevertheless maintains some measure of individual space, itself not ideologically neutral, for agency:

> When we seek to understand a word, what matters is not the direct meaning the word gives to objects and emotions—this is the false front of the word; what matters is rather the actual and always self-interested *use* to which this meaning is put and the way it is expressed by the speaker, a use determined by the speaker's position (profession, social class, etc.) and by the concrete situation. *Who* speaks and under what conditions he speaks: this is what determines the word's actual meaning. (*Dialogic* 401)

Subjects, then, figure prominently into Bakhtin's notion of heteroglossia, since interlocutors are not only subjected to discourse but also subject discourse to their struggle to have it meet their specific and situated needs. Through this struggle, they inject something new into the heteroglot configuration of language. This element of "new" language emanates, then, from both the physical specificity of the subject in the world, as well as the specificity of the situation in which the subject forms their utterance.

But appropriating Foucault's notion of discursive relations adds to what Bakhtin provides, as it enables a more complex understanding of the relation of constraints and possibilities in which the subject is enmeshed. These notions illuminate the inevitable complex of power in which each subject is intrinsically embroiled, a focus not entirely unlike Bakhtin's focus on the ceaseless fluctuating ratio of relation between the centripetal and centrifugal forces in language, a social and political relation that can never be absolute.

Appropriating the notion of discursive relations also allows a distancing from the sort of economic determinism, which according to John Tagg, is often associated with the notion of ideology (21). Foucault, too, writes that the notion of ideology is difficult to use because, he says, "like it or not, it always stands in virtual opposition to something else which is supposed to count as truth" (*Truth and Power* 61). Foucault's conception is that discursive practices are constantly engaged in the dissemination of power from one point in the social fabric to another, which is visually depicted in Figure 9. Such a conception, then, does not correlate with a notion of power as hierarchical, one, for example, based on class. According to Foucault, power does not dominate and repress; it circulates and is thus unstable:

> Power must be analyzed as something which circulates, or rather as something which only functions in the form of a chain. It is never localized here or there, never in anybody's hands, never appropriated as a commodity or piece of wealth. Power is employed and exercised through a net-like organization. And not only do individuals circulate between its threads; they are always in the position of simultaneously undergoing and exercising this power. ("Two Lectures" 98)

Such a conception of power is attractive, Moxey says, due to its flexibility. This notion of power is also attractive in that it is dialogic, since it contains, in addition to the repressive tendency we normally associate with power, positive potential as well, the two of which are constantly in flux. Speaking to the productive quality of power, Foucault writes:

> But it seems to me now that the notion of repression is quite inadequate for capturing what is precisely the productive aspect of power. In defining the effects of power as repression, one adopts a purely juridical conception of such power; one identifies power with a law which says no; power is taken above all as carrying the force of a prohibition. Now I believe that this is a wholly negative, narrow, skeleton conception of power, one which has been curiously widespread. If power were never anything but repressive, if it never did anything but to say no, do you really think one would be brought to obey it? What makes power hold good, what makes it accepted, is simply the fact that it doesn't only weigh on us as a force that says no, but that it traverses and produces things, it induces pleasure, forms knowledge, produces discourse. It needs to be considered as a productive network which runs through the whole social body, much more than as a negative instance whose function is repression. (*Truth and Power* 60–61)

Power, then, says both no and yes, where neither edict is always negative or always positive. Likewise, neither pole, negative or positive, is fundamentally good or bad. It is such a value system that we must relinquish if we are to mine Foucault's notion of power for a critical educational enterprise such as the teaching of writing.

Discursive relations and their inherent aspect of power are fluid and fluctuating, thus their flexibility and panoramic range. Moxey believes that discursive relations, or the notion of power, provides a good model for political interpretation, since "not only is it possible to register the dissemination of dominant values, but it is also possible to discuss instances of resistance and the development of oppositional values" (48–49). There is, then, always an element of fluctuation, which is what provides us a space for resistance, a space in which we can glimpse and critique our situation. Indeed, Dick Hebdige says, "the symbiosis in which ideology and social order, production and reproduction, are linked is then neither fixed nor guaranteed. It can be pried open" (16). John Tagg, too, speaks to a space for resistance, for critique, that Foucault's conception of power engenders:

> Power, then, is what is centrally at issue here: the forms and relations of power which are brought to bear on practices of representation or constitute their conditions of existence, but also the power effects which representational practices themselves engender—the interlacing of these power fields, but also their interference patterns, their differences, their irreducibility one to another. Here, a determinate space is opened up as the effect of recent theoretical debates for which power can no longer be seen as a general form, emanating from one privileged site, uniform in its operations, and unified in its determinate effect. The space is crucial, since it exposes a rift in the causal sequences of deterministic theories of cultural practice and in the general conceptions of representation on which they rest. (21)

A subject's representation of its world, or its discourse as utterance, functions, as the subject itself does, within a network of power relations that make both the subject and the utterance possible. But Foucault's notion of discursive relations also allows a subject's utterance the possibility of constituting an interference. We have with this, then, a space for agency.

Foucault's discursive relations theorize power relations as evident in every aspect of life, and power relations are dialogic as both the positive and negative poles are always in flux. This relation, mediated both through the dynamic of its own impetus as a complex network and through the interventions made possible by spaces open to resistance, is analogous to Bakhtin's conception of all aspects of life being dialogic. The self must mediate its inner and outer self, its relation to the other, and to the world, Throughout all, it must struggle with the centripetal and centrifugal forces in language to create a space to inject its own intention. But while Bakhtin's theory situates the subject in the world and concedes the social and political forces in which and with which the subject is engaged, it does not articulate the power relations that obtain to all aspects of the cultural network. Bakhtin's notion of power relations in space, for example, is restricted to the physical space the subject occupies. Power relations obtain among the spaces that subjects physically inhabit, but Foucault posits that nothing operates outside the complex of power. Power operates through the subject, through discourse, through time and history, and through all space (see Figure 9). Space, even that beyond in which the subject is situated, is thoroughly imbricated in power relations, since the constitution of space is achieved through the discourse of subjects' situated practices. Space must likewise, then, represent a potential site for the production of power relations and thus a space for resistance. It is, therefore, an important focus, for according to Foucault, "space is fundamental in any form of communal life [. . . and] in any exercise of power" (*Space, Knowledge, and Power* 252).

The classic example of the operation of discursive relations in space is Foucault's notion of the *panopticon*, as borrowed from Jeremy Bentham (*Discipline*). As originally coined, panopticon referred to the architectural design of a prison that allowed a prison guard to see all of a prisoner's everyday activities while remaining invisible to the prisoner. The discursive intent of the physical structure enabled a system of surveillance that encouraged not just the normalization of prisoners' behavior but prisoners' self-regulating normalization. Prisoners regulated their own behavior precisely because they assumed that they were constantly under surveillance. The panopticon illustrates Todd May's conclusions regarding Foucault's conception of the political "as an oriented field of power relations, relations wherein actions constrain and are constrained by other actions, not in a haphazard fashion but rather in ways that possess their own logic and can be articulated" (3). Such, then, is the panopticon.

Others have examined the power that circulates through spaces. Henri Lefebvre, for example, asserts that "space is not a scientific object removed from ideology or politics; it has always been political and strategic" (31), while Nigel Thrift writes that both space and time are patently social, which, he says, "are easy enough concepts, perhaps, but the implications are only now being thought through" (49). Edward Soja says our past conception of space as objective has tended "to imbue all things spatial with a lingering sense of primordiality and physical composition, an aura of objectivity, inevitability and reification" (79).

These theorists thus also conceptualize space as social, political, and strategic, impossible to divorce from other discursive relations.

Lefebvre's notion of "representations of space" and "representational spaces" offers a notion of space imbricated in a complex web of relations that encompasses both local social relations and institutional power. There is also an echo of the centripetal and centrifugal tendencies within language itself, where the centripetal or monologic tends toward the orthodox of authority while the centrifugal expands the social and political environment with endless variations of meanings. Nicholas Blomley summarizes Lefebvre's distinction: representations of space, Lefebvre maintains, instantiate the dominant aspect of a culture as expressed by planners, designers, academics, policymakers, and the like, and are thus, Blomley says, "shot through with a formalized knowledge (or *savoir*) that usually implies the exercise of institutional power" (190). In such representations, he says, space is presented as something to be coded, divided, and ordered. Conversely, representational spaces are more loosely structured and function as localized *"connaissances."* This space, then, is imbricated in "the play of local social relations" (190). Important for us, he notes, is that these representational spaces "can depart significantly from the orthodoxy, serving as sites of symbolic opposition and resistance" (190). Blomley thus concludes that space has "a direct bearing on the way power is deployed and social life [is] structured" (xii). Place, he says, as well as movement, is "politically consequential, and discursively related" (xi), so that "how we represent space and time in theory matters because it affects how we and others interpret and then act with respect to the world" (52). The social and political nature of space accrues material ramifications to the subject, to its placement and to its mobility within space.

That representations of space are discursively related and do materially impact movement and place is well illustrated in Minnie Bruce Pratt's following narrative, "Identity: Skin Blood Heart." Pratt writes that:

> as a middle-class and well-educated white person I usually live in the elite bohemian districts of cities, largely residential areas dotted with coffee shops and upscale book and gift stores. Because of my color, I tend to avoid predominately nonwhite areas, often more to avoid rejection than to avoid violence, but

> also to avoid (unthinkingly) carrying on the tradition of imperialism in pursuit of personal pleasures. And as a woman, I avoid going a lot of places, especially when I am alone at night. (12)

Here, then, is a subject whose mobility is affected by the factors of class, race, and gender. Space is saturated with discourses that constitute representations of space which do, necessarily, inform our horizon and our practices and thus how we construe meaning for ourselves, others, and the world. Indeed, "life spaces," Blomley writes, are "rich with personal and cultural meaning" (193).

Another life space imbricated in discursive relations is the workplace. Shoshana Zuboff's historical study to account for the different social constructions of reality that obtain to workers as a result of technological advances speaks to the power of these relations. She writes that "the material alternations in their means of production were manifested in transformations at intimate levels of experience—assumptions about knowledge and power, their beliefs about work and the meaning they derived from it, the content, and rhythm of their social exchanges, and the ordinary mental and physical disciplines to which they accommodated in their daily lives" (xiii). Work, she says, became more abstract, as it was tied to understanding and manipulating information, but she also says that it created new spaces for new types of mastery, so that implicit in the new work was the potential for new meaning. Zuboff illustrates the discursive relations that materially and affectively changed the life space of the workplace and of workers but which also created a space for resistance, for the possibility of new meanings.

But there are many different sorts of potential spaces of resistance. Helene Cixous, for example, argues space as the very possibility for resistance and change with her notion of writing the body. Gendered writing, she says, "has been run by a libidinal and cultural [. . .] political, typically masculine economy [. . .] where woman has never *her* turn to speak—this being all the more serious and unpardonable in that writing is precisely *the very possibility of change,* the space that can serve as a springboard for subversive thought, the precursory movement of a transformation of social and cultural structures" (1235). Susan Jarratt argues for strategies that create spaces for new readings.[30] For example, she explores the relation between the exclusion of sophists and women in order to argue that careful study of the connection between sophistic rhetoric and feminist reading/writing might not only advance studies in the history of rhetoric but also "offer increased leverage" for challenging the patriarchal hegemony established at the time of sophistic marginalization ("The First Sophists and Feminism" 79).[31] bell hooks takes on the politics of location as she calls for the reconstruction of "an archaeology of memory," arguing that memory is return or a form of travel, and thus imperative for understanding "that 'where' is less a place than it is a compilation of itineraries: different, concrete histories of dwelling, immigration, exile, [and] migration" ("Representing" 343).[32] Memory, she says, is a site of resistance, a practice which can "transform history from a judgment on the past in the name of a present truth to a 'counter memory' that combats our current modes of truth and justice, helping us to understand and change the present by placing it in a new relation to the past" (344). Different ways of writing, different ways of reading, and different ways of remembering, then, all offer spaces for resistance to the discursive relations immanent in all the spheres of our lives, in all the networked sites we inhabit.

But how are we, as teachers of writing, to analyze the discursive relations in our choice of writing process and in the space of the classroom? Suggestions from colleagues offer a place to begin, as they provide a rich, discursive source for inquiry to the possible spaces for both the positive production of power and for the critical resistance to that power.

A common refrain from scholars is that we fail to make use of the varied discourses that students bring to the classroom. David Sholle and Stan Denski, for example, maintain that "educational theory must engage with the popular as the background that informs students' engagement with any pedagogical encounter" (307), while Giroux and Simon suggest that the discourse of popular culture must, at the least, be viewed as the background that grounds student voice. Thus, when as teachers we fail to factor students' background discourses, we act to restrict the play of discursive relations in the classroom and instead privilege the institutional discourse sanctioned by the academy. This is not to say that disciplinary discourse should not be primary, but rather to suggest that students' background discourses ought to be respected and valued, for they contribute to students' subjectivities. How can we say that we value students if we do not value their discourse? Metadiscourse in the classroom regarding discourse itself, then, might serve as a catalyst to resistance and thus to a positive production of power. Students' discourses could be legitimized, while the institutional discourse students are expected to adopt could still be promoted.[33]

Another discursive relation that obtains in the classroom of which we should remain aware involves initiation or enculturation. As James Paul Gee argues, education is always the process of initiation of students into various historically situated social practices to insure that they become insiders (291). (Failing to become insiders, they are clearly marked with their failure as outsiders.[34]) As a mitigation of the potential abuse inherent to the act of initiation, Victor Villanueva, Jr. argues for a dialectic approach to the classroom as a way to direct the processes of initiation versus directing students.[35] He suggests that we provide students with opportunities for an increased awareness of the possibility and desirability of changing worldviews. Thus, by juxtaposing tradition with change, he says, students can benefit from altered perspectives, from increased literacy, and from a critical view of the academy. Lawrence Grossberg's notion of affect provides a strategy of resistance to the normalizing process of initiation. This kind of strategy is crucial to the sort of classroom climate that encourages critical initiation while respecting students' cultures. "In everyday life," he says, "we base our decisions not just on rational meanings, but [also] through *emotional and bodily* commitments, commitments understood as falling between 'libidinal economies of desire and affective economies of mood as two different places in which psychic energy is always dispersed'" (285). We cannot, then, appeal only to rational justifications of our curriculum and pedagogy. We must also seek to engage students' commitment to the process. This indicates that we must engage the whole student and not just the mind. Such a strategy seeks to promote genuine reciprocity and to preclude an oppressive imposition of the social practices we would have students adopt in order to become insiders.

Yet another variation of the need to recognize alternative discourses and to view initiation into particular social practices as more than a cognitive event is the need to value difference. This is one of the greatest dangers we face as teachers, for the strongest normalizing tendency of our curriculum may well be homogenization, the leveling of difference altogether. Offering a counter strategy to this situation, Henry Giroux calls for a postmodern discourse of literacy and pedagogy that actually foregrounds difference. He wants, he says, "to develop a rationale, along with some pedagogical principles for developing a politics of difference responsive to the imperatives of a critical democracy" (372). All levels of education, he argues, must be situated within a moral and social context if a politics and pedagogy of difference is to constitute critical democratic discourse. Indeed, it is education for assuming the responsibilities of governing that is the ethical imperative, an imperative that connects difference, education, and democracy ("Literacy and the Politics" 375). But Sholle and Denski offer a useful cautionary perspective, writing that "the affirmation of difference is [often] disconnected from any account of how cultural, political, and economic constraints position various groups in asymmetrical power relations" (305). Each of these recommended strategies is valuable. One points us toward a goal, while the other would have us explore the power relations that make such a goal problematic. Both, however, provide spaces for effective resistance and a positive production of power.

The power relations that embroil us in the academy that legitimizes our relationship with the constituency that provides the rationale for our employment place us in a position of what appears to be hopeless compromise. While we cannot escape our positioning in this relation, we can critically seek to negotiate it. A cautionary argument from Xin Liu Gale speaks to this need. Teachers of all writing process persuasions, she says, attempt to "eradicate institutional authority in their theories and pedagogies," in the mistaken belief that they and their students will thus enjoy an equal relationship (55). This is not possible, however, because the teacher-student relationship is based on the asymmetrical power relations that obtain in society and teachers cannot simply "abandon the institutional authority immanent in the role they play as cultural agents" (55). Teachers' judicial authority over students, she argues, must be conceded as inevitable and institutional authority as indispensable to teaching, while also recognizing the "ever-existing potential danger of its use in the classroom" (57). Such a realization, she writes, "can help teachers avoid assigning all evils to institutional authority, while avoiding using other forms of authority with blind conviction that would likewise threaten to oppress despite their progressive goals in teaching and good intentions for students" (57).[36] Bourdieu and Passeron also maintain that teaching cannot exist independently of institutions because (1) teaching is an arbitrary act and thus requires an institution to legitimate its practice, and (2) the very act of engaging pedagogy requires judicial authority for it to achieve its intended effect. Gale, Bourdieu, and Passeron remind us of the complex discursive relations in which we are inevitably imbricated. We cannot escape this paradox of competing allegiances, but we can use our authority more responsibly, more ethically, and, yes, more effectively, when we critically reflect on our role in these discursive relations.[37] We can, as Gary Anderson and Patricia Irvine suggest, practice critical literacy—and even challenge unequal power relations—if we remain aware of our historical and cultural construction within specific power relations.

Others speak about the power of educational institutions to construct student subjectivity. While I do not believe this is accomplished as unproblematically as some scholars' work suggests, I do believe that our objectives and goals envision a specific subject position we wish students to instantiate into their repertoire of subjectivities.[38] This ideal subject position, however, should not remain tacit and unexamined. We must be reflexive about what we envision in this context of what our pedagogy makes possible. In *Talking Back,* bell hooks relates an experience that speaks to the danger of not reflecting on our assumptions and expectations for student identities. As an African-American student in mostly all-white teacher- and student-populated classes, hooks was troubled by a tendency to equate her "true, authentic voice" to a particular southern black dialect she sometimes used in her writing. "The insistence on finding one voice, one definitive style of writing and reading one's poetry," she writes, "fit all too neatly with a static notion of self and identity that was pervasive in university settings" (11). But the instruments of our pedagogy also contribute to students' subject construction. Kathleen McCormick and Lester Faigley, for instance, argue that issues of student subjectivity play themselves out at the micro-level of institutions in the material form of textbooks and the practices they advocate. McCormick recommends a curriculum that interrogates contradictions, explores repression historically, personally, and culturally, and analyzes the effects of repression so as to create spaces for alternative perspectives that could serve different ends, while Faigley observes that teachers' narratives indicate "success in teaching depends on making a student aware of the desired subject position she will occupy" (129). McCormick's suggestion and Faigley's observation provide alternatives for an ethical negotiation of an ideal student subjectivity, while hooks reminds us of why we must make such ethical negotiations.

Feminist theory and teaching also offers insight for exploring productive and resistant spaces.[39] Joy S. Ritchie, for example, is critical of "academically trained feminists" who prefer to focus on abstract theories of gender construction rather than "explore the immediate implications of those theories for the lives of women students" (249). "Academic life," she says, "often fosters the view that intellectual activity is a solitary undertaking without social origins and political implications" (267).[40] We must, she argues, promote the connection between intellectual activity and the history and experience of people's lives in order to provide an "intellectual practice that allows students to see that we make our own knowledge rather than simply acquire 'the facts,' and that we do so in a reciprocal process of rethinking and reinterpreting the 'word and the world,' in Paulo Freire's phrase" (271). A praxis that values reciprocity, not only between theory and practice but also between experience and knowledge, provides yet an "other" space for the positive production of power and effective acts of resistance.

Kathleen Dixon, however, is critical of much of cultural studies research's focus on the political subject: "I wish to fix my gaze on the underside of the political subject, on the 'personal' or private worlds of human relationships" (257). We must, she says, examine ourselves as subjects overdetermined by processes of enculturation, knowing that our inquiries can represent only partial perspectives. However, she writes, "making this knowledge accessible to our consciousness is taxing and risky work because we don't always know what we are looking for [. . .], nor do we necessarily want to disrupt the habits and assumptions of a lifetime" (256). Dixon's statement regarding the risks of a critical negotiation of power relations implies both material and psychic repercussions; we must remain aware of these risks so as to practice an ethic of care for ourselves.[41]

As teachers/scholars, then, we experience, produce, and reproduce power relations that impact us, students, the academy, rhetoric and composition, and the larger culture. We cannot abdicate the dialogic ethic to which we are bound, that is, to negotiate the recursive relations from our situated, partial, and contingent positions, for to make no effort to negotiate these relations nevertheless constitutes a response. The world addresses us; we must answer. But we must decide whether we will be participants or spectators. Richard Fulkerson's point is well taken in his article "Four Philosophies of Composition," which, he says, advances two messages:

> First, what is now a truism, that teachers who claimed to teach without any philosophy were deluding themselves. It is possible to be unconscious about philosophy, or to be inconsistent, but it isn't possible not to have one. Second, and more important, [. . .] too often teachers were unaware of the philosophy they more or less adhered to and sent contradictory messages in the classroom. They either lacked a consistent view of the ends sought or followed paths that would not reach them. My moral was that the unexamined course is not worth teaching. (410)

I agree. We delude ourselves in assuming neutrality. As C. H. Knoblauch and Lil Brannon write, praxis requires that teachers "scrutinize for themselves the choices they make in the classroom, remembering that they are constantly deciding what to do and how to do it, albeit so routinely that they might well forget the agency that suffuses their work" (8). We have agency and we do participate in knowledge, but this participation can be weighted toward reproductive maintenance of the status quo or it can be weighted toward productive acts of knowledge making. Nowhere is the possibility for knowledge construction more available than in the writing process(es) we choose for our classrooms. All curriculum development is a form of knowledge making according to Louise Wetherbee Phelps, who writes that "all curricula are hypothetical realizations of theses about the nature of knowledge and the nature of teaching and learning. The function of curriculum research and development [she says] is to create curricula in which these are made articulate and explicit and thereby subject to evaluation by teachers" ("Practical" 867). The composition community, Phelps maintains, needs to study itself: its students, choices and their impacts, structures, conceptual bases, and contexts. Part of our work, she argues, is "to make visible [. . .] the ecology of curricular contexts in which any teaching decision is embedded, not merely abstractly but as vivid, particular realities." This requires us "to specify how actions fit together on the programmatic or institutional scale" ("Practical" 867).

As teachers/scholars who make curricular choices that affect the ebb and flow of discursive relations, we are no less than contributors to public policy, and public policy always involves the notion of justice. We can usefully borrow from Iris Marion Young's conception of the political merging with the concept of justice, where the focus is democratic participation, deliberation, and decision making, all of which require a political discourse that situates rhetoric as fundamental to public life. Two values form the framework of this model of justice: "(1) developing and exercising one's capacities and expressing one's experience [. . .] and (2) participating in determining one's actions and the conditions of one's action" (37). Young's model of justice assumes heterogeneity and disallows the notion of objectivity in public policy decisions. In this framework, as in that of Bakhtin, everyone must contribute and must do so from the specificity of their own situatedness. We are all addressed by the world, then, and we must answer for our positions. The ground for public policy, the ground for justice, is participation.

Multiple Epistemologies/Multiple Subjectivities

Epistemology, according to D. W. Hamlyn, is the theory of knowledge, a branch of philosophy concerned with the nature of knowledge, its possibility, scope, and general basis (242). Epistemology, he says, is the study of our right to the beliefs we have; that is, "we start from what we might call our cognitive stances, and ask whether we do well to have those stances" (245). Hamlyn's notion of cognitive stance is relatively inclusive. It includes our beliefs, our knowledge, and our strategies and methods that produce belief and knowledge. Epistemology, then, according to Hamlyn, is "explicitly *normative;* it is concerned with whether we have acted well or badly (responsibly or irresponsibly) in forming the beliefs we have" (245).

Philosophers, of course, have historically theorized knowledge. Hamlyn writes that Locke, for example, argued that ideas come from experience but that not all knowledge derives from experience, since some depends on intuition or demonstration. Locke did believe, though, that experience is the foundation of knowledge, maintaining that the simple ideas of sense are the origin of all understanding (244). That all ideas are derived from sense impressions is the central claim of Hume's empiricism, while Hegel believed objective knowledge could be ascertained through pure reason. Nietzsche maintained the doctrine of the subjectivity of truth, equating truth with power, while J.S. Mill, like others before him, believed that all knowledge derives from experience. A more social orientation of knowledge, however, came from C.S. Peirce, who said the meaning of our ideas is a function of their contribution to rational conduct (244). The basis of knowledge in contemporary discussions is generally conceded to be social, that is, there is no universal truth, no space from which to exercise objectivity, so knowledge is invariably a construction. It is political, as well, since not everyone has equal access to the legitimizing forces of power. A notion of epistemology characterized thusly, as social and political, significantly alters the way in which we conduct an epistemological discussion of epistemology.

A view sympathetic to knowledge as social construction has been illustrated previously in Bakhtin, and this position can also be located in the work of Kenneth Burke, both of whom are critical of a scientist approach to knowledge. Bakhtin characterizes knowledge in two ways: knowledge of the object and knowledge of the subject. Knowledge of the object is scientific and monolgoic, in that the object is comprehended and verbalized by "only one subject, the subject that knows (contemplates) and speaks (utters)" (qtd. in Todorov 18). Here, the knower knows only a "voiceless thing," so there is no communication, thus rendering the situation static and closed or monologic. No knowledge is achieved if the subject is "perceived or studied as if it were a thing, since it cannot remain a subject if it is voiceless; consequently," Bakhtin says, "there is no knowledge of the subject but dialogical" (qtd. in Todorov 18). Where there is no dialogism, the subject is reduced to an object, specifically in order to attain knowledge. Such knowledge, though, is superficial, Bakhtin maintains, or, worse, false.

Bakhtin associates passive understanding with linguistic meaning, which he says is only an abstract aspect of meaning. Passive understanding is monologic because it "remains purely passive, purely receptive, [and] contributes nothing new" (*Dialogic* 281). All it can do is mirror that with which it identifies in the other. This is a peripheral aspect of understanding (*Speech* 141), a state achieved when a subject assimilates only that which is repeatable and recognizable in the other's utterance (143). It is an empathy or a mirroring of cognition and emotion and allows nothing new into the utterance and dissolves the other's personality.

What Bakhtin has described is what Kenneth Burke pejoratively refers to as a scientist perspective to knowledge, and, indeed, Burke avoids discussions of epistemology, even though he acknowledges that it "enters [. . . his] view secondarily," and that his dramatistic view of language is "'scientist roundabout'" (367). Using a reverse proposition, Burke maintains that rather than words being the signs of things, "things are the signs of words" (363). Ironically "roundabout," he posits this reversal as a "heuristic," a strategy that seeks to create new understanding and new knowledge. This heuristic allows Burke to argue for what seems to be a socially constructed epistemology. He says the values of the social group permeate language and language is the medium by which things then materially embody those values (362). The poetic equivalent to this reads: "And how things are/And how we say things are/Are one" (54).

With his heuristic reversal, Burke enacts his notion of circumference (359), that is, he organizes the opposition to his act, seeks to encompass it, sees the "situation anew in terms of it," and, presumably, "arrive[s] thus roundabout at knowledge" (367). Burke admits this theory comprises empirical aspects (362) but maintains that his notion of terministic screens counters the scientist impulse, as its origin lies in the theological doctrine of "believe that you may understand" (47), an analogy that admits the privileging inherent in any perspective, in any terministic screen.

Burke's notion of circumference resonates with Bakhtin's notion of horizon, both of which situate the subject in a partial and contingent position in the social network. The utterance issued by a subject from this position is thus colored by both the opportunities and the limitations of a specific terministic screen. Implicitly, the circumference of any utterance bleeds (overlaps) and renders consensus an ideal. That is why, according to Burke, language cannot be legislated. Rather, the legislation of language must be continually and messily negotiated among/between the terministic screens of individuals and groups.

It is imperative to acknowledge, however, that even with a social constructivist framework, there is not equal access to the legitimizing forces of representations of knowledge. That is, disequilibrium is a mark of any group or network. Another point, garnered from the "self" and "alterity" sites of networked subjectivity, indicates there are multiple ways of knowing, which is not to suggest that they are fundamental and inherent aspects of the subject. Individuals engage in various formal and informal groups (networks), all of which have specific conventions unique to their situatedness. Indeed a group always produces and is produced by what we might call a discursive formation, or in Lyotard's vernacular, a language game, where subjects are normalized to the discursive formation by meeting that formation's truth conditions.

Truth conditions vary among groups, but Teun van Dijk provides a definition of social cognition that captures a part of what we might concur constitutes truth conditions. Social cognition, he says, can be characterized as "socially shared representations of societal arrangements, groups of relations, as well as mental operations such as interpretation, thinking and arguing, inferencing and learning, among others" (258). Although van Dijk concedes we "know little about 'softer' forms of social cognition: opinions, attitudes, ideologies, norms, and values," we know these are valid components of the whole equation (258). Indeed, van Dijk describes what compositionists might refer to as a discourse community, a contested term in the field.[42] I forego the use of the term *discourse community* and elect, rather, a notion of *discursive formation* appropriated from Foucault, and to which I apply equally the notions of epistemology, subject, classrooms, and writing process, all of which I will presently explain.

Hubert Dreyfus and Paul Rabinow write that when Foucault first began his study of madness, he proceeded on the assumption that his object of study, the discursive formation of madness, could be articulated and analyzed by grouping together its significant speech acts. But what he later came to understand is that "discursive formations *produce* the object about which they speak," so Foucault realized madness was not so much an object or an experience that different historical periods had attempted to describe but was, rather, actually constituted through an accumulation and legitimatization of statements "that named it, divided it up, described it, explained it, traced its developments, indicated its various correlations, judged it, and possibly gave it speech by articulating, in its name, discourses that were to be taken as its own" (qtd. in Dreyfus and Rabinow 61). Furthermore, Foucault imagined a circularity from discursive formation to statements and back again to the discursive formation, where statements are subject to the specific truth conditions of the set of statements, or the discursive formation, in which they are used (45). Foucault thus described his task as no longer "treating discourses as groups of signs (signifying elements referring to contents or representations) but as practices that systematically form the objects of which they speak" (qtd. in Dreyfus and Rabinow 62). Discursive formations, therefore, are constructions of truth or knowledge and are thus constantly in flux. They are comprised of discursive relations and so are thoroughly dialogic. This, then, is why I choose to use Foucault's notion of discursive relations. It simultaneously speaks to contingency, reciprocity, fluctuation, power differentials, truth conditions, negotiation, and the said as well as the unsaid. It is social, political, and ethical; it is dialogic.

I suggest we view epistemology in terms of discursive formation, where the discursive relations immanent in various spheres constitute correlative epistemologies. Such spheres are multiple: a subject might approximate insider status in the discursive formations of immediate family, a group of friends, school, church, clubs and organizations, and an internet chatroom, for example. Each of these equates to a discursive formation that, indeed, has its own truth statements for legitimizing participation and knowledge production. Therefore, to the extent that a subject approximates insider status or achieves membership in multiple discursive formations, that subject is subjected to differing epistemologies (see Figure 10). Differing discursive formations thus construct different subject positions each subject must assume to achieve the legitimization of membership. Because differing discursive formations have differing sets of truth conditions, it is likely these sets of truth conditions may conflict. The subject then is characterized by multiple and often conflicting subject positions (see Figure 10).

Insider and outsider status are not absolute terms. A subject may be situated differently, relative to the power centers of its discursive formations. This situatedness is arbitrary in some situations: the subject wishes to enter or to be nearer to the center but cannot gain access. In other situations, however, the subject may choose to remain outside a specific formation or may choose to qualify its membership in the formation, preferring to distance itself from the formation's center. Therefore, there are discursive formations to which we belong of which we are hardly aware, there are those to which we have no access, while there are still others in which we avoid or refuse membership altogether. Also, insider and outsider are not absolute positions, precisely because no one can control the truth conditions that coalesce a formation's center. The relations of the various discursive formations of which each formation member is part enters, at least tacitly, into

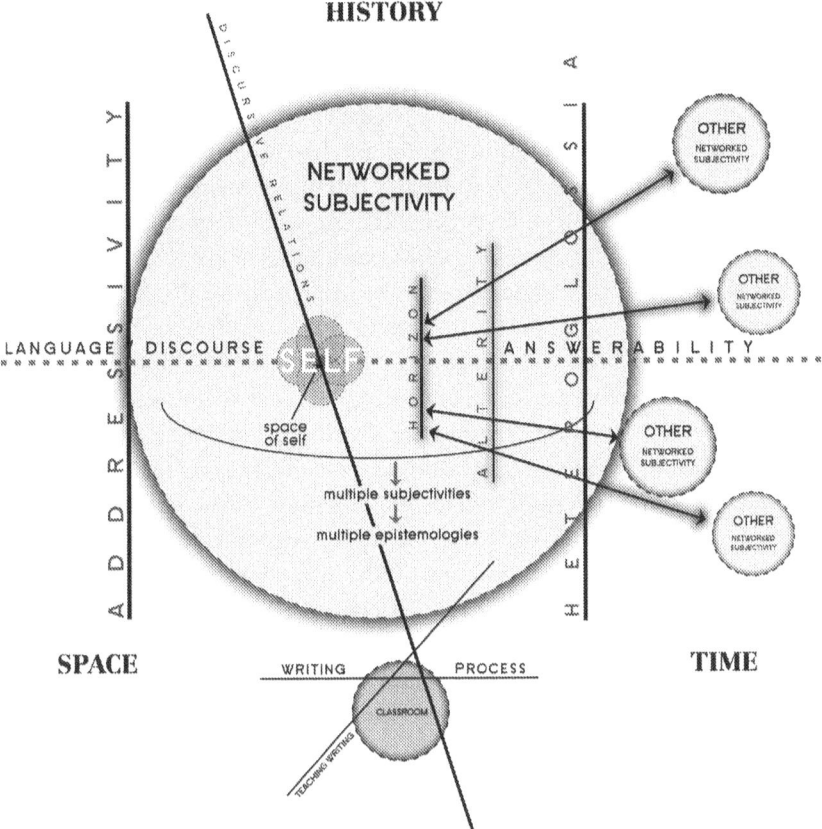

Figure 10. Multiple Epistemologies/Multiple Subjectivities.

the matrix of relations that comprise a specific formation, so the truth conditions, which function toward monologic status remain in some degree of flux. Discursive formations fluctuate and are therefore thoroughly dialogic.

Writing process is also a discursive formation. The statements that constitute it as a discursive formation are subject to the disciplinary truth conditions of rhetoric and composition, whose truth conditions are further subject to the academy, whose truth conditions are subject to the cultural network in which it is situated.[43] This chain thus represents a complex relational configuration of discursive formations. It illustrates Foucault's statements that "these relations are established between institutions, economic and social processes, behavioral patterns, systems of norms, techniques, types of classification, [and] modes of characterization" (62).

This same institutional configuration obtains, for example, to the writing process(es) teachers choose to enact in the classroom. The discursive formation of writing process in classrooms is thus unique to each classroom precisely because the discursive relations that obtain within the classroom environment are uniquely informed by the symbolic and physical aspects of each specific situated classroom context. Students, then, are characterized by multiple epistemologies and thus by multiple and sometimes conflicting subject positions. They come together in a classroom where their multiple epistemologies/subject positions are likely to conflict both with other classmates and with the teacher, who, of course, wields greater authority in this asymmetrical power relation. Likewise, the teacher's epistemologies/subject positions may well conflict with the field, the academy, or the culture. These institutional networked relations are thus complex: we project an ideal subject position we wish students to occupy, which they engage with varying degrees of enthusiasm and effectiveness. They become insiders to the discursive formation in varying degrees. Some do not become insiders at all, while some are situated on the boundary and others still are situated at the very center. The pedagogy we choose contributes to the truth statements by which the student will be initiated or enculturated to the subject position that is our ideal, our goal. It is imperative, then, that we be reflexive of our goals and the pedagogy we choose for our classrooms

Multiple Literacies/Classroom

"Because literacy agonistically and antagonistically inhabits both popular and academic spheres," Darsie Bowden writes, "an uncontroversial definition is hard to come by" (140). Indeed, even within the confines of rhetoric and composition, literacy is broadly and variously conceived.

Many in the field address ideology as a component of literacy. Sidney Dobrin, for example, addresses the influence of literacy theory on the way writing is taught and notes—optimistically, I would suggest—that the field has moved away from a notion of literacy as skill acquisition to a more complex notion of the ways in which the ways we teach, the ways students learn, and the very nature of literacy itself is influenced by social ideologies (*Constructing Knowledges* 119).

Knoblauch and Brannon address the issue of our situatedness relative to literacy. In *Critical Teaching and the Idea of Literacy,* they write that the concept of literacy is embedded "in the ideological dispositions of those who employ it, those who profit from it, and those who have the standing and motivation to enforce it as a social requirement" (15). They note, too, that literacy is never merely a neutral denoting of skills. Literacy is always "*for* something—for professional competence in a technological world, or civic responsibility and the preservation of heritage; for personal growth and self-fulfillment; for social and political change" (15). Fredric Gale, likewise, is critical of a notion of literacy that relies on instrumentalism at the expense of a consideration of the ideology in which even those empowered by it are imbricated, saying that such a lapse "is not a cogent explanation" (152). Richard Ohmann looks at ideology and its function, writing that "literacy is an activity of social groups, and a necessary feature of some kinds of social organization" (226). These social groups are characterized by both conflict and cooperation, he says, so "like language itself, literacy is an exchange between classes, races, the sexes, and so on" (226).

Others focus on literacy as a process. David Bleich characterizes literacy as "an inquiry into how to say what matters to other people that matter" (*The Double* 330), while James Paul Gee says education is always the process of initiation of students into various historically situated social practices to render them insiders (291).[44] Just as Gee's characterization addresses the notion of power immanent in the process of literacy, so, too, does that of Henry Giroux, who in "Literacy and the Politics of Difference," says literacy is political, because the way we read the world is imbricated in power relations, and it is ethical, because people read the world differently (368). He also notes that in its various versions, literacy "is about the practice of representation as a means of organizing, inscribing, and containing meaning" (368).[45] Giroux thus recommends a postmodern discourse of literacy, which he says, "recognizes its own contingency and partiality and elects to exist within an uncertainty negotiated by dialogue and debate" (375). A perspective relative to the issue of alterity is provided by David Sholle and Stan Denski, who write that being literate involves "both having a voice and giving the other a voice" ("Reading and Writing" 315).[46]

It is to specific institutional repercussions that others look in their characterizations of literacy. Patricia Harkin, John Schilb, and John Trimbur say that literacy crises lead to crisis management.[47] Both the institution and rhetoric and composition have sustained themselves, Harkin and Schilb write, in "managing" perceived literacy crises, "by creating new institutions, books, journals, PhD programs, and conferences" (*Contending* 3). Michael Holzman would have us look at specific pedagogical practices relative to institutions as he argues that we must resist our complicity in reproducing the underclass by re-thinking how education takes place rather than focusing attention merely on curriculum and pedagogy. What is needed, he says, is not a hierarchical approach but a lateral one that would help us to re-think this position. Anne Ruggles Gere voices a concern for the (mis)communication between the institution and the public ("Public Opinion"). The resurgence of public interest in teaching writing, she says, parallels literacy crises, which renders the teaching of writing an issue for political dissent. This situation exists in part, Gere argues, because the press fails to acknowledge contested meanings of literacy issues and instead cites monolithic forces that forestall efforts for a fruitful dialogue. She says our priority should be to get these contested meanings into the public realm.

These characterizations of literacy, admittedly, were selected for their affinity to what we might view in terms of dialogic literacy. Any literacy is itself a discursive formation, for it, too, is imbricated in discursive relations and prescribes truth conditions that must be met in order for legitimacy to be conferred. Thus, scholars who speak of literacy in terms of ideology, as process, and as embroiled in complex institutional relations also tacitly addresses a notion of literacy as discursive formation, as dialogic. Literacy as dialogic is analogous to epistemology as dialogic.

Indeed, the dialogic quality that characterizes epistemology is equally pertinent for literacy. Literacy, just as epistemology, is multiple: just as various familial, social, and political groups or discursive formations formulate unique epistemologies due to the truth conditions of their situations, so does literacy. Just as multiple epistemologies may conflict, so can literacies. Just as epistemologies tacitly construct an ideal subjectivity for a subject to assume, so does literacy. Finally, just as subjects are variously positioned relative to legitimacy within epistemological formations, so, too, are they situated in literacy formations. Therefore, we can speak not only of multiple epistemologies and multiple subjectivities, but also of multiple literacies (see Figure 11). Subjects, then, accrue multiple and conflicted subjectivities as

Situating Networked Subjectivity 139

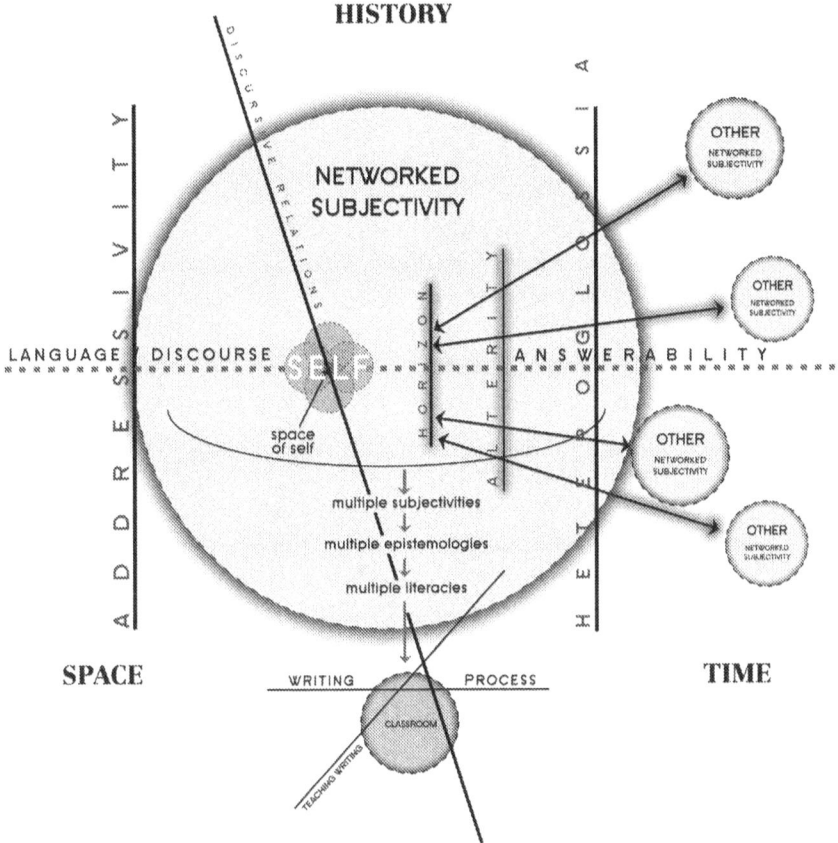

Figure 11. Multiple Literacies/Classroom.

much from literacy as they do epistemology. A subject might, again for example, be situated as a relative outsider to a literacy because s/he is refused access or s/he does not meet the truth conditions necessary for legitimization, or s/he might be situated on the boundary, having met only some of these conditions. Of course, s/he may have successfully negotiated all of a literacy's truth conditions and be situated at the very center of that specific discursive formation.

Obviously, epistemology and literacy are intersecting notions. It is therefore possible for a subject to have mastered the truth conditions of a specific epistemology and yet elect to forfeit membership in a particular literacy discursive formation. This might be characterized as an act of resistance and can and often does occur in the writing classroom.

As teachers/scholars, we must adopt a broad perspective of literacy. Literacies are as multiple and varied as the milieu of discursive formations that exist. Students do not come to the classroom void of multiple epistemologies and literacies. If we ignore this, we confound our own efforts to have them become insiders to the epistemologies and literacies we wish them to both want and to discursively inhabit, for we basically ignore who they are and the contingency of their situatedness. When we choose, for example, a writing process(es) for our classrooms, then, we must consider how this discursive relation will co-mingle and intermix with all that students bring with them. As Cathy Fleischer attests, the writing classroom generally does little to promote and nurture these literacies, a situation that can be remedied by viewing the classroom as a literacy site, "as interactive places where students are encouraged to let their internally persuasive discourses, their own in-formed literacies, serve as the basis for their necessary interaction with academic talk and writing" (186).

As teachers/scholars, we must be reflexive about our choices if we are to exercise our social, political, and ethical obligation to ourselves, our students, our discipline, our institutions, and our culture. The negotiation of these competing interests is not easy. It requires, in addition to reflexivity and evaluation, diligence and perseverance. But we can do no less, for our teaching constitutes part of the authoring we are compelled by the world's addressivity to enact. Authoring, as previously described, is social, political, and ethical: a thoroughly dialogic act.

5 Textbooks, Writing Program Reforms, Institutionality, and the Public

The discursive formation represented by the metaphor of networked process is vast and complex, but using networked subjectivity as a networked-process heuristic provides us with a tool by which to mine the various factors that contribute to networked process. Networked subjectivity can be applied to disciplinary, material artifacts just as easily as it can be applied to disciplinary and institutional sites. An analysis of both in this chapter accomplishes several objectives. First, this analysis demonstrates how the heuristic of networked subjectivity functions; second, it illuminates how a disciplinary artifact (a textbook, *Writing with a Purpose* by Joseph F. Trimmer) and a disciplinary, institutional site (writing program reforms at California State University, Chico) function in the discursive formation of networked process; and, third, it illustrates why and how we ought to reflexively interrogate all of our disciplinary artifacts and sites.

A popular and well-known material artifact that resides in the discursive formation of networked process is *Writing with a Purpose*. The textbook's characterization of writing is described, generally, as "*opportunity*" specifically, as "an opportunity for communication;" and variously as "hard work;" consisting of "formulating and organizing ideas, and finding the right words to present them;" as "both a *solitary* and a *social* act;" and as "a complex mental activity that usually unfolds as a more flexible and 'recursive' sequence of tasks" (2, 4, 6).[48] "Writing is," according to the textbook, "both a procedure of *discovering* what you know and a procedure for *demonstrating* what you know" (13). Elaborating on writing as both a solitary and a social act, the text says that "at times you need isolation and silence to search for words that make meaning. . . . [while] at other times you need community and conversation to see if your words make sense" (4). While writing is characterized by "occasional frustrations" and as a task that may seem "overwhelming," it nevertheless functions to "allow you to express something about yourself, to explore and explain ideas, and to assess the claims of other people" (2).

"Effective writing," according to the book, "emerges from effective decision making," all of which accrues to the writer "rewards [that] make the hard work worthwhile," such as a "gain [in] power" (2). Decisions that student-writers must make involve subject, audience, and purpose, decisions which the book says should serve as *"prompters,"* and as *"touchstones"* but, most importantly, as *"guidelines,"* where "prompters" provide ways to consider the what and how of writing, "touchstones" provide ways to evaluate what has been written relative to the writer's initial goals, and "guidelines," the most comprehensive method, provide "ways to control every decision you make throughout the writing process, from formulating ideas to refining sentences" (7). Writers, the book says, constantly make decisions when writing, some of which "are complex, as when you are trying to shape ideas [while] others are simple, as when you are trying to select words" (7). But "each decision," the book says, "affects every other decision," so writers must continuously adjust and readjust their writing to insure that it is "consistent, coherent, and clear" (7). The evaluation of writers' decisions or the effectiveness of their writing is then to be measured according to the dictum that "in every writing situation, a writer is trying to communicate a *subject* to an *audience* for a *purpose*" (7), and, indeed, "the central idea of this book is that writers write most effectively when they are '*Writing with a Purpose*'" (13).

These representative statements contribute to the discursive formation of writing process that constitutes *Writing with a Purpose*. My critique focuses on these statements, although other illustrative statements will appear in my evaluation as well. However, the controlling question that must be asked of this discursive formation is this: what is writing *not*? To answer this, I first ask *Writing with a Purpose* the following questions:

- What notion of audience is advanced, relative to notions of self and alterity?
- What sort of understanding is promoted?
- What notion of language and discourse is tacitly assumed?

- What notion of context obtains relative to the notion of horizon?
- What notion of purpose is suggested, relative to notions of addressivity and answerability?

Audience, Self, and Alterity

What notion of audience is advanced, relative to notions of self and alterity? To begin to answer this heuristic, we must recall that each of us is bound to the world according to our physical position in space, what Bakhtin calls the law of placement, so that what we see and perceive is contingent upon our physical placement within a context. This insures that each of us orders existence a little differently from all others. The law of placement also insures that we have, simultaneously, both a surplus and a deficit of seeing, relative to all others within a shared context. This, then, renders the self thoroughly dialogic. Therefore, each of us must engage in a sort of reciprocity called alterity, upon which we appropriate both discourse and others' surplus of seeing so as to impose patterns of meaning upon our experiences and give value to our lives. This is a complex activity, one fraught with social and political struggle, as suggested in the notion of the fluctuating ratio that obtains in dialogism and with which we must constantly attempt to negotiate. Without such negotiation—negotiation that gives value to ourselves and to the others with whom we come in contact—our individual development of self is stunted. Alterity, therefore, is fundamental to our achieving consciousness, as well as to our continuing development as human beings. We need others' discourse and surplus of vision, just as others need ours.

Any writing process promotes some notion of alterity. This is evident in *Writing with a Purpose*'s elaboration of its notion of writing as both a solitary and a social act, which requires "at times [that] you need isolation and silence to search for words that make meaning. . . . [while] at other times you need community and conversation to see if your words make sense" (4). In this characterization of writing, writing constitutes both a procedure and an act that is both solitary and social. Although notions of self and alterity allow for alternate solitary and social moments, it is the dichotomy of isolation and community that is troublesome here. Even though we may require "isolation and silence to search for words that make meaning" (4), this search constitutes an appropriation, a veritable struggle, of language from the thoroughly heteroglot social milieu in which it circulates. Meaning-making is thus never an absolutely solitary event. Similarly, the insinuation of social as the need of "community and conversation to see if your words make sense" (4), gives short shrift to a notion of alterity. Certainly, the only way to gauge the effectiveness of our writing is through our audience's response, but this restricted notion of the social, again, elides the interactive and reciprocal nature of alterity and thus seriously reduces the writer's potential to experience a mutually meaning-enriching situation.

More regarding alterity is gleaned from the book's advice regarding audience. The "most inexperienced writers," students are told, "assume that their audience is their writing teacher," a definition which "is naïve and smart at the same time" (10). The book says that "writers must remember that they are writing for multiple audiences, not for a single person" and that "the most immediate audience is *you*. [. . .] You write," it says, "not only to convey your ideas to others but also to clarify them for yourself" (10). A second audience, it says, is comprised of friends, classmates, and teachers, which "are your most attentive audience" (11). They help you through the entire process of writing. "But," students are told, "you must remember that writing teachers and even peers are essentially collaborators and thus are not your ultimate audience" (11). The most significant audience, according to *Writing with a Purpose,* is the one that cares nothing about your writing process, only about the product. The book says it is helpful to imagine a "single significant reader—an attentive, sensible, reasonably informed person who will give you a sympathetic reading as long as you do not waste his or her time" (11).

Ostensibly, the above passage offers a notion of alterity in the way that teachers and peers are equated to collaborators. But the text dismisses either of these as a viable audience, preferring to establish a universal audience, "an attentive, sensible, reasonably informed person," for the student writer. However, on the same page as this passage, more advice follows that, again, seemingly attempts to develop a notion of alterity. "Many times," according to the textbook, "especially as you learn more about your subject, you discover a real-world audience for your writing" (11). Once you know your specific audience, you can "analyze the distinctive features of each group. What do they know? What do they think they know? What do they need to know? The more you know about each group, the more you will be able to direct your writing to their assumptions and expectations" (11–12). Furthermore, students are told, "your decision about audience, like your decision about subject, has to be made in the context of the complete writing situation. Both decisions are ultimately related to your discovery of purpose—what you want to do in your essay" (12).

In this latter passage, the book comes closer to having the writer identify a real-world audience with which to enter into a relationship that alterity necessitates. Certainly, the advice regarding the decision of audience as specific to the writing situation is appropriate, although, the text has not yet discussed specific sorts of writing contexts. But even though the audience analysis questions are helpful, it is important to note that their focus is on the audience's knowledge. For a true notion of alterity, it is necessary that writers engage a reciprocity involving the whole person, not just the person's intellect. So, while the notion of alterity is complicated somewhat here, it nevertheless elides a consideration of the audience's total subjectivity, which renders it at best a diluted notion of alterity.

This elision of a full notion of subjectivity continues, as the text discusses the process of writing a first or discovery draft, an act designed to test an "initial hypothesis" (15). Again, testing an initial hypothesis through a first draft is not bad advice. It is, rather, the nature of a hypothesis itself, which suggests that only a narrow characterization of audience is being factored. Sometimes, the book says, "the discovery draft demonstrates that your hypothesis works, but most of the time, '"you simply cannot prove what your hypothesis suggested you might be able to prove'" (15). The notion of hypothesis, here, "Your hypothesis represents what you want to prove" (15), that is, "*hypothesis*—a working purpose" (14), along with advice about making "your case" and about avoiding "flaws in your reasoning" (15), suggests that hypotheses are more closely aligned with certainty than with speculation. That this discussion of hypotheses is located in the book's generic discussion of writing process indicates that a notion of persuasion is elided in favor of argument as the generic writing purpose of *Writing with a Purpose*. Indeed, such a notion is in sympathy with an appeal limited to the audience's intellect that the text has consistently promoted.

As *Writing with a Purpose* begins to elaborate a writing process, audience is scarcely mentioned. Indeed, in the process as described by *Writing with a Purpose,* it is in the first draft that subject, audience, and purpose are elicited. The book states: "Experienced writers, however, know that their first draft is only a very preliminary attempt at producing a sustained piece of writing. Planning allows them to examine possible topics; drafting enables them to experiment with possible arrangements of thoughts on a topic" (52). Students are told that "you must continue to exercise the 'art of choice,' evaluating your information, arranging and rearranging it, until you compose a coherent draft" (53). Finally, three pages into the discussion on drafting, the book states that "all the choices you make ultimately depend on one question: What arrangement best enables me to communicate my *subject* to an *audience* for a *purpose?*" (54). Through a scratch outline, used for drafting purposes, a student's subject, "although still sketchy," nevertheless "suggests an emerging pattern that is potentially significant, interesting, and manageable" (56). Additionally, "some potential audiences have also emerged" (56). Drafting hypotheses, then, is characterized as involving a struggle to clarify subject, readers, and purpose (58). Thus far, the notion of alterity in this notion of writing process is a fairly impoverished one, for surely the purpose that drives the writer's first draft ought not be divorced from the audience to whom it is directed.

This characterization of writing process changes, however, in the chapter on argument, for students are told here that "in planning an argument, you *select a subject, collect and use evidence,* and *consider the opposition*" (126). This consideration of the opposition holds promise for some notion of alterity, but relative to the "Argument" chapter's introduction, such an assumption is premature:

> But because their primary purpose is to convince others—to accept a proposal, to challenge a situation, to support some cause—formal arguments must be developed according to rules of evidence and logical reasoning. These demands may seem formidable, but in many ways they are simply extensions of what you have learned about those elements that govern the writing process.
>
> You begin composing an argument by planning, by investigating a variety of sources so that you can discover a subject. Next, you organize your argument into a draft so that it most effectively and fully expresses your subject to persuade your audience. Fi-

nally, you examine your test [hypothesis] to revise those features that obscure the clarity or weaken the credibility of your purpose.

As you move through these stages, you will expand your appreciation of other arguments (particularly those of the opposition), develop your authority to present those features of your argument that matter most, and increase your understanding of those aspects of your argument or your opponent's argument that might be negotiated or that might never be resolved. (126)

The notion that formal arguments must be developed only according to logical reasoning elides a full notion of subjectivity, of other, of audience, as does the characterization of "other" as opponent. Indeed, though the chapter section on rhetorical appeals provides some caveats for all three appeals, there is little complication of any of them. The exception may be emotional appeal, which the book says, some people find "suspect" since "it relies on the feelings, instincts, and opinions of readers" and is often associated with "the devious manipulations of advertising or politics" (140). Affective appeals, suggested to be suspect, are thus tacitly excluded. Even the notion of *ethos,* though it tacitly permeates the text, is not explicitly complicated as an issue with which students ought to grapple. For example, statements alluding to students' expanded appreciation of their opponent's arguments throughout the writing process suggest that an understanding of the opposition's arguments is necessary for "winning." The chapter on argument offers no sense that an effort to truly understand represents a particular *ethos* or that a genuine reciprocity that characterizes alterity ought to inform the writing process.

An agonistic characterization of alterity continues as *Writing with a Purpose* says that "*a formal argument must focus on a subject that can be debated* [and that] such subjects are open to interpretation because opposing opinions can be supported with evidence and the audience is free to consider both claims and to choose sides" (127). Students are then instructed that "to convince your readers that yours is the right side (or at least the better side), you will need to support your position" (127). This advice does little, however, to have students genuinely engage opposing opinions. It does not seek a perspective that would inform their writing and thus accrue to their reader an equal opportunity for the exercise of broader interpretation. Rather, a "right/wrong" and/or "win/lose" mentality, arguably the lowest common denominator of argument's purpose, severely constrains this notion of writing process. Even this statement, which might, at last, allude to a notion of alterity—"You are trying to establish a partnership of mutual inquiry" (135–36)—is situated in the section, "Organizing the Argument: *Drafting*," rather than in the planning phase of the writing process. This "partnership of mutual inquiry" becomes yet another technical ploy to win an argument, rather than an act of reciprocal inquiry and meaning-making characteristic of alterity.

Last, another overture to a notion of alterity appears in the chapter on argument, titled "Accommodation": "accommodation takes your audience's hesitations into account [so that] instead of trying to win the argument, you try to improve communication and increase understanding" (139). This would constitute an overture to a notion of alterity, if not for its being situated as a subsection to "Arranging the Evidence." Therefore, although this strategy "to improve communication and increase understanding" ostensibly suggests some sort of mutual meaning-making event, its context within instructions for arranging evidence belies its pragmatic purpose as advice for the *appearance* of accommodation as a tactic for winning.

This analysis indicates that, while there are statements that seem to suggest alterity, there is no genuine notion promoted by the book. Rather than an "acting with," there is instead a consistent insinuation of an "acting upon." This assessment gains strength in the following sections' discussions.

Understanding

The heuristic of "What sort of understanding is promoted?" leads us to a consideration of Bakhtin's distinction between shallow understanding and responsive or active understanding, both of which are necessary to a notion of alterity. Shallow understanding, represented by a passive redoubling of the other's experience, serves as a bridge to responsive understanding, which translates experience into an altogether different axiological perspective. Responsive understanding can either resist or support discourse, but it always enriches discourse. Responsive understanding requires evaluation and is thus active. Therefore, Bakhtin says, understanding and evaluation constitute an integral act that serves to reveal the multiple meanings available in dialogism. This integral act of responsive understanding thus strengthens alterity, opening discourse to different levels of meaning and value.

Understanding is pivotal to any notion of writing process, both in how students understand the writing process itself as well as the understanding they must achieve to engage in acts of writing. Both types of understanding are addressed in the textbook. For example, in a section titled "The Stages of the Writing Process," *Writing with a Purpose* describes planning as a process of "developing your ideas and giving them shape" and as comprised of "*a series of strategies designed to find and formulate information in writing*" (5). This is necessary, students are told, because "you need to discover what is possible within the confines of the assignment—to explore a variety of subjects and invent alternative ways to think and write about each subject" (5). Students are thus instructed to anticipate planning strategies in a later chapter designed, the book says, "for generating information you can transform into a first draft" (5). Granting that understanding can be marked by degrees of intensity, this passage speaks to a notion of responsive understanding, although, perhaps, in a somewhat diminished degree. I say this because what is missing is the exigence that would drive responsive understanding. Still, the advice to students to "invent alternative ways to think and write about each subject" would, if executed, contribute to active, responsive understanding.

Expecting to find a notion of exigence factored in the section, "Determining Your Purpose," I examined the following excerpt for a more complex characterization of responsive understanding:

> When *purpose* is considered as an element inside the writing situation, the term has a specific meaning: *Purpose is the overall design that governs what writers do in their writing.* Writers who have determined their purpose know what kind of information they need, how they want to organize and develop it, and why they think it is important. In effect, purpose directs and controls all the decisions writers make. It is both the *what* and the *how* of that process—that is, the specific subject the writer selects *and* the strategies the writer uses to communicate the subject most effectively. (13)

It is difficult to ascertain from this passage the degree of responsive understanding this notion of purpose engenders. While purpose seems overdetermined by technical features, it also includes the writer's sense of why her/his purpose is important. Nevertheless, purpose does appear to be heavily weighted toward "the what and the how," rather than "the why" of writing.

Another passage that describes the writing process also heavily alludes to "the what and the how," of writing, again eliding "the why" or exigence that would drive the process. Such a notion of writing process cannot thus engender a high degree of knowledge-making potential for students. Rather, the concern focuses on the communication of knowledge, which is driven by a series of decisions. The book maintains that the decisions student-writers must make involve subject, audience, and purpose, and that these decisions should serve as "*prompters*," or ways to consider the what and how of writing, and as "*touchstones*," or ways to evaluate writing according to initial goals, and, most importantly, as "*guidelines*," or ways to control every decision of the writing process (7). In this description of writing process, there is a focus on the art that leads to communication. Absent is any notion of genuine inquiry; rather, the tacit assumption is that information is to be collected, organized, and arranged in a manner that will translate this information as seamlessly as possible to the audience. In Bakhtin's characterization, this translation constitutes merely a shallow understanding, a redoubling of someone else's experience, when what is called for is the responsive understanding that can lead to mutual knowledge-making and to reciprocal engagement.

An opportunity for responsive understanding to inhere in *Writing with a Purpose*'s writing process might have been located in the chapter on planning, specifically in the section titled, "Reading," but, this potential is once again thwarted by a variation on the banking notion of education, as the student is told that "you must be a critical consumer—*selecting, analyzing,* and *evaluating* what you read for one purpose: to help you write" (37). Students are then told to "think of reading as another form of interviewing—a way of talking to people who have already thought and written about your subject" (37). That this notion of consumer is then extrapolated to the act of interviewing likewise diminishes the potential reciprocity of this additional form of inquiry. So, while both reading and interviewing contain much potential for achieving responsive understanding, the implied subject position of consumer mitigates this potential at the same time.

The particular notion of purpose and inquiry promoted in *Writing with a Purpose* focuses on the communication of information and the technical procedures that would render this communication as static-free as possible. As a result, the possibility of responsive understanding is diminished. There is little sense that students ought to be agents, acting through the information they seek and assimilating it to arrive at a place different from the one they occupied at the beginning of the writing process. There is little space in this notion of writing process for students to experience responsive, active understanding.

Language/Discourse

The heuristic of "What notion of language and discourse is tacitly assumed?" would have us acknowledge that a notion of language and discourse is fundamental in any conception of writing process, although it may not often be, if ever, directly addressed. A dialogic conception of language posits that language is marked by degrees of sameness and difference. A pole of sameness is characterized by a centripetal force within discourse that renders it monologic while a pole of difference is characterized by a centrifugal force that renders it dialogic. Discourse is thus both thoroughly social and political, as every utterance is marked by the inherent struggle between these two forces. The unique nature of each utterance, along with this inherent struggle, however, makes language/discourse dialogic. The continually fluctuating tension between opposing centripetal and centrifugal forces constitutes the ratio that distinguishes discourse as dialogic. Dialogized heteroglossia can never be exhausted because it continually reconceptualizes the world.

Relative to the constitution of consciousness, language always lies on the border between ourselves and others. It becomes ours only as we struggle to appropriate it and to infuse it with our intentions. Language does not exist in a neutral or impersonal realm; it exists in other people's mouths, in other people's contexts, serving their intentions and it is from here that we must appropriate language and attempt to make it our own. It is this struggle that renders language, dialogism, both social and political.

In *Writing with a Purpose*, language is most explicitly addressed in the areas we would normally anticipate finding such discussions: a chapter on diction and a chapter on style. In chapter seven, "Diction:

The Choice of Words," one of the writing assignments foregrounds the importance of the right word with the use of a quote from Mark Twain: "'The difference between the right word and the nearly right word is the difference between lightning and a lightning bug.' Compose a narrative essay about the consequences of your inability to select the right word(s) to explain your behavior on an important occasion" (253). In chapter ten, "Tone and Style," effective communication is addressed as students are instructed to question themselves thusly: "Do I find my writing clear, unambiguous, and likely to engage my readers? Have I carried out my purpose at every level; that is, am I satisfied that the *how* of my writing—its attitude, organization, and the language—conveys the *what* of my ideas?" (268).

The problems in the passages above are associated with what is not addressed by *Writing with a Purpose,* which is the struggle each of us must engage in our attempts to make our intentions understood by others. Yes, I agree with the book regarding the importance of the right word, of effective communication, and with the notion that the "how" of writing cannot be separated from the "what." What is troublesome is the phrase, "your inability to select the right word(s)," along with the insinuation that the "why" of writing is not pertinent to this discussion. There thus exists a tacit notion that language unproblematically represents thought, so that students' inability to select a right word has less to do with their struggle to appropriate a heteroglot word than with their lack of ability to *choose* the correct word.

This assumption permeates the text. In the general discussion of writing process, students are told that "confusion occurs when you know too little about your writing project; contradiction occurs when you think too little about what you know" (7). There is no sense that confusion and contradiction can emanate from a felt dissonance, a struggle to appropriate language, and/or a struggle to successfully negotiate genre conventions, so, again, confusion and contradiction are characterized to be the sole result of the writer's deficiency. While a tacit concession seems to be made as *Writing with a Purpose* states that the writing process is sometimes "a disorderly, contradictory procedure," this concession is immediately undermined when we read that "experienced writers know that [this] disorder and contradiction are probably inevitable but temporary disturbances" (7).

However, writing that seeks to achieve responsive understanding is rather very likely characterized by contradiction and disturbance. Furthermore, the suggestion that this state is temporary elides the often very difficult situation a writer negotiates, as s/he struggles to achieve the moment of necessary *stasis* at which writing can even begin. While it is necessary that a commitment to some specific perspective of understanding be made in the act of writing, it would seem appropriate to counsel students that their perspectives may well change even after they have produced a text. This is the nature of responsive understanding. It is necessary to acknowledge this struggle rather than undermining it by insinuating that "disturbance" is something that ought to be mastered into oblivion. Rather, the mastery ought to be directed toward the productive negotiation of disturbance, one that results in the sort of responsive understanding that renders students as makers of knowledge, as well as merely communicators of knowledge.

A correspondence theory of language inheres in this writing process, as writers, the book says, constantly make decisions when writing, some of which "are complex, as when you are trying to shape ideas [while] others are simple, as when you are trying to select words" (7). But "each decision," the book says, "affects every other decision," so writers must continuously adjust and readjust their writing to insure that it is "consistent, coherent, and clear" (7). Certainly, consistency, coherence, and clearness are admirable qualities, but advice given so unproblematically diminishes the struggle writers engage in their attempts to achieve responsive understanding and thus become makers of knowledge.

Language, in *Writing with a Purpose*, is unproblematically presented to students as representing thought. If only they collect sufficient amounts of information, students will then be in a position to choose the words that can accurately transmit this information. There is no sense of the struggle we must all negotiate in our attempts to have language serve our intentions. A failure to successfully negotiate this struggle is attributed solely to deficiencies in the writers' procedures, which can easily be remedied through a more faithful attention to the book's advice. This perspective assumes writers, at the least, have the potential to achieve complete autonomy.

Context and Horizon

What notion of context obtains relative to the notion of horizon? This heuristic would have us consider the notion of horizon as issuing from both a strong sense of reciprocity and the physical constraints of subjects in the world. Because two bodies cannot simultaneously occupy the same space, each subject structures the setting of the world, as well as the position of all others, according to their specific placement in it. Subjects' shared context is characterized as environment, indicating that the place, or context, of perception shapes the meaning of that perception. The place of perception unique to each subject due to the physical constraints of space, however, is called horizon, as this is the context from which each subject authors her/his unique utterances. Horizon inevitably encompasses, in addition to the unique perspective afforded by a subject's unique physical placement in the world, conceptual and physical aspects of a common context shared by participating interlocutors: the spatial horizon of the common physical context, as well as interlocutors' knowledge, understanding, and evaluation of this common context. Profoundly characterized by reciprocity, horizon thus engenders the perspective that each subject view the other as not merely a duplication of itself but as a mutual opportunity to co-experience the other's life that enriches the context and, therefore, the lives of all participating interlocutors. Utterances, then, are thoroughly social, as they are, in effect, the products of interlocutors' interaction.

In my conclusion, I address horizon in its broader context, but, presently, I examine it relative to students' relationship with the textbook's notion of writing process, specifically to students' writing contexts. Horizon is addressed in *Writing with a Purpose* as the writer's environment, which the book says is key to establishing rituals and habits of writing that enable writers' productivity.

Environments are connected to writing habits, which the book defines as "the conditions and tools they [writers] believe they need whenever they write"; as the "enabling conditions that allow you to enter and complete your writing process"; and as the "physical and psychological setting for the central action—the mental procedures you perform as you move through the stages of the composition" (3, 5). Here then, the setting necessarily encompasses the spatial horizon of the physical context, the writer's unique physical placement within it, and the writer's knowledge, understanding, and evaluation of all that constitutes the setting. The "enabling conditions" to which *Writing with a Purpose* alludes are both "physical and psychological," requiring knowledge, understanding, and evaluation of the "mental procedures" a writer performs while moving "through the stages of the composition" (3, 5). These "enabling conditions" are or should become habits, some of which *Writing with a Purpose* says are formed by "chance," while "most come about almost unconsciously and conform to a writer's other personal habits" (3, 4). Some writers, the book reports, view these writing habits "as rituals, procedures to be followed faithfully each time they write" (4). Although "each new piece of writing will inevitably contain new challenges," the book explains, experienced writers "believe the habits that have worked before—composing in a special environment, maintaining a disciplined schedule, and using familiar tools—will work again" (3).[49] So, although experienced writers may allude to "inspiration" or "good luck," they do not depend on such "mysterious forces," the book warns, for "effective writing emerges from effective decision making" (3). The book thus definitely promotes the notion that the effective decision making required of writing is enhanced by the writer's physical and conceptual horizon. Conceptually, according to the book, experienced writers possess the knowledge, understanding, and evaluative capacity necessary to identify and solve problems. Experienced writers can recognize obstacles, use strategies to overcome these obstacles, and discern when to repeat a previous stage of writing (3). *Writing with a Purpose*, therefore, admonishes every writer to "*develop writing habits that work for you and trust in them*" (3).

The habits and rituals of the writing environment are, then, undoubtedly factors in each writer's horizon. These habits and rituals allude to a specific context, which influences and shapes the writer's perception. The text suggests that the habits and rituals of writing are as unique as each individual practicing them. So, again, while the writing context is characterized by physical objects, this context is also acknowledged as requiring the writer's knowledge, understanding, and evaluation, at least to the extent required by the habits and rituals of writing.

But this is also the limit to which a notion of environment in *Writing with a Purpose* speaks: the habits and rituals of writing, unique to each writer, function in the writer's environment to elicit her/his knowledge, understanding, and evaluation of the writing process. A notion of horizon, however, would include this but would likewise maintain that the writing process ought to become an interlocutor in this context. In other words, it should, to the extent that a textual representation is capable, recognize the physical context of the student-writer and, most importantly, interact knowledgeably and understandingly with this mutually shared context. I do not see this writing process participating as an interlocutor to students' partial, situated, and contingent contexts, a participation that would require some degree of understanding regarding the power/knowledge relations in which a student functions and which then influences the manner in which the student can and will engage the writing process. Therefore, while the book addresses the issue of environment, it nevertheless fails to sufficiently complicate this notion to achieve the fuller notion of horizon.

Purpose: Addressivity and Answerability

We must return to the concept of dialogism to address the heuristic "What notion of purpose is suggested, relative to notions of addressivity and answerability?" As previously discussed, dialogism represents the ratio of social and political tension that ensues from the struggle between centripetal and centrifugal forces that obtains in heteroglot discourse. The social aspect of dialogism is called addressivity, because each of us is addressed by the world and each of us, responsible for our unique physical position in space, has no recourse but to answer, for this is a necessity by which to achieve consciousness as well as an ethical obligation to engage in acts of alterity that enrich life's meaning. Addressivity is thus a quality of every utterance since every utterance is directed toward some notion of addressee, whether it is an immediate subject with whom we are in dialogue, a "public," contemporaries, like-minded people, opponents, etc. Bakhtin says both the composition and, especially, the style of the utterance depend upon who the addressee is, how the writer senses and imagines the addressee, and the force of the addressee's effect upon the utterance. Addressees, then, are the equivalent of the world and our responses constitute an "authoring" to which we are compelled to answer for our unique position in the world's space. This ethical necessity is also referred to as having no alibi in existence, since even no answer paradoxically constitutes an answer.

Answerability, or the act of authoring, is also equated to a performance, since answerability constitutes our struggle to impose form upon our own time and space. Meaning occurs in tandem with answerability and value accrues to our lives as patterns of meaning likewise accrue. Answerability as an act of authoring also constitutes an architectonic, a construction or building, as well as an aesthetic, since both notions involve the relation of parts to whole. Answerability thus not only speaks to the shaping of our personality and our social and political imbrication in the whole culture, it also speaks to the ethic of situating that shaping from partial and contingent positions. Due to this ethic, it is the process rather than the product of answerability or authoring that is most important, although neither is, of course, discrete. Each is a necessity of the other so that they constitute a relation. Our existence in the world is thus neither a given nor a privilege but a responsibility. Therefore, we must author our lives both for ourselves and for the world.

Writing process, of which the authoring of a product, a text, is part, is thus not unlike the authoring of a life. Certainly, any notion of writing process constitutes its own version of addressivity and answerability, and all the components thus far evaluated in *Writing with a Purpose* contribute to its specific notion of addressivity and answerability. As indicated in the textbook's title, purpose drives its notion of writing process, and this self-professed tenet—*Writing with a Purpose*—is telling, regarding its notion of the circumference of purpose in its notion of writing process: "The central idea of this book is that writers write most effectively when they are '*Writing with a Purpose*'" (13). The notion of effectiveness is not, in itself, a negative. As a controlling criterion of purpose, however, effectiveness disproportionately weights this notion of writing process toward the end-product, the produced text. A focus on the strategies and procedures needed to produce the product elides the writer's sense of exigence that would, in the first place, compel him/her to utilize the recommended strategies and procedures to transform one sort of understanding into another, that is, a transformation of information (experience) into knowledge (value).

An examination of the book's treatment of purpose illuminates its attitude toward addressivity and answerability. "As you begin writing," the book advises students, "you start to acquire a general sense of your purpose" (14). A body of information is acquired and is then examined for a specific perspective, "an interesting angle from which to investigate your subject," any of which can be used "to form a *hypothesis*—a working purpose" (14). One hypothesis, however, must eventually be chosen, and how you choose this hypothesis, the book says, "ultimately emerges from your temperament, experiences, and interests, and also from the requirements of the context—whether you are writing for yourself or on an assignment" (14). This is one of the few allusions in the text to exigence, but it is significant that no strategies are offered in this writing process by which to propel students toward the location of an exigence unique to the context of their situatedness. Thus there is no sense that the goal in seeking information should issue from the writer's horizon; the goal issues, rather, from its necessity to fulfill the expectations of effectiveness in the context of a class assignment. Here, then, purpose is seemingly imposed upon information, an act for which students are, indeed, coached by this writing process.

That purpose is to be imposed also follows from the expectation of this writing process that purpose is derived during revision: "You must," students are instructed, "eventually arrive at a final decision about your purpose. You make that decision during revision, when you know what you want to do and how you want to do it" (15). Notably, the final decision regarding purpose is described as being made in tandem with a decision regarding a thesis. The text goes into some detail to explain the distinctions between purpose and thesis:

> One way to express your purpose is to state your thesis. A *thesis* is a sentence that usually appears in the first paragraph of your essay and states the main idea you are going to develop. Although the thesis is often called a purpose statement, thesis and purpose are not precisely the same thing. Your purpose is both contained in and larger than your thesis: it consists of all the strategies you will use to demonstrate your thesis in a sustained and successful piece of writing. Your thesis makes a *restricted, unified,* and *precise* assertion about your subject—an assertion that can be developed in the amount of space you have, that treats only one idea, and that is open to only one interpretation. [. . .] In many ways the difference between a hypothesis (a working purpose) and a thesis (a final assertion) explains why you can speculate about your purpose *before* you write but can specify your purpose only *after* you have written. (15–16)

Only now, only at the point of revision, are students instructed about a thesis, the commitment they must make in their writing, a decision that coincides with a final decision regarding the purpose of their writing. The connection between speculation and specificity, the tension the book describes as obtaining between the writing process and the writing purpose, requires that students frequently pause and evaluate their progress, to prepare them for this moment of final decision making. The guidelines offered to students at this point of revision for determining purpose and thesis include the following questions:

1. What are the requirements of my writing project? If writing for an assignment, do I understand the assignment? If writing on my own, do I have definite expectations of what I'll accomplish?

2. As I proceed with this project, what do I need to know? Do I have a good understanding of my subject, or do I need more information? Have I considered the possible audiences who might read my writing?

3. What hypothesis can I use as my working purpose? How many different hypotheses can I formulate about my subject? Which of them seems to direct and control my information in the most effective manner?

4. What purpose have I discovered for this writing project? Has my purpose changed as I learned more about my subject and audience? If so, in what ways? Have I discovered, by working with a hypothesis or hypotheses, what I want to do with my writing?

5. "What is my thesis?" (16)

These questions are not, of themselves, poor questions, nor are they necessarily moot at the point of revision. Questions regarding the quality of understanding and sufficiency of information, for example, are certainly pertinent. But I am puzzled regarding questions of possible audiences, at least to the extent that this consideration may have surfaced only at this late point and the same concern applies to questions regarding a hypothesis or working purpose. There is a difference between allowing that decisions can be changed throughout the writing process and encouraging deferral of decision making until the time of revision. I am inclined to infer that this encouragement of deferral constitutes the book's notion of writer exigence, which would make exigence bestowed upon the writer rather than emanating from the writer's own horizon.

Speaking further to a notion of exigence is the book's discussion of students' location of a subject about which to write, along with suggested writing assignments. Student writers, the book says, often complain that "finding a subject" is their "biggest problem," so *Writing with a Purpose* offers students a "sampler of writing assignments," with the instruction that "as you browse through each assignment, consider how the subject is defined and how you are expected to develop it" (8). These instructions mitigate a notion of addressivity, as there is nothing that would suggest the alterity or responsive understanding that could constitute a response of legitimate answerability. This is further confirmed in the steps students are instructed to take "to find a suitable subject": First, students are instructed to select something they know or can learn about; second, they are told to select something that can be restricted; and, last, they are advised to ask themselves if it is significant, interesting, and manageable (8–9). "Ultimately," however, students are told that they "must develop [their] own methods for answering these questions" (9). Essentially, then, students are instructed in what to do to locate a suitable writing subject, but they are not told how to do it. The text, however, provides students with a default for finding a subject to write about in its offering of a variety of writing assignments at the conclusion of each chapter.

Each chapter concludes with ten writing assignments, which appear to be a mix of traditional composition modes and Bloom's taxonomy,[50] with the "collaborate" section included to address the contemporary composition issue of collaboration. The headings of assignments conform across chapters and read as follows: 1. Narrate; 2. Observe; 3. Investigate; 4. Collaborate; 5. Read; 6. Respond; 7. Analyze; 8. Evaluate; 9. Argue; 10. Argue. I examine three different types of assignments—investigation, evaluation, and argument—taken from three separate chapters.

The first assignment, taken from chapter two, "Planning," would have students "investigate." The assignment reads as follows:

> Interview someone on your campus or in your community who is involved in managing information—a reference librarian, a newspaper writer, an advertising designer. Ask your subject to describe the procedures he or she uses to discover, store, and reproduce information. Then write a profile of this information manager, focusing on the procedures he or she uses to overcome the anxieties certain types of information induce. (50)

Exigence is short-circuited here. Although a context for writing is provided, the guiding issue, "the anxieties certain types of information induce," is not explored in the context of either the student's experience or interest. Instead, the inquiry is prescribed: the assignment calls for an interview of an information professional; the interview questions are dictated; and the genre is specified. Audience, notably, is not addressed at all. There is no sense of addressivity or answerability in this assignment, as the parameters, the nature of the inquiry, and the genre of the final product are all given to students.

A second assignment, taken from chapter seven, "Paragraphs: Units of Development," is designed to have students "evaluate." Here, students are instructed to:

> Reread the paragraphs on the status of the American family in this chapter [Philip Slater, page 167; Jane Howard, page 169; Jane O'Reilly, page 169]. Reexamine Ellen Goodman's argument about the stresses and strengths within the American family. Then argue that (a) the power of the American family was always more an ideal than a reality, (b) the American family is breaking up beneath the forces of contemporary culture, or (c) the contemporary American family, though changed in character, is as strong as it ever was. (193)

The subject, the American family, is provided, as is the focus of inquiry, "the stresses and strengths within the American family." Moreover, the sources of inquiry are prescribed, as is the tacit genre of exposition while, again, a consideration of audience is elided. No greater sense of addressivity and answerability thus inheres in this assignment than it did in the one previously discussed. In fact, this assignment even more egregiously usurps writers' exigence, as students are ostensibly to exercise their ability to evaluate, yet they are denied the challenge of locating and presenting their own conclusions. Rather, they are given a choice among three pre-packaged hypotheses. Such a limitation elides any "other" perspectives students might be compelled to assume on the basis of their own exigence.

The last assignment I examine asks students to "argue" and is taken from chapter nine, "Diction: The Choice of Words." This assignment is interesting not only for its prescription of exigency but also for its tacitly reductive notion of language/discourse and of the knowledge/power relations that characterize cultural formations. It reads as follows:

> When the emperor asked Confucius what could be done to restore harmony to his troubled land, the wise man replied, "Purify the language." Select an example of language that needs purifying from, for example, a political speech or a product warranty. Identify those places in the text that need revision. Then write a letter to the appropriate authority using your revisions to illustrate how effective diction can create social harmony. (254)

I should note that this assignment does not correspond to any reading in the chapter. Its context truly is the Confucius anecdote. The focus, then, is language, language that needs purifying; the prescribed genre is a letter; and unlike the previous two assignments, the audience, an "appropriate authority," is now likewise indicated. Exigency is again usurped: students are told to argue that "effective diction can create social harmony." Presumably, their theses are left to their own discretion. But I for one am confounded by the notion that "effective diction can create social harmony." What exactly would "purifying" an example of language actually entail? Must the student attempt to strip language of its heteroglot baggage? And were this even possible, how, exactly, would this stagnant language then contribute to achieving social harmony? This assignment is troubling not only for its reductive notions of discourse and of addressivity and answerability but also for its reductive approach to what might well be complex systemic social problems. Even conceding that language can be purified, the notion that such a purification might bring about social harmony is not only ridiculous but ethically impoverished as well.

The world compels us to answer for our place in it because each of our places is unique. We are ethically obliged to share our own privileged perspective, and we must, therefore, author our partial, contingent, and situated perspectives. This reciprocity simultaneously enables our own capacity to author as well as the capacity of "others." Because the learning situation of the classroom is a component of the architectonic of subjectivity, the authoring that writing process encourages ought not be divorced from it. *Writing with a Purpose*, however, does divorce these types of authoring, with its designated primary criterion of purpose: effectiveness. Effectiveness is a legitimate criterion of purpose, but by itself it diminishes the social and political responsibility, that is, the ethic, of students to practice answerability.

How then does the writing process of *Writing with a Purpose* compare with a conception of networked process as analyzed through the use of the networked subjectivity heuristic? Relative to a notion of language and discourse, *Writing with a Purpose* subscribes to a correspondence theory of language, where language is represented as unproblematically corresponding to thought. If students collect a sufficient amount of information and think adequately upon it, they will then have the knowledge they need to write. Through the use of strategies and procedures designed to insure the effectiveness of their final documents, students are then enabled to accurately transmit the information they have collected and organized. A failure to achieve static-free communication is attributed to a deficiency in the writer: either s/he has not collected sufficient information, s/he has not thought about it adequately, and/or s/he has failed to follow the book's advice and instructions for writing, instructions that rely heavily on descriptions of the writing processes of professional writers. Absent is any notion of the heteroglot nature of language and the dialogic struggle we must all undertake to make language serve our intentions.

Writing with a Purpose's notion of the self is extrapolated from its notion of language and discourse. With a correspondence theory of language, subjects are not theorized to be subjected to ideology and knowledge/power relations that circulate throughout discursive and nondiscursive formations. There is a tacit assumption that subjects are fully rational, coherent, unified, and autonomous, and are able to control language and have it correspond perfectly to thought. There is no space in this writing process for multiple subjectivities, epistemologies, and literacies. Agency is thus overdetermined in this conception, yet it is notable that this writing process is nevertheless structured to repress agency.

The notion of "other" is also attenuated in this notion of writing process, as the implication is the management of "others," so as to increase one's power. There is no genuine notion of alterity since students are not encouraged to engage in reciprocal acts by which to accrue meaning and value to all participants. Manipulation of "others," an acting upon rather than an acting with, also agitates against a notion of active, responsive understanding required to transform information or experience into value or knowledge. Agency is thus neutralized.

The repression of agency is also apparent in the book's notion of environment, which never extends to the more comprehensive theory of horizon. *Writing with a Purpose* does acknowledge that the habits and rituals of writing are unique to each writer, but the book lacks notions involving the subject's unique placement in the world, which indicates that each person's perception and perspective is contingent upon that placement. The absence of a notion of horizon corresponds to a lack of alterity. The necessity of sharing individual perspectives in order to mutually transform these perspectives is not acknowledged either. *Writing with a Purpose*'s notion of writing environment requires the writer's knowledge, understanding, and evaluation, but these, too, are theoretically constrained by the individual writer's rational control of the writing process itself. There is no sense that an "other" is necessary to the individual's acquisition of knowledge, understanding, and the ability to evaluate. The writing process tacitly sets itself up as serving the writer as a self-sufficient construct by which to produce a text.

Finally, the notion of authoring—of addressivity and answerability—inheres in *Writing with a Purpose*, most notably in its notion of purpose. Purpose, however, is also linked to notions of exigence and of agency, so that all of these elements—authoring, addressivity/answerability, purpose, exigence, agency—are so tightly imbricated as to be almost impossible to discuss discretely. Because we appropriate language from "others" and because we engage in reciprocal acts of meaning-making, or alterity, we experience addressivity as a sort of exigency that compels us to author a response. To author a response, however, we must have a sense of purpose relative to the exigency. These states cannot be imposed from outside but must emanate from our unique horizons.

But *Writing with a Purpose*'s notion of purpose, of which the primary criterion is effectiveness, cannot incorporate the sort of authoring associated with addressivity and answerability. This attenuated notion of purpose also confuses agency since on the one hand, autonomy is assumed in the notion of language and discourse promoted in this writing process, while on the other hand, agency is repressed through its restricted boundary criterion of effectiveness. Therefore, exigency is a mitigating factor in this writing process, as the focus is on the communication of knowledge rather than on the making of knowledge.

This is well-illustrated in the writing assignments that prescribe many of the decisions this writing process presumes, leaving students to negotiate the collection, organization, and arrangement of information, along with its seamless communication. Such a notion of authoring impoverishes the notions of addressivity and answerability.

Authoring our lives is the strategy by which we come to have a conscious life and by which we impose meaning upon experience, and assign value to our lives. None of our experiences is exempt from the ethic of authoring, including experiences that occur in the context of the academy and of the classroom. However, not all experiences are equal in their potential to impact the addressivity and answerability that compels us to the act of authoring. We might then, perhaps, think of the potential for experiences to impact our lives as characterized by degree. As for the efficacy of writing processes, it would seem that we need to attempt to evaluate their potential to affect the lives of our students on the assumption that a writing process can change our students' lives. To the degree that our chosen writing process(es) promotes or hinders the process of authoring—or has no effect whatsoever—the exigency represented by the addressivity and answerability of our students' lives, that is, the architectonic that is subjectivity ought then to guide both our evaluations of writing processes and our decisions about the processes we promote in our classrooms.

But a critique of the material artifact of the textbook alone is not sufficient for gauging our choices, for the textbook is but one factor, one discursive formation, in the institutional web of discursive relations within which networked process exists. The textbook functions in a teaching/learning context of a classroom in which we desire students to experience the world's addressivity and respond with the sort of answerability that would constitute a meaningful act of authoring for both the classroom and the world.[51] This also promotes our ideal, which is to prepare students to be students within the academy, to be productive and ethical professionals in the workplace, and to be active and responsible citizens. However, it is unrealistic to expect that any textbook could accomplish the goals of this ideal by itself. If, as Foucault maintains, "discursive formations [do] *produce* the object about which they speak," then we must look beyond the discursive formation of only the writing process textbook to other situated institutional discursive formations in which the textbook functions, along with the students and teachers imbricated in these relations.

I want now to conceptualize such a group of statements specifically as a discursive formation, comprised of both discursive and nondiscursive relations, and to speculate upon how such a reformulation might affect institutional contexts. In the process, many of the institutional relations with which networked process is imbricated will be illuminated. Without a concrete, situated context to critique, however, all I can do is to abstract from Foucault, who tells us we exist in a webbed relation of power—that institutions exert, appropriate, diffuse, commodify, and discipline and that subjectivities are inevitably affected by these power relations. I can say that a change of statements regarding writing process has the potential to change institutional structures, which can then change practices, which can then change the nature of networked process. The subject position we offer to students can become a transductive sort of circularity that represents a sort of praxis. The strength of such assertions, however, pales without the advantage of a concrete referential context. I have, therefore, elected to approximate a concrete context through a published article by Judith Rodby and Tom Fox titled "Basic Work and Material Acts: The Ironies, Discrepancies, and Disjunctures of Basic Writing and Mainstreaming." This article reports on writing program reform at California State University, Chico, and speaks to the role of institutional relations in which writing process is imbricated and which thus ought to be part of our conceptual configuration of what writing process is.

Introduction to "Basic Work and Material Acts: The Ironies, Discrepancies, and Disjunctures of Basic Writing and Mainstreaming"

This article is illuminating for not only what the authors specifically address but also for what can be gleaned regarding subjects, writing process, and institutional relations. The authors foreground the dialectic between material conditions and theory and practice, arguing that a critique of basic writing need not be confined to postmodern theorists, that writing program administrators and teachers can practice this critique themselves. I would add that writing program administrators' and teachers' critiques need not and, indeed, ought not be limited to basic writing. Instead, they can and should extend to the institutional relations in which all teaching and learning practices of writing are imbricated. This article is especially appropriate for my notion of networked subjectivity; it speaks to institutional economy, subjectivity, resistance, statements that lead to practice, physical and conceptual structures, material practices, and writing process pedagogy.

In the following section, I provide the authors' abstract of "Basic Work and Material Acts: The Ironies, Discrepancies, and Disjunctures of Basic Writing and Mainstreaming." The discussion that follows the abstract is a synthesis of both the authors' observations as well as my own. I should note that I am, in this analysis, not interested in locating points at which I might take issue with the authors' interpretation, but rather in using their institutional context and then synthesizing some of their observations with my own critique. Ultimately, I propose to illustrate an example of the relations that ought to be factored when making an evaluation of writing process according to the networked subjectivity model.

Abstract of "Basic Work and Material Acts: The Ironies, Discrepancies, and Disjunctures of Basic Writing and Mainstreaming"

> "Basic Work and Material Acts" summarizes what we have learned from mainstreaming basic writers in first-year composition at California State University, Chico. We found that "basic writing" as an institutional structure (defined by the State of California as remedial and granted no baccalaureate credit) created basic writers. Once basic writers were in the context of first-year composition, "basic writing" as a concept and as a practice disappeared. Two related principles about learning to write emerge from this experience: 1) one learns to do college writing by being in the context of college writing, not in some other context; and 2) literacy learning does not come in discrete levels. Drawing upon these insights, we go on to describe the ways that our program supports writers in first-year composition through adjunct workshops. The material circumstances of our program support students' college writing in ways that lessen the punitive nature of basic writing and are coherent with recent research in literacy studies. (84)

Critique of Institutional Relations in "Basic Work and Material Acts: The Ironies, Discrepancies, and Disjunctures of Basic Writing and Mainstreaming"

Fundamental to an understanding of the web of institutional relations relative to the writing course is the economy in which both teachers and students are imbricated. Within this webbed relation is an economic rationale: the exchange value of a product produced by the work of students for grades, which are institutionally legitimized and for which the institution confers to teachers the authority to designate. From a strictly economic viewpoint, then, students are required to provide the institution with labor, which is commodified by both the academy and academics, alike. For example, students' labor is commodified by the academy into institutional capital, e.g., to acquire funding, achieve competitive stature, elevate public opinion and cultural perception, increase its own ability to legitimize, etc., while it is likewise commodified by academics to maintain work contracts, achieve tenure, gain promotions, serve as grist for publication, confer legitimacy to vitaes, etc. The fundamental prerequisite of the academy's survival is, unquestionably, students' work. It therefore follows that the fundamental prerequisite of academics' survival is also students' work, since academics are themselves legitimized by the academy.

The insights of Rodby and Fox include the recognition that the university economy of giving credit for course work had commodified the activities of both basic writing and first-year writing courses, so that classroom practices were defined by their purchase power, that is, graduation credit. Significantly, no graduation credit was given for basic writing, while for first-year writing it was. Students, therefore, complained about the "worthlessness" of basic writing, that they were "'sick of writing' and that writing and reading had become a punishment," while teachers of basic writing complained of students' lack of motivation to invest in the course and feedback from faculty in first-year writing was that "basic writing students were not adequately 'prepared' for work in their classes, even though this was also the case for many of the students enrolled in first-year writing" (86). The environment of the basic writing course, according to Rodby and Fox, had thus "backfired," as students resisted any investment in the course and thus in their writing, which led them to conclude that "basic writing classes had produced basic writing" (86).

Ironically the course had emanated from a genuine desire to increase marginalized students' access to the university. While the writing program administrators understood that the economy of the basic writing course was a factor in students' resistance, they also speculated that a part of students' discontent might involve the curriculum itself. The initial concern had been that the basic writing course curriculum ought to be simpler than that of first-year writing, as basic writing would serve as preparation for first-year writing. The course was, according to the authors, standard: modes were used with the assumption that those such as expressive and descriptive were more easily managed by basic writing students, who, it was believed, should be made to "feel comfortable and achieve fluency" and should therefore write "what they knew" (86). But this curriculum had obviously not worked, for "in this environment, all too often students did not use writing and reading for gaining or making knowledge, for communicating with their instructor or fellow students, or even for expressing their multiple senses of self" (86). The writing produced in the basic writing course thus constituted only "basic texts with minimal goals, purposes, topics and language" (86). "Writing and reading," the authors say, "were neither acts nor actions" (86).

Writing program administrators thus attempted to "rehabilitate the scene" of basic writing, making it more challenging by essentially implementing the same curriculum in the basic writing course as that of first-year writing. The basic writing curriculum effectively disappeared although the basic writing course as a physical and institutional construct retained its viability. In tandem to the curriculum change, writing program administrators attempted to argue that students deserved credit for the basic writing course, as they were, in fact, doing work at the level of difficulty of first-year writing, but they found that "while the basic writing courses changed, the economy legitimizing them did not" (87). No graduation credit was thus forthcoming for basic writers enrolled in basic writing courses.

I am led to conclude that while the curriculum of the basic writing course had changed, the subjectivity construct of the basic writer had not. Basic writers continued to be marked first by their initial low-scores on placement tests and second by their involvement in the physical, institutional space of the basic writing construct, a space that was created to accommodate low-scoring students who might otherwise have been denied access to the university. In this instance, a change in curriculum altered neither the institutional construct of basic writing nor the subjectivity construct of students in the basic writing course. The economic sanction associated with the institutional construct of basic writing also did not abate: in return for allowing access to students who would otherwise have been denied, no graduation credit was to be conferred for the course, regardless of the rigor of its curriculum or the quality of work produced. Such was the power of the institutional relations set in motion by the genuine concern for access.

Moreover, similar to the institution's refusal to acknowledge a change of legitimacy for the basic writing course, the authors report that students' opposition to the course "was not quelled or even tempered," regardless of the curriculum changes (87). Indeed, "cynicism grew as the tautology underlying basic writing became more and more apparent" (87). So, in spite of some faculty's conviction that "basic writing students needed to be challenged and that they would work harder and appreciate the course more if the course content were more demanding," along with writing program administrators' and faculty's hope that students would "see the connection between basic writing and the demands of future writing courses" (86), these convictions and hopes were dashed in the face of strong student resistance. I would maintain that students were resisting the economy of the basic writer subject position, which in this genuine effort to achieve productive reform nevertheless condemned students to expend even more work effort to produce even higher quality writing in exchange for no graduation credit. Students understandably rebelled against a basic writing subjectivity they had no vested interest in occupying.

A second reform initiative thus ensued: "to mitigate the growing discontent, we allowed students to petition to skip one or more basic writing courses, based on interviews, evidence of motivation, teacher recommendation or writing samples" (87). Writing program administrators speculated that "if basic writing was produced and reproduced by the context of basic writing courses, perhaps basic writing would disappear if students were asked to write and read in the context of a regular first-year writing course" (87). It was through this process, the writers say, that they learned low-testing students could succeed in first-year writing courses, that "they didn't need to learn something basic first" (87). Only a year later, basic writing courses were eliminated altogether, as most, according to Rodby and Fox, had simply vanished, along with the assumption that students needed to learn basic writing before they could do first-year writing.

Obviously, institutional relations had reified the basic writing construct and along with it the construct of basic writer subjectivity. Rather than direct more energy toward reforming the construct, then, writing program administrators had chosen an option that subverted these institutional relations by offering low-testing students an alternative subject position. As the basic writing course vanished, so too did the subject role associated with it. So, while students continued to be marked by the status of their low placement test scores, they were nevertheless placed in a context, the first-year writing class, for which their efforts were institutionally legitimized with exchange value, a grade that would accrue graduation credit. Institutional economy and a concomitant alternative subject position thus played significant roles in the success of this second reform effort. But these were not the only institutional relations that factored in this success.

With the construct and the structure of basic writing eliminated, students entering first-year writing with low-test scores were also enrolled in an adjunct writing workshop. The economy, notably, was more equitable in the writing workshop than the basic writing course but not so much as in the first-year writing class. Students received one non-graduation credit for the workshop, which could be applied to either financial aid or to athletic eligibility requirements and which was conferred only on the criteria of attendance and participation. Rodby and Fox concede this was not an ideal arrangement, as low-scoring students were still required to complete a course for which they received no graduation credit, but it did represent their best compromise, given their current institutional climate. I would add that students may have found the adjunct workshop a much more equitable economy than basic writing, as they did receive exchange value for a reduced institutional expectation of labor. But both the structure and the nature of the adjunct workshop also contributed to its institutional success (86% of students in workshops passed first-year writing the first time).

Structurally, adjunct workshops were designed to support low-test scoring students taking first-year writing. Workshops met twice a week for fifty minutes and were capped at twelve students. Each workshop comprised students from different first-year writing sections and because California State University Chico's writing program did not subscribe to a common syllabus, each student was often working with a different first-year writing syllabus. Adjunct workshops ostensibly had no curriculum independent from the work students were doing in first-year writing.

Workshops functioned in various ways, which is depicted in the authors' report of a typical workshop day. Observing a current workshop session, Rodby and Fox found students recording on the blackboard the assignments they were currently working on: one student had not yet started a paper, another was revising a paper and had brought copies for everyone, another was revising but was experiencing no problems, and two others reported problems with a reading by bell hooks, as well as the writing assignment attached to it. Everyone, they say, participated to determine the day's agenda. Students first reviewed a paper being revised, analyzing its problems and volunteering solutions. They then moved to discuss the bell hooks's reading, as the workshop teacher guided them in unpacking a particularly difficult passage. Once students understood the reading, they discussed the writing assignment based on the reading. But, in addition to the structure of the workshop, Rodby and Fox also speculate about the nature of the workshop or about other practices the workshops made possible. In so doing, however, they first looked to a critique of practices in first-year writing itself.

Noting problems of practice in first-year writing, Rodby and Fox concluded that "the writing process" in the class did "not capture the ways in which real life, everyday writing practices are stretched over time and space and involve activities, tools and interactions that may not even appear to be about literacy at all" (94). The result, they say, was that "students often cannot learn enough about literacy practices through direct observation (if there even is anything to observe)" (94). Writing program administrators and workshop teachers also recognized the usefulness of Urs Fuhrer's notion that the "need for understanding is aroused by perception of an incongruous event, [so that] it [understanding] is developed and supported by dialogue and peer group approval and it flourishes if [/when] mental modeling is unhindered by the immediate need for a definitive solution to the problem" (qtd. in Rodby and Fox 94). The significance of this critique to a notion of authoring is crucial, a point to which I will return momentarily.

The practices the workshops made possible were pivotal to the workshops' success, as well as to the facilitation of students' learning. These successful practices included Fuhrur's notion of the role of dissonance in triggering a need to understand as well as the role of dialogue and social approval in understanding. For example, in the workshops, students discussed various ways of executing the writing practices required of them, which often led them to construct a mental model of what writing in new contexts would actually entail. Students might borrow a model from another writing context with which they were familiar and attempt to modify it, the success of which was "in large part determined by the social relationships and the interactive context that constitutes the literacy practice itself" (94). Additionally, some workshop teachers had students explicitly describe the practices they would enact and plan the time and space they would work in. Rodby and Fox report that interaction and dialogue among students, as well as among students and teacher, were crucial to students' implementing these new writing practices. This change in the writing program's approach to the process of writing thus represented a significant change from the previous, traditional curriculum.

Most significant in this alternative situated set of writing process practices was the freedom of students to identify their own sense of dissonance and to engage in inquiry meaningful to them within the supportive social context of teacher and peers. These practices supported the sort of responsive understanding Bakhtin views as necessary to a genuine notion of alterity, which is a prerequisite to achieving a situated, partial, and contingent meaning in the context of an individual's specific experience expressed in the act of authoring the architectonic of networked subjectivity. This capacity for the quality of students' experiences in the classroom points to the need to "re-see" the practices that comprise students' writing processes. Rather than having students (re)act rote upon the curriculum imposed upon them, which was the situation in the previously critiqued first-year writing course, students in this reconfigured institutional environment have a space to act through the curriculum. Thus the first-year/adjunct workshop institutional complement approximates the world that addresses students and to which they author a response because of the dissonance that demands answerability. Additionally, the authors say, the nature of the workshop made possible yet another significant space, one for productive conflict.

Indeed, conflict and struggle were actually embraced in the workshops in an effort to have it channeled productively. Rodby and Fox say the decision to do so was based on research that students' experience of cultural conflicts constitutes a central feature of writing instruction and that the tendency to eliminate or reduce this conflict is detrimental, since discursive acts issue from conflict and struggle. Many scholars, for example, have written that the use of collaborative groups tends to produce resistance to the class, that students resist the teacher's authority and even critique her/his behavior in their groups. This resistance, however, is usually denied agency in the classroom because it is not allowed voice. But because the workshop did not function as an adjunct to a specific class or teacher, Rodby and Fox say, it retained an important autonomy from the first-year writing class. It thus created an institutionally legitimate space aside from the first-year writing class. The workshop teacher was not an extension of the first-year writing teacher and the criteria of the workshop grade were different and independent of that in the first-year writing class.

This space thus allowed students to take on different roles from the ones they could assume in the larger first-year classroom. For example, if they were quiet in the first-year class because they did not understand the purpose of the course or the relevance of the readings, they could express this resistance in the workshops, where teachers then attempted to reframe the resistance by helping students come to new understandings. Workshop teachers believed that because the workshop was not graded in the same way as first-year writing, and because students were not in the workshop with others with whom they were competing for grades, they were then "'free' to express confusion, despair, anger, and opinions that they could not raise in their first-year writing class because it [was] graded" (97). Rodby and Fox conclude that workshops provided the possibility that classroom writing might then "not be always already a commodity, that the workshop may complement the first-year writing course as students enter into conflict and dialogue and experience agency with respect to the curriculum" (97). The nature of the workshops thus created spaces for students to practice resistance that could be channeled into productive writing practices.

Spaces for resistance nourish a real sense of addressivity. Frequently, though, students do not have the capacity, the knowledge, the skills, the literacy, to dialogue with the course curriculum. In this situation, whatever writing students produce is, indeed, commodified, as it achieves nothing more than economic exchange value: a product for a grade. In the workshop, however, students' resistance was encouraged, as they were then directed to frame their resistance productively, in effect, to dialogue with the curriculum, their peers, and their teacher in order to achieve active, responsive understanding. For example, resistance to the bell hooks's reading was legitimized as worthy of inquiry, as the workshop teacher modeled a legitimate academic critique, thus enlarging the possibility that students could develop the critique into something they could write for their first-year writing course.

In the space of the workshop, then, a specific epistemology was promoted, developed, and practiced in the context of students' real-life situations, in this case the real-life situation of the workshop. The focus upon the acquisition of this epistemology, along with the institutional context in which it was practiced, acted to individualize students' epistemologies and their reservoir of literacies. The result was a context that nourished the addressivity and answerability that constitutes the authoring necessary for networked subjectivity.

The workshop construct has thus far been illustrated to successfully function due to its more equitable economy, its structure, and its nature in providing a safe haven for students to enact new writing practices and to express resistance in productive ways, all of which produced an alternative subject position in which students were more likely to voluntarily invest. Workshops, then, represent a sort of ideal we might all indulge, if we had the resources to do so, for all of our first-year writing students. There was an absence of curriculum in workshops and a mitigation, if not total absence, of institutional authority. Students thus obtained greater agency in this context, as they achieved a heightened degree of dialogism and alterity than they did in the first-year classroom, where a much more monologic reality existed (this, again, due to the increased institutional stakes associated with economic exchange value).

But there were other repercussions. According to the authors, the workshops provided an institutionally sanctioned forum for students to openly discuss with others anything and everything about the first-year writing class: "the instructors' teaching practices—down to the concrete details of their assignments, their responses, their reading choice, their grading, even their classroom demeanor" (97). The structure of the workshops thus increased first-year writing teachers' visibility, making "their failures to communicate, their misfired responses, their terrific assignments, their passion, and their unintended slights [. . .] all pubic, all open to comment and critique" (98). So, as the workshops functioned to deprivatize the first-year writing classroom, the force of first-year teachers' authority was altered, as students who might otherwise have been reluctant to raise issues in class were more free to do so in the workshops. The result was that some first-year writing teachers viewed the workshop as a threat to their authority, so that tensions did sometimes arise between workshop and first-year classroom teachers. The authors, however, say this tension was not necessarily a negative, and, in fact, maintain that it can be "enormously helpful, provided [first-year] instructors see resistance as constructively pressuring their teaching practices" (97). Teachers' vulnerability to critique Rodby and Fox write, "may make teaching a little more stressful, but it certainly also makes teachers more consistently self-critical" (98). The space of the workshop, then, exerted pressure on the first-year writing class, rendering it more public and thus more open to critique. This situation also pressured first-year writing teachers' personal behavior and their professional choices and practices.

Other theoretical insights emerged from their experiences, the writers say, which developed into principles used to structure the curriculum of the first-year writing program. First, "one learns to participate in a particular writing practice by being engaged in that practice and not by learning some other writing practice with the idea that the latter prepares writers for the former" (88). In other words, they realized that "different writing practices may or may not share conceptual and or procedural knowledge bases" (89). With this understanding of writing as a practice, skills cannot be viewed as discrete and static but rather as sets of actions which apply knowledge to particular contexts: "whether one knows how to read and write is not an absolute value; what one knows and does changes radically from situation to situation" (89). With this understanding of writing as practice, writing was then perceived to be an activity, which, they say, is not best taught and learned in levels, for writing practices cannot be parsed into convenient, developmental gradations. It is more appropriate "to imagine writing in actual scenes, [so that] a 'narrative' emerges as the genre because the situation calls for a story" (90). "Levels of discourse," they continue, "especially as they are inappropriately related to levels of ability, make little sense" (90).

This reformulated writing process curriculum speaks accurately to the notion of addressivity and answerability from which authoring emerges. Indeed, a subject simply is in the world; there are no gradations to being so.[52] Answerability for our places in existence is very much an activity, as each response contributes to the architectonic that constitutes networked subjectivity. To suggest that addressivity and answerability ought to be parsed by "levels" is tantamount to suggesting that alterity ought likewise be parsed, an act which would attenuate the writer's ability to construct new experiences and achieve new meanings. Students best learn to assume responsibility for their written responses to the world in real-world scenes.

Other configurations of institutional relations in the California State University Chico writing program merit note. One configuration involves the institution, which, with the construct of basic writing, managed to absorb cultural critiques of student access. I use the word "managed" to suggest that this absorption was not some insidious institutional goal but was, rather, an outcome of a complex network of various relations. Ostensibly, the academy would provisionally accept low-scoring students, provide them with unprecedented opportunity, but then undermine the potential success of that opportunity with a curriculum made moot by the economy in which the curriculum operated. Moreover, in the context of basic writing, the academy fully absorbed students,' teachers,' and writing program administrators' resistance. Students resisted the basic writing course, based on its economy and its practices, which produced a subject position in which they had no vested interest. Teachers resisted the course because they were unsuccessful in having students occupy the desired subject position of their curriculum objectives and goals: to become better writers, well prepared for first-year writing. Writing program administrators resisted the program, as they realized that the construct of basic writing itself was confounding their efforts to provide equitable terms for both access and success. This illustrates that "a discourse of good intentions," that is, a commitment to broader access, can be tied to a set of material practices that neutralizes the goals of its original intentions. The institutional structure is thus strengthened not because it provides access, but because it *seems* to provide it. The academy provides access, on the one hand, while undermining it on the other, all the while absorbing resistance and becoming increasingly strengthened in the process.

But the writing program also neutralized resistance. The program attempted with the first set of reforms to subvert students' resistance, as well as the institutional constraints that provided viability to the basic writing construct. Neither attempt was successful. Students continued to resist and the institution refused to legitimize with credit value what standardized testing had delegitimized. Statements with greater weighted legitimacy were thus those that maintained the institutional status quo of the basic writing construct. Statements of institutional eligibility and statements of standardized testing outweighed statements of the curriculum itself, at least in the space of the basic writing classroom. Statements thus produced a practice that institutionalized a specific space that could not be easily negotiated. Indeed, as previously discussed, the academy effectively absorbed the writing program's first exercise of resistance—that of students, teachers, and curriculum planners.

But writing administrators' second reform effort achieved a much more positive outcome. The authors say that eliminating the physical space of basic writing eliminated the course and thus the construct of basic writers. Still, testing was in place that marked students' abilities according to institutionally sanctioned standards, and the department used these test scores to differentiate among students. But, the department had chosen a new set of statements to construct those with low test scores, so that they, the department, as much as the economy of the institution, were influential in eliminating the construct of basic writers. But the new statements also included a new curriculum and a new physical construct, material changes that impacted the nature of the discursive formation of basic writing itself. A less authoritative discourse (dialogic discourse) characterized adjunct workshops, which created a space for students to express subversive discourse. Yes, this subversive discourse was absorbed by the institutional structure, but it was done so in a meaningful and productive way, in a manner that allowed and encouraged students to make meaning for themselves in expressions of alternative readings, but to do so within the parameters of institutionally sanctioned discourse conventions. Student subversion, then, was controlled, but it was controlled in such a way that would both draw students more securely into the discourse community of (institutional) choice and have them assume a persuasive, dialogic subject role rather than an ineffective, monologic subject role. This appropriation, this near-production of docile bodies, constituted a positive, productive use of power. But, as teachers, we can achieve such an ethic only through strenuous critical reflexivity of our practices and our networks of institutional relations.

The role of workshops to achieve a positive, productive use of power entailed an absence of institutional authority that provided a space for students to claim greater degrees of agency. So, ironically, while workshops contained no curriculum, they were nevertheless a part of the curriculum. This non-curriculum, functioning in tandem with the reformatted writing process curriculum in first-year writing, did more to realize the goal of students learning to write. It also better approximated the world's addressivity and exigence for answerability and provided students with real opportunities for authoring.

Addressivity is always structured in context, so the context of the writing classroom represents only one more such situation of addressivity. But, in the classroom, there exists the institutional addressivity of the course, along with the addressivity of our curriculum. Students often experience a greater exigency relative to institutional addressivity and to the tacit economy that obtains within it than they do to the addressivity of our classroom curriculum, which is often appropriated and subverted in order to adequately answer to the institution. This is what occurred in the basic writing course at the California State University, Chico. Our challenge as teachers, then, is to devise a curriculum that not only calls for answerability relative to the curriculum's institutional situatedness but that also elicits a strong exigency for answerability relative to students' specific world contexts. We do this by valuing the differences, subjectivities, epistemologies, and literacies that students bring to the classroom and by creating spaces where student agency and the exigency of answerability can flourish.

We cannot deny that in the economy of the academy, the programmatic, curricular, and pedagogical choices we advocate are always commodified by the institution that dispenses legitimacy to our teaching and to our students' learning. Perhaps our question is how we can best satisfy the demands this economy places on us while honoring a particular ethic to ourselves, to students, and to the broader culture. There is no definitive and static response to this question, for the response constitutes nothing less than the responsibility and ethic of answerability to which we are compelled by the world's addressivity.

6 Networked Process and the Long Revolution

The process/post-process tension within the field is very much an issue of identity, a tension that revolves around the issue of naming. Naming is, after all, a politically charged act, one that seeks to draw and define the very parameters of identity. But perhaps the term naming is also misleading, as it carries with it a hint of autonomy. I use it, though, with the caveat that I consider it not as a single act but as a discursive and non-discursive relational process involving all manner of people, places, and things. The issues involved in this challenged naming coalesce around professionalization and disciplinarity. Again, I do not suggest that these issues follow a lock-step cause-effect pattern; rather, I broach them as existing within a set of networked relations where they pressure and are themselves pressured to produce the situation in which we now find ourselves.

The arguments of post-process proponents have been shown to be by no means monolithic. Some claim that post-process is little more than a logical extension of process, some argue that the limitations and pressures of process have hopelessly compromised both its appeal and its method, while still others deny the viability of any process formulation whatsoever. While I have previously delineated process and post-process positions and their namings, I want for the moment to think of post-process not so much as a position but as a sensibility, one that inexplicably yearns for rupture. I say rupture, because there has been a failure to engage writing process discourse, either with its early proponents, who, I believe we could say, never imagined process the way it is now often construed and summarily dismissed. I also say rupture because this yearning is reminiscent of the one that both constructed and demonized current-traditional rhetoric. Hindsight suggests that we demonized the old to construct a conceptual rupture with its terrain, only to eventually recognize that no such dichotomy, however attractive at the time, really existed. Nevertheless, the dichotomy forestalled genuine dialogue between the two, so that while a conceptual rupture occurred, there was, arguably, never an equally correlative rupture in practice. Thus, the legacy of demonizing one perspective to valorize another continues to haunt the field and doubtless fuels the sensibility from which many critiques of writing process now issue.

Nevertheless, there is a difference in the nature of this historical moment, for the current-traditional/writing process tension centered around writing and the teaching of writing, which was reflected in the questions that gave birth to the field, mainly—What does it mean to write?; What does it mean to teach writing?; and Why does what we do matter? The difference now is that the post-process sensibility finds the latter two questions imminently suspect. While it would be easy to dismiss this sensibility as elitist, we would do ourselves a disservice in doing so. Perhaps we might also simply ignore these process/post-process rumblings if—in spite of our teaching now being more theoretically informed, more compassionately authoritative, and more thoroughly reflective—our best efforts did not often fail to translate into effective learning and practice by our students. We cannot claim that process has been a panacea or that the historical moment does not call for pushing boundaries. The field's terrain is obviously changing and, yes, needs to change. But if we are to avoid a rupture based on a particular pedagogy's superiority to some other pedagogy, we would do well to first take a stark look at some of the seeds of discontent that may fuel this desire. Perhaps it is not so much process that the post-process sensibility finds objectionable as it is the institutional factors that circumscribe its delivery, mainly, the first-year composition course. The ethical, disciplinary, and professional issues of first-year composition have, for the most part, been well rehearsed in our literature, but they do bear revisiting in the context of an institutional inertia so great as to render any notion of change almost quixotic.

The first issue is the universal requirement of first-year composition and its status as a service course. Complaints about the first-year composition course are part of our heritage and our contemporary reality, voiced in recurring calls for both the abolition of the course and for various types of reform (Connors "The New"; Crowley; Fleming "The End"; Goggin and Beatty; S. Miller; Petraglia; Russell *Writing*). Some, particularly Sharon Crowley, have argued against the course's mandatory status ("Composition's Ethic"; see also Brannon, Connors

"The New," and Schuster). Given that our disciplinary identity is so thoroughly enmeshed with first-year composition, it is not surprising that the course continues to be the focus of so much energy and attention. This focus has been challenged by those such as John Trimbur, who concede that while we "have derived a powerful sense of mission from the first-year course," we ought to question "whether such an attachment to a single course has been a good thing or whether it has brought its own peculiar pathologies" ("The Problem" 10; see also Harris; Crowley; Berlin; Goggin; and S. Miller). One of these pathologies might be said to include how the course has and continues to be variously conceived, but another, Trimbur says, is that "our professional questions may be skewed because they are being asked of only one course" (11), a course that is also generally viewed as a "service" course.

The service issue, compounded with a focus on a single course, has also been critiqued as contributing to rhetoric and composition's lowly status. Sharon Crowley takes issue with this. In "Composition's Ethic of Service," she reports that according to Burton Bledstein, the rise of professionalism led to the development of many American disciplines, whose justification rested largely on a service ethic. Crowley thus argues that rhetoric and composition is not the only discipline to have a strong service mission. Nevertheless, most disciplines first created and accumulated a body of knowledge to which a service course(s) was either attached in tandem or was subsequently attached as a way to disseminate said knowledge to a broad audience and to recruit neophytes into the fold as majors (see Mahala and Swilky). A primary difference between rhetoric and composition and other disciplines, though, is that our service mission, realized in the material reality of the composition course, preceded the development of our disciplinary knowledge by almost a hundred years. This set in motion a host of difficulties, with which we continue to contend. Not the least of these are the thorny labor issues associated with the majority who teach composition, along with the development of a thriving testing industry.

We know, for example, that this course emanates from perceived literacy crises, which fuel the public's imagination and demand for it. The impetus for the course, then, is based on a punitive notion of lack. There is a need to measure lack, a need around which has mobilized an industry of standardized testing. These two industries, first-year composition and standardized testing, thrive through responses to perceived literacy crises. Both are industries because both generate tremendous revenue; indeed, first-year composition is frequently referenced as a virtual, institutional cash-cow (see Crowley "Communication").

But composition's status as an institutional cash-cow comes at a cost that is ethical, professional, and disciplinary. For example, there is the chronicled exploitation of the adjunct faculty who mostly teach the course; indeed, an online issue of *The Chronicle of Higher Education* reported that most composition courses are taught by nontenured instructors at 85 percent of the institutions that require it.[53] That this exploitation is real is not, I believe, seriously challenged. In fact, many conversations these days about composition revolve around the issue of unfair and unethical labor practices. Certainly, that these practices do exploit huge numbers of instructors is a deplorable situation.

But what a focus on labor exploitation obscures in the conversation of rhetoric and composition and the adjunct labor mostly responsible for its delivery are issues of disciplinarity and professionalization. The field's lecturers and adjuncts are, doubtless, comprised of mostly concerned, motivated, conscientious, and skilled instructors. But it is also true that most lecturers and adjuncts do not have the disciplinary knowledge that the field believes teachers of writing ought to have. In other words, our field's lecturers and adjuncts are not, at least not *yet*, comprised of under-employed PhD's, which is the situation for some disciplines that also rely on contingent labor to deliver introductory courses. But, with the discrepancy between the real and the ideal, we are faced with a conundrum, mainly a contradiction between what our disciplinary knowledge indicates and the reality of the everyday practices in which the course that bears half of the field's name is delivered. Moreover, I think we have to admit that even if economics were not a factor and institutions were to have only tenured and tenure-track teach the course, it would be unrealistic to pretend that a sufficient number of faculty could be produced to do so. According to C. Adelman, first-year composition is now "the most required course in American higher education" (qtd. in Fleming, "The End" 112). It seems, therefore, to be an untenable situation, when the material conditions of the delivery of first-year composition not only frustrate disciplinary knowledge but also exploit those who actually do deliver it.

While not a "cause" of the current state of affairs, we know that textbooks do play a role and that they played a role in the current-traditional rhetoric/process dichotomy, as well (see especially Crowley *The Methodical Memory* and Connors "Textbooks"). During the emergence of the process movement, the majority of the labor force, who selected and purchased textbooks, did not share this knowledge, and many textbooks simply grafted a process approach onto what they were already doing. Process became immensely popular, and the textbook industry complied to produce and provide what instructors demanded.[54] It is not, therefore, an exaggeration to say that process was commodified, as it was easily appropriated to serve a variety of philosophical approaches.

Together, this set of relations, comprised of three industries—publicly and institutionally sponsored composition, the testing industry, and the textbook industry—have created a tension with disciplinary knowledge. This tension challenges notions of professionalism, which then pressure how we conceive ourselves as scholars and teachers of writing, along with how we conceive the field. Seemingly, the situation of first-year composition undermines professionalism and challenges disciplinarity even as it and we are virtually powerless to alter the institutional realities that condone and underwrite unfair labor practices. Perhaps, we should not be too surprised, then, that some might simply want to disassociate the field and themselves from this situation.

But even in the face of what seem to be insurmountable odds, the field has responded to this conflation of events through the discursive construction of writing program administration (WPA), which conceives a conceptual basis for writing-program administration as intellectual work. As reported by David Blakesley in *The Chronicle of Higher Education,* graduate programs in writing-program administration have been launched at Purdue, Syracuse University, and the University of Arizona (McLemee). I doubt that anyone believes that writing-program administration can be the salvation of first-year composition, but the phenomenon does represent the field's desire to mediate the institutional complex that first-year composition has become. There is reason, then, for at least a guarded optimism about WPAs' ability to productively intervene in the institutional complex of first-year composition.

Such optimism, however, is not shared by all of the post-process sensibility. Indeed, Lynn Worsham stated in the *Chronicle of Higher Education* article that she is troubled by the "fairly huge investment in the subject of writing-program administration," made by the field, that "for the past 30 years, people in the field have tried to define [composition studies] as an intellectual discipline, not a service component of the university" (McLemee). There is in this sentiment at least a tacit assumption that Ph.D. programs in writing program administration are training students to corroborate with the institution rather than training them to be scholars in the discipline.

Admittedly, I have in this part of my discussion perilously entertained a dichotomy between the post-process sensibility and "everybody else." I have done so in order to make the point that underlying the post-process sensibility lurks a desire for a conceptual and material distancing from first-year composition. But the "everybody else" in this equation are, of course, quite diverse in their regard of the issues I have raised: some are content with the present state of affairs; some find themselves in an ethical, intellectual, and professional quandary; some are earnestly attempting to actively intervene to effect improvement; others may prefer to simply ignore the situation, altogether. But other institutional developments are now occurring that bear thoughtful consideration, for they may further complicate our relationship with first-year composition, and, by extrapolation, complicate our sense of disciplinary identity.

Institutional Place(ment)

The most potentially productive development occurring with rhetoric and composition today is the ever-increasing trend to alter the institutional space we occupy.[55] Understanding that space is socially and politically constructed and thus never innocent or neutral, we are compelled to seriously interrogate the repercussions of our placement in English departments. Certainly, the status of rhetoric and composition and the litany of abuses suffered in English departments, both well-rehearsed in our literature, issues in great part from the historical hegemony of literary studies and the colonization of rhetoric and composition.[56] But there has not been an intellectual and affective investment in the active pursuit of change.[57] The reasons for this are as complex as with any hegemony, but certainly the situation could not exist if we were not complicit with our own oppression. Taken alone, the intellectual reasons for our placement in English departments have historically been persuasive. For example, we study discourse; literary studies also studies discourse. We value and promote literacy; literary studies also values and promotes literacy. Together, we represent two sides, consumption and production, of the same discursive coin. Our perspectives about the nature, constitution, and purposes of discourse(s) and literacy(ies) are, however, very different, just as are those of the disciplines of communications and linguistics, which have long since declared their independence from English departments to pursue their professional and disciplinary agendas unfettered by the normative influence of the hegemonic structure that literary studies simply *is*.[58]

Even some rhetoric and composition pioneers believe that we could function more effectively outside of English departments. At the Watson Conference held in October of 1996, Randy Cauthen conducted a group interview with some of these folks, focusing on the issues of professionalism and inter-disciplinarity. He asked them to complete the sentence: "If I knew then what I do now. . . ." Richard Young responded by saying that with one exception, he would make no changes to the way he had conducted his career. The exception: when he went to Carnegie Mellon to establish their rhetoric program, the dean gave him the option of doing so inside or outside of their English Department; he chose to do so within. He said:

> Looking back over the almost 20 years in the English Department, I find it has been a constant uphill battle, and we in rhetorical studies have never quite been able to shake ourselves loose from the definitions that have been imposed upon us. What's the discipline of English? What's our place in the discipline? If you look at the history of rhetoric in MLA, what you see is a contest over whose definition of the enterprise is going to be the one that is institutionalized and that drives professional practice. We, that is rhetoricians around the country, might have grown in a more desirable way and the shape of our discipline might be less problematic today had we been able to step outside the English Department, which I have found to be constraining in all kinds of ways. For example, rhetoric is still defined by many around the country chiefly in terms of the freshman course. [. . .] Had we taken another direction and developed outside English departments, we might have done better, since we might well have begun with a larger definition of

the discipline. And look at the problems we have by staying in English. For example, over the last generation, there has been an extraordinary proliferation of knowledge about [. . .] writing and the teaching of writing and about languaging in the world. But how do you teach classical rhetoric or any other sophisticated rhetoric in a 15-week course? Current-traditional rhetoric worked, but largely because it was so simplistic. We have a kind o[f] knowledge now that does not fit well within the institutional framework, which is extremely difficult to change. (Cauthen 208–09)

Having definitions of identity imposed upon us and having an institutional structure that virtually ignores our body of disciplinary knowledge were not Young's only disciplinary concerns, however. "There is," he says, "a deep current of Platonism that runs through literary education that places a high value on dissociating oneself from the world," whereas rhetoric is precisely about making connections with the world (212).[59] Young also reported that in a conference session attended earlier, he had heard Lee Odell articulate a new area of rhetorical studies, which based on his own observations of English departments, would make it extremely difficult to tenure anyone working in the area Odell described. The area, Young said, is "alien to the focus of attention and the values" of "traditional English faculties" (211).

Peter Elbow and Janice Lauer did not necessarily concur with Young, but both expressed concerns that have everything to do with our placement in English departments. Peter Elbow did not speak specifically to disciplinary placement, for example, but he did endorse (a) Young's complaint of the 15-week composition course as an inadequate curriculum for teaching writing and (b) Young's assessment that rhetoric needs to be in an environment that encourages expansion, as he said that our graduate students "really need to be encouraged to take advantage of the potential for breadth in rhetoric and composition" (213). Janice Lauer, who directed the development of the rhetoric and composition graduate program at Purdue, said that she had "an ambivalence about being in the English department," since the program had flourished there and she believed that "the effort to remain in English departments ha[d] helped to change the field of English"; however, she also conceded that "one of the trickiest problems ha[d] been the recognition of our types of research when it comes down to the reward system" (209).[60]

Andrea Lunsford viewed the English department as an inadequate site for the sort of inter-disciplinarity that composition could achieve, saying that "what we need to find is a site [for an inter-disciplinary enterprise]—and increasingly I don't think it is going to be in the English department" (210). Attacks on the field's advocacy of professionalism, often issued by our own departmental colleagues, were discussed by Joseph Comprone, Andrea Lunsford, Lisa Ede, and Janice Lauer. Such attacks have everything to do, of course, with rhetoric and composition's connection with the world.

Others have also spoken for the need of rhetoric and composition to claim departmental independence.[61] This need is, again, based on the belief that we are fundamentally at odds with the hegemonic structure of our present departmental homes, a situation that retards our ability to not only develop the breadth and depth of scholarship we are compelled to conduct but also, especially, to disperse to students the knowledge emanating from this scholarship. Even if we were to enjoy the same status as literary studies, some question what that would really mean for rhetoric and composition. Kurt Spellmeyer, for example, relates achievements of rhetoric and composition that have rendered us disciplinary status, concluding that, relative to our literary studies colleagues' estimations, we must "surely [. . .] *have* arrived" ("Education" 79). But our colleagues' estimations are not, as it turns out, Spellmeyer's preoccupation; rather, it is the status of our colleague's discipline to which we are fettered by association. He writes: "But I still find myself haunted by doubt: where exactly does *arrived* put us? The truth may be that we have fought our way out of steerage only to claim a chair on the deck of a sinking ship, while we are eagerly waving our young protégées into the chairs beside us" (79). A similar view of literary studies' state of health is expressed by Todd Taylor, who says that "relative to other so-called disciplines in the humanities, our future is bright. Sure, composition teachers may occupy the basement but the penthouse is not looking so attractive at the moment" (148).

Personally, I think these reports of literary studies' demise are premature. They do, however, signal a disjunct between the rationale and missions of the two disciplines. Spellmeyer articulates this in his article, "Education for Irrelevance? Or, Joining Our Colleagues in Lit Crit on the Sidelines of the Information Age," where he says that the humanities, in general, have been wrong-headed in the presumption that they are and should be the "leader, the conscience, and the judge of the whole society," a vision, he says, that "has become manifestly unachievable" (83). This enterprise, he continues, "was doomed from the start," since its proponents "lacked an adequate *systemic* understanding of how their knowledge fit within a larger constellation of knowledges" (83). The knowledge enterprise of rhetoric and composition is precisely about understanding knowledges—how they come to be, how they are maintained, how they can be changed, what they mean to individuals and to larger cultures, etc. Specifically, we study this from the angle of written discourse, which as Charles Bazerman reminds us in "A Rhetoric for Literate Society," no other discipline does.

Susan Miller offers a scathing critique of our own complicity with the hegemonic values of literary studies. In "Why Composition Studies Disappeared and What Happened Then," Miller writes:

> Following Plato in the *Republic,* not Aristotle's *On the Soul,* many [in rhetoric and composition] think writing instruction has the power to overturn family wisdom and to untie students from community, religious, occupational, economic, and regional heritages whose positive impact on academic history we largely deny. No early English journal or professional debate denies this divisive social-cultural mission. All assume that writing teachers mediate relations to higher culture and to a higher status, that the interior lives of students can be enhanced by composition's more and better ways of moving them toward Idealist realities. [. . .] We embody and privilege a better, writing life, an ineffable quality of experience. We hereby slight specific knowledge in ways that undercut our hotly voiced demands that teachers be compensated equitably in institutions that do reward demonstrations of expertise but do not usually prize the unrealized value of personalities. Composition studies thus enforces evaluative judgments while rejecting as common opinion, as mere *doxa,* the respect already accorded them as having knowledge of the increasingly secret secrets of producing traditional texts. It focuses on selected readings, not on rhetorical actions that

> warrant wars, laws, and consent to them. It equally admires but names an aesthetic, and thus mystified, the control of language production that enriches imagination, for whatever purposes. (51–52)

Certainly, part of her point is that this situation is a result of the socially and politically infused space we occupy. That this space shapes and constrains is thus undeniable.

What independent, departmental status would provide rhetoric and composition is the space to develop *differently*. It would also confer a legitimacy to our body of disciplinary knowledge that we do not currently enjoy in our present institutional spaces. Independent, we would no longer have valuable time and energy, better spent elsewhere, pilfered in arguing for that legitimacy; rather, it would be an institutional assumption.

The Writing Major

David Fleming, writing in 1998, captures the situation that has long existed regarding the curriculum of rhetoric and composition. He says, "at one end, [there is] a fifteen-week course on writing for incoming freshmen; at the other, [is] a multi-year program of advanced study for PhD students. Between the two, there is little or nothing" ("Rhetoric" 173). This situation is related, in great part, to rhetoric and composition's lack of departmental status. However, this is slowly changing, as writing majors are beginning to be developed in traditional English departments.

This development, in itself, is pressuring change for first-year composition, as it must be relationally configured to the full writing studies curriculum. For those who have been critical of the sole disciplinary status of the course, this is welcome news. For example, Maureen Daly Goggin argues that in adopting a curricular approach that "instruct[s] students in the complexities and richness of literate practices as they occur in a variety of situations and for a variety of purposes," we can finally "let our pedagogy emerge out of our discipline rather than let our discipline be ruled by an ill-conceived and rotting pedagogical structure" ("The Disciplinary" 43). We can, as some have suggested, offer disciplinary courses that are about writing that will inevitably help students navigate courses in the practice of writing (Bazerman,

"The Case"; Crowley, "Composition's Ethic"; Cushman, "Vertical"; Fleming, "Rhetoric"; Russell, "Activity; Trimbur, "The Problem").

Another benefit of the writing major has to do with our disciplinary relationship beyond the confines of our own fellow rhetoric and composition faculty and writing major students. A recurring refrain in our professional literature bemoans the discipline's effectiveness in getting the word out in the academy and in the larger culture regarding our current understandings about writing. Despite our best intentions, writing is still largely reductively conceived as a skill, which once acquired can be unproblematically transferred across varied personal, academic, and professional rhetorical contexts. Indeed, our list-servs are replete with anecdotes attesting to the need and to the difficulty of making arguments for a more complex notion of writing not only to fellow faculty across our campuses, but also to our own departmental colleagues. It is, admittedly, difficult to imagine how this situation might be remedied.

Writing concentrations or, more precisely, writing major students, constitute our best hope for accomplishing what has so far escaped our efforts to influence. Initiated to rhetoric and composition's body of knowledge, students are then likely to perpetuate that knowledge in their personal, professional, and civic lives. In this scenario, rhetoric and composition's disciplinary knowledge thus becomes one (more) terministic screen by which they inevitably come to view the world and act therein. This changing student perception of writing carries the potential to effect cultural repercussions and to alter the public's perception of writing.

RE-VISIONING RHETORIC AND COMPOSITION

I began this chapter talking about the issue of naming as an inherently political act, and I offered the metaphor of "networked process" to better represent our contemporary disciplinary identity. I wish now to endorse the suggestion that we also alter our discipline's name to fit the identity we can forge if we embrace professionalism, disciplinarity, and departmental independence. Such an altered identity is more accurately captured with the name, Rhetoric and Writing Studies.

Many who have called for disciplinary re-naming cite two main reasons: to resist the institutional baggage that accompanies the term composition, a term that imposes a limiting disciplinary identity; conversely, others resists composition because its traditional focus on the first-year composition course no longer represents the far-reaching theoretical and pedagogical interests the discipline currently and regularly engages. Almost all agree that we need to distinguish between composition and writing. Ellen Cushman reminds us that "composition and writing are not the same thing," with the proposition that "if *composition* is relegated to the remedial, the first-year, the disenfranchised, underemployed, and the exploitive, then *writing* opens up the possibilities of teaching courses about the literacies that various professional, community, and organizational members practice" ("Vertical" 121). For Sharon Crowley, "composition is an institutional term" that not only imposes the discourse of student need onto our disciplinary identity but also negatively influences that identity due to its "saturat[ion] with the discourse of formal correctness." Writing, she says, is the term that best "names the practice that we study and teach" ("Composition's Ethic" 237).

Susan Miller, Maureen Daly Goggin, and David Bleich view a disciplinary re-naming as engendering different disciplinary possibilities. Miller, for example, views the naming *writing studies* as holding intellectual potential as a viable mode of disciplinary inquiry, and she is particularly emphatic that *writing studies* clearly indicates a consonant focus with our disciplinary mission: the production rather than the consumption of texts ("Why" and "Writing"). She thus recommends "'writing studies' as both the content and a name" ("Writing" 41), which, she maintains, carries with it the additional benefit of a claim to disciplinary expertise. "If we claim expertise about relations between specific writers, their processes and their texts," she writes, "we easily grow and successfully divert out-worn attempts to marginalize our teaching and research" ("Writing" 52). Optimistic with what a re-naming could portend for disciplinary content, Goggin believes the potential of Rhetoric and Writing Studies is a more concentrated focus upon "a rich framework of theories and practices that have been concerned with the reciprocal relationship between discourse and social, political, and cultural contexts" (qtd. in Fleming, "The End" 118), while David Bleich believes a renaming would lead to a conceptual change in the way language is conceived, that is, "from a *transparent medium for* to a *material constituent of* social [and political] relations" ("Materiality" 39).

Disciplinary naming is intimately tied to disciplinary identity. Ours is not only being challenged from some within the discipline, it is also being pressured by the numerous developments that have occurred and are occurring within the discipline. Added to this are institutional and cultural events that are creating spaces for us to possibly reconceive who we are, what we do, and how we might go about doing it. No, we cannot change our name every time we experience a disciplinary shift. But calling the events with which the discipline is currently grappling a "shift" is truly an understatement. We can seize a unique opportunity to alter our disciplinary perception to ourselves, to the academy, and to the public, or we can take the more conservative path and thereby maintain the status quo. One option capitalizes on *what is;* the other capitalizes on *what is possible.*

A name is needed for the discipline that can better serve to not only describe what our fundamental object of study is but also better serve the goal of inclusiveness. Goggin and Beatty (as well as others) have persuasively argued in their edited collection *Inventing a Discipline* that the viability of rhetoric and composition as a scholarly enterprise, both within the academy and in the public, has been compromised by the failure of disciplinary insiders to agree on what it is (39). This failure has stemmed from a tendency to privilege some *aspect* of rhetoric and composition—theory, the art of "textual" production, pedagogy—to the detriment of the whole. Therefore, a name is needed that represents *all* aspects. Adopting an inclusive disciplinary name does not ensure that the *privileging* of a particular disciplinary aspect will not continue to occur and that we will not continue to lament the repercussions of such privileging, but it can serve to name a value we commonly share.

Disciplinarity

Disciplinarity is a significant institutional development about which some in rhetoric and composition remain deeply ambivalent. This is not surprising, given that rhetoric is a master discipline (some would call it a meta-discipline), fundamentally inter-disciplinary by its very nature, while the historical conception of composition studies embodies a strong trace of resistance, with its overt anti-establishment and anti-authoritarian impulse to which many continue to cling. Nevertheless, rhetoric and composition has achieved disciplinary status[62] at a time when the academy is undergoing significant change. Therefore, some who might otherwise be uncomfortable with claiming disciplinary status claim instead a particular disciplinary sensibility (e.g., rhetoricality).

I am sympathetic to this desire to remain aloof to the inevitable disciplining to which rhetoric and composition is and will be subjected, but I also believe that such a desire is inherently conservative and even self-serving. As a field/discipline, we seem to harbor an extraordinary need to play the part of the perpetual adolescent, desperately wanting to be likable, liked, and included by any and all. Embracing disciplinarity would necessarily indicate a degree of boundary setting and establishment, which we are too often loathe to do. We pay a price for our self-indulgence, however, which in another discourse might be called our complicity with the very structures that de-legitimize and marginalize us. The more subversive act available to us is to embrace disciplinarity, even as we seek to re-define what that is, and to let our ethos articulate and enact that discipline. Many post-process advocates also desire to see us assume a responsible disciplinary role, but some also appear to want to do so by leaving our history and ethos behind.

Rhetoric and composition is, however, indivisible with its history. To speculate about a disciplinary future, then, we must remain mindful of this history (see Berlin; Connors; Crowley; Johnson; Kitzhaber; S. Miller; and North). For example, we understand how our disciplinary identity is, in great part, planted in the seeds of classical rhetoric, and we understand how the nature and domain of rhetoric has waxed and waned in the last 2500 years. We understand how our disciplinary evolution has been affected by the United States' appropriation of the German model of the university, with its demarcated and discrete disciplines so antithetical to the robust nature and function of rhetoric. We understand how English departments were born to serve a social, political, and nationalistic agenda to inculcate the chosen, with a particularly fervid discourse of social correctness and spiritual morality no less impassioned and zealous than the explicitly religious discourse whose role had been compromised with the adoption of a public and thus profane educational model.[63] We understand how the establishment of English departments disciplined individuals' idiosyncratic reading practices, which flourished with the mass availability of reading material made possible by burgeoning publishing venues; we understand how the values of rhetoric were debased in this institutional and disciplinary climate; we understand the social and political nature of the literacy crises that further reduced the richness of rhetoric to the compulsory and remedial first-year composition course. We understand the intermittent calls for reform and abolition of the course; we understand the confluence of events (additional literacy crises; national and international political events; the successful advocacy for federal funding to support research on writing; the tireless efforts of a group of people dedicated to the study of writing for a democratic benefit and thus to the establishment and development of rhetoric and composition by way of professional conferences, societies, research agendas, journals, and graduate programs[64]) that set in motion our very disciplinarity. We understand how English departments benefit from and thus perpetuate unfair labor practices associated with first-year composition; we understand how our own disciplinary status is complicit with these unfair labor practices, given the paradox that they contribute to sustain our disciplinarity even as they undermine the status of that disciplinarity; and we well understand how our disciplinary identity and development have been impacted by our placement in English departments. We understand much and, yet, our everyday practices often indicate a sort of willful amnesia.

It is quite likely that some question why we ought not just live with the tension between process and post-process, why we ought not just be content to revel in the passivity of plurality.[65] After all, we are a diverse field, historically tolerant of a plethora of interests, methodologies, and theories dealing with everything from the composing process of a single student to the machinations of power in institutional networks. We concede that our disciplinary knowledge is partial, situated, and contingent, a reality that spurs our disciplinary imagination. We revel in the experience of inter-disciplinarity, even as many of us chafe at the disciplinary hegemony that undermines that experience and that marks the reality of rhetoric and composition's institutional situatedness in many universities. We entertain, if not actually invite, the ideas of most anyone expressing an interest in our interests, blurring considerably our disciplinary boundaries of insider and outsider. We are, in short, a broadly generous, inquisitive, and tolerant discipline. It would seem, then, that we might well take the advent of post-process in stride, assuming that the field would merely expand to allow yet another perspective its own disciplinary space. A movement that names itself "post-process" and that subscribes, especially, to a strong notion of the term is not merely situating itself, however, in an attempt to multiply the terms of disciplinary discourse. In the "post" of post-process knells the faint ring of paradigm hope.

History indicates that process, too, once shared this same paradigm hope, but hindsight also indicates the exaggerated optimism in such hope.[66] Nevertheless, it is no exaggeration to say that process has functioned as a controlling metaphor in our field[67] in much the same way Louise Wetherbee Phelps indicates, as she writes that the field has historically been variously organized around different methods, one of which is key concepts. She equates such efforts with "strategies of dominance that attempt to impose a unifying order on the discipline based on structural divisions and a hierarchy of value that," she says, "have real consequences" ("Composition Studies" 129). Furthermore, if and when a key concept is accepted, she says, it privileges "certain directions in scholarship" over other alternatives and may even "devalue" prior scholarship to the extent of possibly "ruling out some altogether." A key concept that functions as a metaphor for a discipline's identity might thus be said to exert a certain will to power. That such a metaphor has material influence is undeniable. That the stakes are high for whatever metaphor dominates is equally undeniable.

Certainly, we have only to look at our disciplinary history to understand the degree to which the metaphor of process has functioned to shape our identity; how the metaphor of post-process might shape a future identity is questionable, but a few have legitimately questioned whether there would even be a future with this identity. Again, given rhetoric and composition's disciplinary ethos of generosity, inquisitiveness, and tolerance, we might also question the wisdom of embracing *any* disciplinary metaphor. After all, do we really need or want a metaphor that functions to delimit, similarly to disciplinarity, while our ethos functions to enlarge? I think we do—I think we must—for the two potentially function in tandem as the ground of possibility for a re-imagining of disciplinarity itself.

A disciplinary metaphor and disciplinary ethos indicate the sort of competing notions of compartmentalized rhetoric and intertwined rhetoric characterized by James Porter. While compartmentalized rhetoric maintains "strict boundaries between itself and other disciplines, arts or practices," intertwined rhetoric "accepts as natural and as enabling points of overlap between itself and other disciplines, arts, and practices" ("Developing" 213). The rhetoric we promote at any given time, Porter says, is contingent on our local circumstances and should thus be used strategically according to specific needs and purposes. He argues that we should promote a compartmentalized rhetoric when clearly delineated disciplinary boundaries are needed, such as when we must compete for institutional resources or when, I would add, our goal is to acculturate students through their core doctoral studies to become disciplinary insiders. This would not be the time, Porter says, to foreground our interdisciplinary nature, since we would need to effectively present ourselves as having a distinct disciplinary identity from other fields and disciplines. But, at other times, we would want to promote an intertwined rhetoric. We juggle these different rhetorics, then, according to local need and purpose, understanding that to "become too diffuse," "to overlap too many other areas," is to "risk losing our identity" altogether, while to build "rigid boundaries," is to risk the "irrelevance" of "becoming overspecialized, arcane" (213). These competing rhetorics are not absolute, but together they usefully describe the nature of rhetoric and composition's disciplinary identity. Therefore, we might usefully conceptualize our disciplinary metaphor as representative of a compartmentalized rhetoric and our disciplinary ethos as an intertwined rhetoric, both of which we strategically negotiate.

The metaphor I nominate to name the strategic negotiation of compartmentalized and intertwined rhetorics is "networked process," which describes the constituency that occupies the largest space on a rhetoric and composition continuum of process and post-process. This space represents the complexity of multiple networked process sites and signals both an intellectual and a material (re)negotiation of our professional and disciplinary status conducted, significantly, with the assumption that we are indivisible with our history.

Rhetoric and composition is precipitously poised. Various options exist, not the least of which is to continue functioning as we are, a position that effectively supports the status quo. But, we can also elect other options, e.g., to claim intellectual independence, to agitate for departmental status, to develop undergraduate majors, to embrace a mature notion of disciplinarity. However, with such acts come risks, both personal and professional. We do have an obligation, though, to make the attempt. As Anne Ruggles Gere reminds us, we must dare to engage Raymond Williams notion of "'the long revolution'" [which he identified as] the historical process by which individuals interact with changing government, industry, and culture to participate in the creation and negotiation with new realities" ("The Long" 119). We have the opportunity to (re)make a new reality. As both conceptual/material heuristic and as disciplinary metaphor, then, networked process has the potential to realize a new day.

Notes

¹ I use the term "heuristic" in the sense that Janice Lauer describes in her book, *Invention in Rhetoric and Composition:* "Psychologists characterized heuristic thinking as a more flexible way of proceeding in creative activities than formal deduction or formulaic steps and a more efficient way than trial and error. [. . .] Neither algorithmic (rule governed) nor completely aleatory (random), they prompt investigators to take multiple perspectives on the questions they are pursuing, to break out of conceptual ruts, and to forge new associations in order to trigger possible new understanding" (8–9).

² Mark Taylor writes in his book, *The Moment of Complexity: Emerging Network Culture,* that "complex adaptive systems can help us to understand the interplay of self and world in contemporary network culture" (26) and that "the notion of complex adaptive networks illuminates the ways in which symbols, concepts, myths, and theories transform noise into information, which can be organized in meaningful patterns to inform thinking and guide action" (26–27).

³ In his article, "Process Pedagogy," Lad Tobin writes that by the early 1980s, process had become "a kind of disciplinary shibboleth" for the field (4).

⁴ Lad Tobin speaks to this generational issue in *Taking Stock: The Writing Process Movement in the '90s,* writing that "in the 90s, advocates of writing process pedagogy are now being caught between conservative teachers, parents, and administrators who never liked the movement in the first place and contemporary critics who, interested in separating themselves from the process generation, believe they have moved beyond it" (7).

⁵ For a more comprehensive review of Kent's theory of paralogic hermeneutics, see Sidney Dobrin's *Constructing Knowledges: The Politics of Theory Building and Pedagogy in Composition,* particularly pages 76–88.

⁶ See Kent's "Beyond System: The Rhetoric of Paralogy," "Paralogic Hermeneutics and the Possibilities of Rhetoric," "On the Very Idea of a Discourse Community," "The Hope of Communication," "Formalism, Social Construction, and the Problem of Interpretive Authority," and "Language Philosophy, Writing, and Reading: A Conversation with Donald Davidson."

⁷ Reed Way Dasenbrock has also written extensively on Donald Davidson, some of which he has explicitly targeted for rhetoric and composition. See *Inquiries into Truth and Interpretation,* "A Coherence Theory of Truth and Knowledge," "A Nice Derangement of Epitaphs," *Redrawing the Lines: Analytic Philosophy, Deconstruction, and Literary Theory,* "A Response to 'Language Philosophy, Writing, and Reading: A Conversation with Donald Davidson,'" "A Rhetoric of Bumper Stickers: What Analytic Philosophy Can Contribute to a New Rhetoric," *Literary Theory After Davidson,* "The Myths of the Subjective and of the Subject in Composition Studies," and *Truth and Consequences: Intentions, Conventions, and the New Thematics.*

⁸ In "Process and Post-Process: A Discursive History," Paul Kei Matsuda writes that "Atkinson locates the origin of the term [*post-process*] in Trimbur's 1994 review article in *College Composition and Communication*" (65).

⁹ In *Taking Stock: The Writing Process Movement in the '90s,* Lad Tobin registers a similar response: "At a recent conference I heard progressive composition theorists—that is, theorists committed to cultural studies, social construction, oppositional politics—make statements that sound eerily similar to those made twenty years ago by traditionalists" (6).

¹⁰ Lad Tobin concedes in *Taking Stock: The Writing Process Movement in the '90s* that "the field seems on the verge of another major shift" but believes it will not be so much "away from the premises and pedagogies of process" as it will be toward "a reconceptualization of those premises" (9). Bruce McComiskey, in his book *Teaching Composition as a Social Process,* also takes the position that post-process constitutes not a break with but rather an extension of process.

¹¹ For an interesting historical discussion of the term *current-traditional,* see Robert Connors' *Composition-Rhetoric,* pages 4–7.

¹² Certainly, Lester Faigley argued this in his book *Fragments of Rationality.*

¹³ I am, admittedly, using Jameson's notion of cognitive mapping in only a very partial sense. For a view of what Jameson's work might contribute to composition studies, see Patricia Bizzell's 1993 article, "Commentary: Fredric Jameson and Composition Studies." Jameson, of course, argues for an aesthetic of cognitive mapping; Bizzell, suggesting that pedagogy can function as art, writes: "I would like to examine the possibility that pedagogy, like art, can assist at the formation of cognitive mapping, and precisely by attempting to restore a sense of history" (484).

For an interesting critique of Jameson's project of cognitive mapping, see Kathleen M. Kirby's *Indifferent Boundaries: Spatial Concepts of Human Subjectivity,* especially chapter 2, "Lost in Space: Establishing the Limits of Identity." Here, Kirby compares the form of subjectivity in Enlightenment individualism to that of postmodern "*sujet en proces* (roughly, the subject 'in process/on trial')" through a comparison of the journals of two American explorers and that of Fredric Jameson, whom she calls "a contemporary cultural pioneer" (7). She ultimately concludes, however, that Jameson's project of cognitive mapping remains an exclusionary practice, as his praxis maintains the contours of the Enlightenment individual.

[14] In *The Art of Wondering: A Revisionist Return to the History of Rhetoric*, William Covino expresses very well the position I presume to take relative to Berlin. He writes: "A certain security comes from the fact that one always begins within a context of 'received' assumptions, the security that every 'counterinduction' derives somehow from 'the culture of reference,' and for this reason the innovator sustains a dialogue as well as a tension with that culture, never cut loose altogether from communal exchange, never isolated in an entirely private subjective world. But also, never capable of 'pure' observation, only of seeing things in some measure as others have seen them" (126).

Covino also writes that "rhetoric has little to do with the survey of established categories; rather, it is an activity at once logical, political, philosophical, and psychological" (25). Thus, I have chosen not to critique Berlin's specific categories of writing process because it is the cognitive maps by which these writing process categories are derived that I read as being "at once logical, political, philosophical, and psychological." Taking from Derrida, I believe the critique of Berlin's cognitive maps represents potential space for the proliferation of perspectives, or play, as Derrida would call it. This play can begin only with "the means at hand," which is to admit "the necessity of borrowing one's concepts from the text of a heritage" ("Structure, Sign, and Play" 282–285).

[15] Kathleen Kirby, in *Indifferent Boundaries: Spatial Concepts of Human Subjectivity*, says that maps constitute space according to the mapper's cultural matrix. For example, early American explorers mapped in response to the features of the new world, but they could not preclude imposing into this new space the logic of Europe. They failed to recognize the efficacy of Native Americans' maps because these did not coincide with the logic of European mapping standards. The relationship of Native Americans to the land was thereby rendered invisible to Europeans, who then suffered no compunction in taking the land from the Natives. (54–56)

[16] A caveat: I agree with Berlin that we should, even in a networked process world, be able to recognize and justify our writing processes along with their implications. I also agree with Berlin's attempt to complicate this requirement for teachers of writing beyond the reductive process/product opposition that lingered and lingers in the field's imagination. I readily concede that classification systems improved upon this opposition, enlarging the conceptual framework in which we could contemplate rhetorics and writing processes. Certainly, classification systems can be beneficial in that they observe tracings, marshal strands, and impose coherence, providing a common terminology and conceptualization around which to focus and further

professional discourse. But classification systems can be detrimental, too, in that they obscure subtleties, level differences, and collapse multiple aspects. These tendencies restrict their usefulness to a call so complex as that issued to teachers by Berlin. I maintain, therefore, that a disjunction inheres between the call and teachers' ability to meet it.

[17] A counter position is offered by Michael Murphy in "After Progressivism: Modern Composition, Institutional Service, and Cultural Studies." Modernist strategies of resistance, he says, will not effect radical change in composition theory and pedagogy; what can constitute this change, he believes, is a transformation of composition through a postmodernism that focuses on cultural studies. Composition's historical alignment with the American myth of progress and service, Murphy believes, has eroded over the last thirty years and could see its demise with the advent of cultural studies. His problem with much cultural studies pedagogies, though, is that their critiques of progressivist pedagogies are themselves progressivist, so that Murphy worries that cultural studies may be co-opted and reduced to just another of "composition's long line of ultimately moderationist liberalisms" (214). To illustrate, Murphy takes Berlin's "Rhetoric and Ideology in the Writing Class" to task: "The progressivist discourse of educational democracy—along with its allied senses of duty ("our responsibilities as teachers and citizens") [493] and social welfare ("the greater good of all") [490]—is so fundamental a part of the language of composition scholarship that it can effectively underwrite the work of even as guarded an anti-foundationalist as Berlin" (215). Another culprit is "the contemporary theoretical fetishization of ethics," which he says is "only the latest in a long line of powerful essentialist mystifications" (218). He charges us to a diligent self-consciousness about the implicit and powerful sway that composition imposes in its requirement of an articulation to a commitment to the social.

There is much I agree with in Murphy's argument, but I would contend that his characterization of "progressivism" is itself essentialist, so that he ultimately falls into the same trap for which he takes so much of the field to task. I will elaborate my position in chapter three.

[18] Berlin's insistence that rhetorical theories do not differ due to "the simple undue emphasis of writer or audience or reality or language or some combination of these" ("Contemporary Composition" 765) is a motif that runs throughout much of his work in the period: In "Writing Instruction," he writes, "Rhetorical schemes differ from each other, I am convinced, not in emphasizing one of these elements [reality, writer, audience, language] over another" (2) and in *Rhetoric and Reality,* he contends that "The difference in these rhetorics is not [. . .] a matter of the superficial emphasis of one or another feature of the rhetorical act" (3). The historical context to which these statements are directed has to do with Berlin's observation in 1982 that recent scholarship addressing "various approaches to teaching composition"

share and promote the erroneous assumption that because all approaches are necessarily concerned with the same composing process elements—writer, reality, reader, language—disagreements, must, therefore, involve which element(s) should receive most attention. "Differences in teaching theories, then," he writes, "are mere cavils about which of these features to emphasize in the classroom" ("Contemporary Composition" 765).

I would argue that these statements are Berlin's way of distancing himself from the context in which differences of rhetorics/writing processes/teaching approaches have been couched. He argues that it is the deeper structure and its assumptions that merit attention, not "mere cavils" about the obvious features of rhetorics. Whether his characterizations, e.g., "simple undue emphasis" and "superficial emphasis," are directed at degrees of applied emphasis or toward those who would argue the efficacy of any such emphasis is, perhaps, unclear. What I will argue, however, in chapter three is that an emphasis, of either commission or omission, on a specific element does distinguish rhetorics differently. Whether this emphasis is applied by one "simply" and/or "superficially," by which I would infer a lack of thoughtful reflexivity on the part of the "one," is not, in my view, crucial, as an emphasis of a rhetorical feature(s) changes, in tandem, the underlying structure, regardless of one's awareness of it.

[19] Rorty writes in the *Philosophy and the Mirror of Nature* that "we understand knowledge when we understand the social justification of belief, and thus have no need to view it as accuracy of representation" (170). This is the position toward which Berlin has moved and makes explicit in later writings.

[20] Various scholars have taken Berlin to task for this tension, one that continued to haunt his theory and practice: how do you at once assume that a student is fully constructed and yet grant the agency that would have him/her elect to change his/her ideological sensibilities? Marshall Alcorn, in "Changing the Subject of Postmodernist Theory," for example, writes: "Berlin claims to understand the subject's constructed nature and inability to be rational and free, but he advocates a pedagogy that is absolutely dependent upon the subject's ability to be rational and free" (339).

[21] Seyla Benhabib, in "Feminism and the Question of Postmodernism," writes: "The study of culturally diverse codes which define individuality is not the same as an answer to the question as to *how* the human infant becomes the social self, regardless of the cultural and normative content which defines selfhood. In the latter case we are studying *structural processes and dynamics of socialization and individuation;* in the former, historical processes of signification and meaning constitution" (217). A full approximation of the two processes that Benhabib describes is required for a viable notion of the individual subject who writes.

[22] Joseph Harris reports that at the 1966 Seminar on Teaching and Learning of English at Dartmouth College, James Britton maintained English could not be defined by simply defining its subject matter. It would be defined, instead, by asking what the function of English is in the curriculum and in the lives of our students. Britton, Harris says, was not interested in how the subject matter of English was defined but found more compelling the notion of "what we want our students to do" (141).

Lester Faigley also speaks to teachers' tacit notions of what they would have their students *be* relative to curriculum, as he writes that "even if assumptions about the subjectivities that student writers should occupy are not as singular or as well understood as expressive realism, I argue that shared assumptions about subjectivities—the selves we want our students to be—still shape judgments of writing quality" (*Fragments* 114).

[23] Some might characterize Foucault as subscribing to a totally subjected subject. I do not read him this way, a position I will expand upon in chapter four.

[24] This map is a conceptual representation of phenomena and practices not easily articulated. While its articulation is not arbitrary, the visual representation of this articulation is.

[25] See Tzvetan Todorov's introduction to *Mikhail Bakhtin: The Dialogical Principle* for a discussion of difficulties related to issues of authorship (Voloshinov and Medvedev), chronology, publication, and access. For a discussion related to issues of ideology (Marxism, Christianity, and West European philosophy), see Michael Holquist and Vadim Liapunov's introduction to *Art and Answerability: Early Philosophical Essays by M. M. Bakhtin.*

[26] Bakhtin's interests included biology, physics, linguistics, psychology, theology, politics, and literary analysis, all of which he believed must be reconciled to philosophy if philosophy is to be a meaningful discipline. Bakhtinian scholar Michael Holquist says that Bakhtin's writings encompass linguistics, psychoanalysis, theology, social theory, historical poetics, axiology, and philosophy of the person. Bakhtin also wrote specific works on the subjects of vitalism, Formalism, Dostoevsky, Freud, Goethe, and Rabelais (vii). Katerina Clark and Michael Holquist, eds. *Mikhail Bakhtin*. Cambridge: The Belknap Press, 1984.

[27] This represents a process, however, as the architectonic is always a work in progress. Order and form are ideals.

[28] Bakhtin, however, does allow the metaphysical to stand, on the basis that faith is a form of knowledge.

[29] Again, Bakhtin does not generally concede that monologism can be absolute. He does say, though, that madness would approximate this absolute non-coincidence with one's self. In the "axiological void," he writes, "no utterance is possible, nor is consciousness itself possible" (*Art and Answerability* 123–24).

30 Another strategy for locating spaces for new readings is offered by T. Denean Sharpley-Whiting in "The Dawning of Racial-Sexual Science: A One Woman Showing, A One Man Telling, Sarah and Cuvier." Here, Sharpley-Whiting enacts a historical re-reading of space, as she tells the story of Sarah Bartmann, a South African woman, whose person, specifically, her sexuality, was commercially co-opted by the European community and later scientifically and culturally co-opted by French anatomist and naturalist Georges Cuvier in order to serve an eurocentric goal to demonize Africans. As a result, she writes, this historical narrative has figured prominently in Western sexual-racial science and French cultural history throughout the nineteenth and into the twentieth century.

Bartmann was exhibited in England and France and, during her life, became the subject of cartoons, a popular vaudeville show, and a nude painting. She constituted an exotic product which stimulated European consumers' erotic impulses, while simultaneously, she served as "other," invisible, and thus endlessly open to ideological inscription. The most influential was "scientific," the result of Cuvier's anatomical study of Bartmann, following her death of smallpox. This endeavor, as well as the writings that emerged from it, are rife with bias and stereotyping. Cuvier associates black femaleness with the bestial and primitive by associating Bartmann's sexuality with an excess emanating from primitive origins. His norm, of course, is the idyllic beauty and form of classical antiquity. He uses phrenology to validate the European prejudice that Africans are fundamentally different, pathologically, and his interpretation places Africans in the space of the missing link. Sharpley-Whiting argues that science thus served as handmaiden to eurocentric prejudice, the effects of which are still with us today.

31 Historical new space is also charted by Susan Jarratt, who explores the relation between the exclusion of sophists and women in her chapter "The First Sophists and Feminism: Discourses of the 'Other'" to argue that careful study of the connection between sophistic rhetoric and feminist reading/writing might not only advance studies in the history of rhetoric but also "offer increased leverage" (*Rereading* 79) for challenging the patriarchal hegemony established at the time of sophistic marginalization. Her conclusion is that although the sophists may not have been feminists, feminists enact sophistic strategies which create space for the recovery of historically marginalized voices in rhetoric through a correlation of feminist theory/literary critical practice to the sophists' democratic rhetoric.

The focus of Jarratt's exploration is intellectual marginalization, which begins with Plato and Aristotle, whose philosophy established the binary logic that privileges hierarchical epistemological structures that "coincide on many counts with the cultural stereotype of the 'feminine' operative in the West for centuries" (65): truth/opinion; soul/body; science/practical knowledge; eternal/temporal; speech/writing. Associated with this is the reduction and denigration of "style," relative to sophists and women, to a code that translates to persuasion through deception.

Gayatri Spivak characterizes the process by which sophistic rhetoric/woman has been historically situated negatively in relation to the privileged pole of philosophy/man as "the production of a discourse of man through a certain metaphor of woman" ("Displacement" 169; qtd. in Jarratt, *Rereading* 65): irrationality, magical power, subjectivity, emotional—these are equated with the feminine; rationality, objectivity, detachment—these with the masculine. The main difference, Jarratt says, between sophistic rhetoric and the "metaphor of woman" is the agonism of the former compared to the passivity characterized with women. "Suppression of difference is," Jarratt says, "crucial to the operation of philosophy" (66).

Jarratt discusses the intersecting role of rhetoric, deconstruction, and feminism in exposing exclusions. Derrida locates in Nietzsche three sites for women, which also correlate to different historical perspectives of rhetoric: woman as falsehood; woman as instrument of truth; and woman as emancipator. The latter position equates woman and rhetoric with the instrument of deconstruction. But the apolitical nature of deconstruction as textual exercise is criticized for its failure to engage the material conditions of textual production. It is not enough to deconstruct *logos*'s transcendent conceptions of presence, idea, and speech, it is also necessary to deconstruct *logoi*, "'laws in the normal sense'" (67). Only by so doing can the intersection of rhetoric and feminism illuminate political realities.

Turning attention to deconstruction and feminism, Jarratt recaps three evolutions of feminist politics/theory: first, there was the discourse of equality; next came the discourse of difference; last is the discourse of deconstruction. These last two positions, however, when isolated, prove to be unsatisfactory to a feminist enterprise. A discourse of difference is essentialist, which plays into the hegemonic hand, while the antifoundational precept of deconstruction denies essence and sexual difference altogether. Additionally, deconstruction posits a feminine other as a generic for "otherness" (67), a textual location that does not account for a material woman, much less for material women. Readings of "otherness," Jarratt concludes, are contingent upon their rhetorical situations.

Rhetorical feminism accommodates the three irreconcilable feminist discourses by allowing them to "co-exist in contradiction," definitely a sophistic strategy. Acknowledging that human agency is overdetermined, each person must, nonetheless, make a choice, take a position, realizing that such situatedness exacts a political price. The sophists, as well, understood "the imperative of rhetoric to formulate kairotic discourse—that is, suitable for the time" (70). Spivak suggests we change the question of "'What is woman?'" to "'What is man that the itinerary of his desire creates such a text?'" (70). Jarratt says this approach offers potential for the connection of feminist reading practices to the history of rhetoric.

Discussing how feminist sophistics can revise logic through narrative, Jarratt cautions against a binary, essentialist notion of man's and woman's logic. The point is, rather, "to locate legally and historically the falsely naturalized logic of patriarchy (as emerging from a particular set of *nomoi*) in contrast to an alternative experienced historically by women and creating necessarily different discursive products" (76). Spivak recommends acknowledged "'misreadings'" based upon "'suitable allegor[ies]'" (76). Nancy K. Miller suggests the use of narrative as a way to revise logic, a strategy that "'overread[s]'" an "underread" text (77). The goal is to both locate feminine texts and to identify the reality of their production.

Jarratt, then, effectively constitutes a new space with this historical rereading. Significantly, she also offers a methodology by which to chart new spaces with additional readings.

[32] In "Representing Whiteness in the Black Imagination," bell hooks explains her rationale for "an archaeology of memory." She writes: "The discourse of race is increasingly divorced from any recognition of the politics of racism"; indeed, contemporary society displaces racism with concepts such as pluralism and diversity, which allow for "assimilation and forgetfulness" (345) and for continuing white racist domination. hooks calls for critical interventions into the historical legacy of white domination, into its physical and psychological impact. Although black people, she says, remain relatively silent about representations of whiteness in the black imagination, the "representation of whiteness as terrorizing" (341) is experienced by black people who are often unable to articulate the ways in which they are terrorized for fear of reprisals in the form of accusations, such as reverse racism or demands for special treatment. She stresses this representation of whiteness is not a reaction to stereotypes, but is instead "a response to the traumatic pain and anguish that remains a consequence of white racist domination, a psychic state that informs and shapes the way black people 'see' whiteness" (341).

White people's amazement that they are watched by black people "with a critical 'ethnographic' gaze" is, itself, a manifestation of racism, hooks says (339). hooks's critical gaze emerged from classroom discussions about the issue of recognition: whites, she says, "imagine that they are invisible to black people," that whites assume "the right to control the black gaze," the right to "deny the subjectivity of blacks" (340). hooks appeals to memory to counter institutionalized ignorance of black history, culture, and everyday existence, so that black experience can be theorized. She calls for the reconstruction of "an archaeology of memory" (343) for uncovering, restoring, and deconstructing these memories in order to avoid reification. Memory is return, a form of travel; the theorizing of travel is, she says, imperative for understanding the politics of location, "that 'where' is less a place than it is a compilation of itineraries: different, concrete histories of dwelling, immigration, exile, migration" (343). Michel Foucault characterizes memory, she says, as "a site of resistance," maintaining that "the process of remembering can be a practice which 'transforms history from a judgment on the past in the name of a present truth to a "counter memory" that combats our current modes of truth and justice, helping us to understand and change the present by placing it in a new relation to the past'" (344).

Critical intervention, hooks says, holds radical possibilities. Gayatri Spivak explains that "'what we are asking for is that the [. . .] holders of hegemonic discourse should de-hegemonize their position and themselves learn how to occupy the subject position of other'" (346). Only then, hooks says, can black people decolonize their minds and their imaginations. Such is the possibility for resistance, then, in hooks's notion of "an archaeology of memory," a methodology she offers for exploring the politics of location.

[33] An example of a classroom in which students' discourses were valued is related in the article "Informing Critical Literacy with Ethnography," by Gary Anderson and Patricia Irvine, who foreground the need to contextualize applications of critical pedagogy, a consideration that is often not articulated by its proponents. Their classroom illustrations focus on choices of language. Students researched their native language from a variety of perspectives and, ultimately, decided for themselves to what degree they would modify their own language practices. These were socially and politically informed choices; here, students decided to maintain their native language practice for specific writing situations, while assimilating to the dominant discourse in order to situate themselves in specific, desired spaces. This pedagogy is both sensitive and responsible. Of course, this application is somewhat complicated when the classroom is comprised of multiple native language variations.

Another salient point they make is that change in self-esteem, although empowering, is necessary for, but not equal to, social action. I agree, although I concede that this observation challenges teachers and students alike. However, the students that Anderson and Irvine describe engaged social action. The action taken by a class in Albuquerque, New Mexico, was very impressive. Native Spanish-speaking immigrant children in middle school wrote books in Spanish and English for Nicaraguan children who had few educational resources due to the U.S. boycott. Over 5,000 of the books were sent.

This is an excellent narrative of students' native discourses existing dialogically with institutional discourse and both discourses being equally valued for their use in specific, but different, contexts.

[34] The historical backdrop Michael Holzman provides in "Observations on Literacy: Gender, Race, and Class" for explaining the origins and motivations of literacy/illiteracy is crucial to understanding the issue of insider/outsider status today. He makes a cogent argument for the role the issue plays in

our culture, arguing that discussions of literacy occlude the issue of racism. Holzman attempts to contextualize this discourse of the underclass according to race, gender, and class, so as to complicate the literal issue of illiteracy and to focus attention upon it as its representation as symbol. Viewing illiteracy as a symbol of a problem, Holzman maintains, allows us to sidestep it as a manifestation of inequity.

For example, ideology perpetuates the notion that there is a correlation between literacy, economic success, and social status; thus the poor have become a symbol of illiteracy. Holzman counters this assumption with historical data from both national and international sites. He follows with two literacy stories: the efforts of the Swedish and the Soviets to force literacy upon populations—the former's motivated by religion, the latter's by politics. It had become unfeasible, he says, to rely on orality to perpetuate hegemonic ideology, so literacy provided an alternative. With the marriage of the social/political, the entire domain of the population became the targeted goal. Pedagogy was instituted and its effectiveness gauged against this goal. Although the U.S. doesn't have one dominant ideology but rather multiple and varied ideologies, these various coalitions do cohere toward a common economic ground. Not all groups are, however, represented in this ideological coalition: the underclass, for example, serves its economic interest, but does not have a voice in shaping the ideology. In this scenario, the underclass is necessary for the preservation of the ideological coalition, a situation Holzman sees reflected in our schools' exemplary job of reproducing the structure of society by literally educating the underclass into illiteracy. It is no coincidence, he says, that this underclass is predominantly black.

Illiteracy, however, is not the goal. What is necessary is an economically superfluous segment; in this country, this segment is overwhelmingly female and overwhelmingly black. The underclass is "other," marked by the interstices of gender, race, and class. One of its distinctions just happens to be illiteracy. Holzman does complicate the tensions between economic reality and gender, race and class prejudice, and his complication of these relations resists a simplistic cause/effect rationale of domination. Holzman says that we must work to change educational complicity in reproducing the underclass. This can begin in the English classroom, K-12 and beyond, by re-thinking how education takes place rather than focusing attention on curriculum and pedagogy.

While I agree with most of Holzman's argument, especially with his assertion that we need to re-think how education takes place, I also do not believe this can or should be divorced from a focus on curriculum and pedagogy. It is far too easy for us to emotionally and intellectually concede the inequities inherent in educational enterprises, yet continue to support those practices unwittingly because we have not reflexively examined how our curriculum choices and pedagogical practices function relationally to support this status quo.

[35] Villanueva argues for a dialectic approach to the classroom in "Considerations for American Freireistas" as a way to direct processes, versus directing students, a strategy he says that provides students with opportunities for an increased awareness of the possibility for changing worldviews. He believes that juxtaposing tradition and change in the classroom benefits students by offering them altered perspectives, increased literacy, and a critical view of the academic community.

Villanueva offers a variety of experiences that confirm the need and viability of his argument. First, he disperses some autobiographical snippets, in narrative form, to focus attention to the issues. It is a story of the double bind of oppressor/oppressed. It illuminates the workings of hegemony, which Villanueva says we must understand if we are to effect real change, and it recommends counter-hegemony, which, as this article proves, "cannot be easily sold" in the classroom (251). His story effectively illustrates his thesis: "that history and culture alone do not make for a political sensibility, that such a view is reductive of the complex combinations of cultures and histories in American minorities, and that multiculturalism alone can be deceptive, in that it suggests a friendly pluralism that does not exist outside the classroom" (249).

Next, Villanueva discusses empirical research he conducted, an ethnography of a Writer's Project classroom where the teacher, Floyd, Freire-trained and Freire-committed, nevertheless succumbs to hegemony. Villanueva's critique of Floyd's curriculum/pedagogy/classroom management leads him to this insight: "I have observed something of the fulfillment of an American Freireista's fantasy and have seen its limitations" (251). The flaw in Floyd's curriculum, he says, is "superimpos[ing] a cultural concern on a class-structural model, discussing culture in classlike terms" (252). According to Freire, the newly literate, critically conscious, must attempt to transform the class system precisely because the marginalized exist only within the structure, not in the domain of the class system at all. America's class system, then, co-exists with a caste system, the latter to which one is consigned by birth. Castes consist of racial minorities and Hispanics, he says, whose cultural memories carry traces of colonization and slavery. It is not sufficient, then, to understand our culture; we must understand our culture in context to other cultures. We must understand that these cultures conflict. No one in America, Villanueva says, can exist as monocultural. Floyd is also criticized for his pedagogy, which is described as "traditional." As a result, his students fail to achieve their individually determined goals, "literacy of the kind that leads to certification [. . .] to the middle class" (258), while Floyd's goals are eclipsed by a method characterized as "explicitly propaganda" (256).

Finally, Villanueva discusses a curriculum he developed with Dolores Schriner at Northern Arizona University, which works toward the goals of his argument: "tradition and change for changes in tradition" (258). This curriculum introduced the dialectic by juxtaposing tradition (Hemingway) with change (Buchi Emecheta) and by having students attempt to relate the readings to their own experiences. Friere admits that this isn't going to "overturn tradition," but it can "provide the means for access, acknowledging the political, the while avoiding propaganda" (260).

Villanueva's point that culture cannot be approached from a class perspective is interesting. Even though minorities have made it to the middle class and beyond, they are never fully "enculturated," first, because the dominant do not allow it, and, second, because their inherited ideologies, carrying the traces of colonialism and slavery, inevitably conflict with their adopted ideologies. But what is to be done? Awareness is no panacea, and I do not see any recommendation for action forthcoming from Villanueva. Understanding hegemony conceptually and experientially, he says, constitutes the possibility for change, echoing Freire, who says that awareness is a prerequisite to change. It seems to me the counterpart is absent: advocating an understanding of hegemony by those within the dominant ideology. The assumption seems to be that the dominant have a clear understanding yet refuse to act due to a conflict of self-interest. This is not entirely untrue (although clear understanding is an overstatement), but it is reductive. Are we so sure that hegemony works the same way for all groups? I do not think it does, and until we explore and address this question, we cannot expect to see substantive change.

[36] Delores Schriner's article, "One Person, Many Worlds: A Multi-Cultural Composition Curriculum," is a rich example of Gale's argument that institutional authority is both inevitable and indispensable to teaching. Frankly, this article interests me most for its negotiation of ethical liability. A large Midwestern university receives a grant from the Ford Foundation, a veritable pillar of dominant hegemony. The grant is designated to improve the "enculturation" process of minority students, namely Native Americans, at a small southwestern satellite university. The grant is used to create a curriculum that flirts with subversion of the very hegemony that enabled it. The article's limitation, however, is that students' responses to the curriculum, couched in the neutral terms of self-discovery, do not allow the reader much insight as to how the curriculum correlated to its goals. Nevertheless, its narrative is instructive.

"One person, many worlds," was the theme of a new curriculum, Schriner says, fashioned after the program at the University of Pittsburgh, implemented at Northern Arizona University in the late 1980s. The goal was to have students recognize that everyone exists within multicultural social realities; *world* rather than *culture* was used in an effort to encourage students to see beyond what they might typically consider to be within the domain of culture, so as to encompass the wide range of human experience. The impetus for the curriculum was the high attrition rate (90%) of Native American students, caused, in part, by their difficulty in negotiating the discourse conventions of the academy. The university targeted the English Department as a resource to address the problem, and with a grant from the Ford Foundation, Schriner, among others (she thanks Victor Villanueva in a note for his contributions to the development of the curriculum), developed a curriculum with these goals: to have students understand (1) that everyone is multicultural, with experiences that move them among borders; (2) that in the nature of this movement, they are both created by and creators of these multicultural social realities; and (3) how the practices of accommodation (resistance/opposition) work to shape subjectivities. The realization of these goals, it was believed, would ideally give students a framework from which to "politicize their lived situatedness in dominant or subordinate cultures" (qtd. in Schriner 98).

Comprised of writing/reading components (seven writing and seven reading assignments), the curriculum was divided into three series that corresponded to the curriculum's three goals. The first series asked students to consider notions of individuality, the second that they consider social and cultural factors that enable/restrict experiences, and the third that they reflect on this intersection of private/public. Additionally, the curriculum was designed to foster interpretive and thinking skills grounded in students' experiential contexts.

Another component of curriculum implementation was teacher training, which necessarily included addressing the curriculum's theoretical framework and goals. Generating and maintaining class discussions, evaluation of and feedback to students' papers, and becoming more culturally aware and sensitive were major areas of concentration in teacher training. Part of the result was that teachers began to deconstruct their pedagogies and to become more reflexive about their own roles in the university. Schriner concludes by stressing that this curriculum is not a prescription, that any curriculum must be contextualized to the demographics of the student population it is designed to serve.

This article, then, is instructive on many levels. It illuminates how the literacies students bring to the classroom can be valued and used to promote new understandings. It provides an illustrative case for a critical examination of how education is conducted with a simultaneous reflexivity of pedagogy and teachers' institutional roles. Finally, it serves as an example of a critical navigation of institutional power relations that both constrain and enable.

[37] Dale Bauer and Susan Jarratt exhibit great self-reflexivity regarding their classroom authority, offering an alternative to the power dilemma in the classroom in "Feminist Sophistics: Teaching with an Attitude." They argue

that rhetorical and feminist theories offer a way for students to develop counterauthority in their own discourses. By reading feminist theory through a sophistic rhetorical lens, they "devised a pedagogy linking civic responsibility for public discourse to personal experience" (150). This article describes their course, its sophistic foundations, resistance to the course, and successful instances of students' counterauthority.

The goal of this summer graduate seminar of fifteen was to provide students a way to argue from a feminist rhetorical perspective. It was the students' resistance to history, Bauer and Jarratt say, that most surprised them; they argued for "a liberatory politics [that] requires a discourse that locates bodies (ignored or devalued in Platonic metaphysics) in time, space, and material conditions" (153). Bauer and Jarratt attribute this resistance to an inability of students to see themselves as potential agents of change within historical narratives, yet they contend that historical knowledge is crucial to understanding social processes/problems as well as to imagining any sort of transformation. "One has to be placed, in space, in time, and in a vision of social order, the last of these making possible 'attitude' as an aggressive challenge to social hierarchies" (154).

Bauer and Jarratt used a process pedagogy that encouraged counterauthority through the connection of singular and collective histories. They also focused on the historical situation of the feminist rhetor and her students. Reactions to feminist sophistics led Bauer and Jarratt to propose the link between private and public discourse and for the foregrounding of ethics and politics in the classroom. It is important, they contend, that feminism not be viewed as "just another skeptical philosophy, cynical deconstruction, or ahistorical theory, replacing the liberal humanist principles of free will, open dialogue, truth in advertising, and tolerance of other views" (159). The relationship of the classroom to society must be complicated as well as the multiple social positions occupied by both teacher and student.

Their classroom practices included requesting students to adopt a situated but provisional position as transformative intellectuals in the culture, a position that required an explicit location of the body relative to race, class, and gender in history. They did not request personal narratives, rather their implicit request was manifested through the modeling of their own historical attitudes in their interactions with students. Team teaching was beneficial because it mediated a teacher-student tension; Bauer and Jarratt made a point of stressing their differences of opinion so as to avoid the acceptance/rejection binary of teacher authority. Equally important was Bauer and Jarratt's modeling of self-reflexivity regarding their own evolving locations relative to history and difference. This difference, a counterauthority, is generated, they say, when students "confront or recreate their own histories and present locations as social beings" (160). The impetus for this transformation was a request for students to respond to any of the essays in bell hooks's *Talking Back*.

Students were to write in their own voices (Bauer and Jarratt emphasize the plurality of voice) their reactions to the kinds of pedagogies hooks advocates. Excerpts of students' mediations were then presented and analyzed, which the authors found somewhat disappointing.

Nevertheless, Bauer and Jarrett conclude by reiterating the importance of Bakhtin's term *heteroglossia,* "since it suggests how authority is not only internalized but also challenged by one's personal history in dealing with authority" (163). "Feminist dialogics becomes a feminist sophistics when the dialogue is centered on persuasive power, not to enhance the personal authority of the teacher (as in some views of the Sophists), but to work at understanding the processes by which linguistic and social power work" (164).

Bauer and Jarratt's methodology for the negotiation of teacher authority represents an ethical and situated response on their part. That their goals and objectives were not fully met in this class does not mitigate its potential.

[38] Because students are comprised of multiple discourses and use multiple discourses, they therefore possess multiple epistemologies and literacies (see Figure 9). It is to this that I refer relative to multiple subjectivities. An opposing viewpoint to the notion of multiple or fragmented subjectivity is offered by Masud Zavarzadeh and Donald Morton, who critique the curriculum reform in English and Textual Studies (ETS) at Syracuse University. The authors complicate its successes by illuminating its very complicity with capitalist structures while at the same time critiquing the politics of reform in academe. The impetus for curricular reform, they say, was the change in contemporary capitalism and the labor force, which now requires a worker more capable of abstract thinking, a worker whose subjectivity is shaped by a postmodern conception of consciousness.

The curriculum responded by instituting theory, which the authors contend has always been historically necessary for the training of the labor force. They fault the ETS curriculum for occluding materialist pedagogy, a situation they believe to be caused by the postmodern discourse of fragmented subjectivity. This represented, they say, a shift in the same old humanist position. Humanism was not displaced; it merely absorbed the dissonance through a politics of inclusion. Resistance was thus neutralized. Outsidedness was delegitimized, authorized, they say, by those such as Foucault and Derrida, whose theory precludes the very possibility of outsidedness. The result was "bourgeois reformism" (79), which operates through strategies of coalitions and consensus. Thus, they say, there was no substantive change. The academy simply worked as the handmaiden to capitalist hegemony, foregoing its opportunity to inspire radical collective change.

In my opinion, Zavarzadeh and Morton undercut their rich and thoughtful critique by treating their opposition's positions reductively; they frame political options in the form of a binary, that is, either you work within, and thus swallow, dominant hegemony or you remain outside of it in an effort to effect truly radical change. What they advocate is ideal, but its very impossibility conflates their radicalism with an ultraconservative idealist impulse.

[39] I would add that feminist historiography, as evidenced in Susan Jarratt's article "Sapphic Pedagogy: Searching for Women's Difference in History and in the Classroom" also offers insight for exploring productive and resistant spaces. Here, the themes of gender and difference, learning and desire, and the uses of history are pursued by Jarratt, who uses Sappho as an example by which to explore the nature of difference relative to gender in the classroom. Using textual evidence and a literature review of secondary sources, Jarratt argues for Sappho as an analogue for teaching. By reflecting on Sappho's poetry, Jarratt says we can learn something about difference and desire that will beneficially inform our pedagogy.

Like others, Jarratt argues for "a *feminist* pedagogy of difference from the *feminized* classrooms that challenge institutional authority"; she argues for the "idea of the authoritative feminist teacher" (79). Granting that claiming an authority we would deny men is problematic, Jarratt uses Joan Wallach Scott's analysis of difference in a contemporary sex discrimination case against Sears to justify the use of difference. Sears's implication was that "'difference'" is categorically and absolutely opposed to "'equality'" (79). Scott's reply was that difference is not an absolute category, that it must be contextualized and examined as being historically specific. The case, Jarratt writes, "demonstrates the necessity that feminist theory interrupt the opposition of equality-versus-difference as complete, opposed, and mutually exclusive categories" (80). Both difference, which implies norms and positions, and equality, which is not the equivalent of sameness, must inform feminist politics and practices. Jarratt endorses Scott's characterization of difference "'as the very meaning of equality itself'" (Scott 144; qtd. in Jarratt 80), which, again, she says, is not the same as a radical pluralism. She then recommends a process for politics and the writing of history. Having thus made the case for a feminist pedagogy that is both different and equal, Jarratt moves to Sappho's poetry to explore the issues of power/passion relative to gender difference/equality in teacher/student relationships.

Support, affection, and bonding, just as in Classical times, continue to characterize academic mentoring relationships, she says. Called "'filiation'" by Said and "'good old boys'" network by Jarratt, these relationships signify "the fraternal affective structure of academic life: the comfort men experience in same-sex groups, the tendency to discover and nurture promising students who are male" (Said, *The World*, qtd. in Jarratt 81). Jarratt questions where women fit into such a pedagogical system since "for the female teacher, stepping into the Socratic role more radically challenges gender and familial narratives" (82). Looking again to Greek history, Jarratt looks for both a mentoring model that could include women and to the difference that would mark this cultural form.

Jarratt looks to scholarly readings of Sappho that seek new meanings by which to mark her difference by reading her sexuality contextually. Jarratt takes issues with these readings, even though she is sympathetic to the impulse "to remake masculinist culture from the inside out" (83). By ignoring or glossing Sappho's desire for power in the lover/beloved relationship as well as her persuasion, which is connected to pursuit and coercion, these scholarly readings reflect a desire for radical difference, which Jarratt says is parallel to the anxiety over women's authority in the classroom, to the "overstepping" of gender lines, to the concern of "'politicizing'" the classroom (83). But how, Jarratt asks, is an agenda that encourages students to change the way they think any different from the hegemonic process of transformation that humanists seek? She suggests the authority of the feminist teacher can be counterhegemonic "when she argues for the gendered construction of 'human natures,' culturally specific forms of reasoning, and multiple determinants of subjectivity" (84). Jarratt suggests readings of Sappho that explore difference as the meaning of equality can thus increase our understanding of feminist authority in the classroom.

Jarratt acknowledges using Sappho as an analogue for feminist teachers may make some nervous; she also says she is "persuaded by reading Sappho to acknowledge that learning involves currents of erotic desire and exercises of power, no less if a woman teaches than a man" (86). Desire, she says, is inherent to learning, so to deny sexual tension is to forfeit a "vital energy" for our teaching. Current narratives of female power, she maintains, are insufficient to the realization of an alternative construction for feminist, teacher authority. The maternal role is constraining, older women are routinely demonized, and sisterhood has proven to be limiting. Sappho, she says, offers an alternative: "a woman's community, laced through with power and desire, affection and loss, celebration and beauty, separate from but also within a male-dominated society" (87). Jarratt writes she doesn't recommend this as a prescription but offers it only for rumination.

[40] Barbara Bee works as an adult literacy teacher with socially and educationally disadvantaged women in Australia. She is an academic who does not focus on abstract feminist theory that ignores its own social and political implications. In her article "Critical Literacy and the Politics of Gender," Bee says she believes that genuine emancipation for women is only available through economic independence, which can only be achieved when women understand the "structural arrangements within society which subjugate them and maintain their economic, political, and social inferiority" (105). She advocates the personal/public epistemological approach, focusing on issues of self-identity, the politics of both house- and paid-work, the vocational and occupational status of women, and child care.

Throughout, Bee weaves stories from her teaching experience to illustrate and embellish her theoretical perspective. Bee works not only with women, but with the most marginalized of women—older immigrant women, whom much of society believes should be, if not content, at least resigned to their roles within the nuclear family. Governmental policy addresses these women only as adjuncts of their husbands, which is to say they are not addressed at all. Bee relates an experience of writing three words on the board and asking each woman to articulate just one sentence about it. The words were *mother, wife,* and *woman.* It is telling that the women had no problem with sentences about mother and wife but were genuinely puzzled and quiet about woman. Bee says they reverted to sentences about mother and wife, unable to contextualize themselves outside the contexts of these identities.

The different materials Bee used are interesting; she, like Mike Rose, advocates using experientially relevant material. One example is a visual map that traces a day's activity of a woman who is also a wife and mother. The women wrote sentences describing the activity in each frame and then practiced reading them. The critical element in this strategy is the frame that appears about one-third of the way through the collection of visuals depicting the woman, cooking, delivering children to school, doing laundry, grocery shopping, etc. In this frame, the woman's husband says to a male friend, "My wife doesn't work." Bee does not attempt to simplify how these materials and the subjects they enable play out in either the classroom or in these women's lives, but she does offer anecdotal evidence of how some of the women are able to effect some measure of change for themselves.

[41] The experience of Richard Penticoff and Linda Brodkey, as described in their article, "'Writing About Difference': Hard Cases for Cultural Studies," speaks to the issue of risk when teachers attempt to transgress traditional institutional discursive formations, for the following described course was cancelled before it ever began. The dean of Liberal Arts, they say, "sent the English department a memo announcing his decision to postpone the implementation of 'Writing about Difference' to address "misunderstandings about the course expressed with the university community" (126).

In 1990 an ad hoc group of faculty and graduate students at The University of Texas at Austin created a syllabus for a first-year writing course required of all students, titled "Writing About Difference." The impetus for this curriculum was the realization that many who teach composition are ill-prepared to do so, a situation that often reduces composition pedagogy to an obsession with correctness. In such an institutional context, the content of student writing is eclipsed. The topic of difference was adopted, they say, because it "challenge[d] the culturally and socially sanctioned practice of imputing extraordinary human value to some people by diminishing the worth of others" (124).

The theoretical framework of the course was Stephen Toulmin's method of argument, the primary focus of which was his notion of warrants. This method better supported a pedagogy of inquiry, which represented, the authors write, a balance between intellectual and pedagogical imperatives. Toulmin's claims, grounds, and warrants were the criteria by which readings were to be analyzed as well as the principles of invention that would generate student writing.

The subject position assumed for both students and teachers was that of transformative intellectual, a position that assumes dominant hegemony is susceptible to both internal and external critique and that intellectual activity is potentially transformative. The notion of rhetoric was also reconfigured, that is, rhetoric as inquiry was assumed to transgress disciplinary boundaries, so that inquiry as a goal was privileged over the mastery of content or skill. It was also assumed that the course's single topic would provide a focus to this inquiry.

Penticoff and Brodkey reflect on the pedagogy, conceding that only an empirical study could have illuminated the efficacy of their curricular decisions. The rights of students to voice personal opinions and to use personal experience was denied in the course on the grounds that free speech is not an absolute right but is, rather, contingent on rights and responsibilities that obtain within the classroom. Ultimately, this pedagogy would, they say, transform the classroom into an intellectual culture where arguments could be evaluated as arguments.

The course fiat at The University of Texas at Austin represents an extreme case of institutional power, since little, if any, negotiation took place. There were, moreover, repercussions that extended beyond the domain of just that institution.

[42] For a succinct tracing of the genesis, development, and criticism of the term, *discourse community*, see Peter Vandenberg's entry "Discourse Community" in *Keywords in Composition Studies*, pages 67–70, and/or M. Jimmie Killingsworth's entry "Discourse Community" in the *Encyclopedia of Rhetoric and Composition*," pages 194–196.

[43] Janice Lauer in "Composition Studies: Dappled Discipline" provides the anatomy of a discipline and thus a map of its truth conditions.

[44] In "Postmodernism and Literacies," James Paul Gee discusses the process of meaning in a postmodern climate and speculates how moral judgments and resistant action can be legitimized in the face of postmodern rejections of exclusivity and privilege. Ultimately, he would have us view meaning as the result of sign systems derived from the historically situated social practices of particular groups. The ramifications of this view support, he says, a position that there are many literacies, all of which are tied to social practices, so that fluency in any one must be determined relative to its given social practice. Because education constitutes an initiation of students into specific literacies, educators must reflect on those they support both explicitly and implicitly. Otherwise, we create "insider" and "outsider" positions. The basis on which we can morally disapprove of this inequity and can advocate re-

sistance, Gee writes, rests on two principles that characterize ethical human discourse. The first principle is this: "that something would *harm* someone else (deprive them of what they or the society they are in view as 'good') is *always* a good reason (though perhaps not a sufficient reason) *not* to do it" (292). The second principle is this: "one always has the ethical obligation to try to explicate (render overt and conscious) any social practice that there is reason to believe advantages oneself or one's group over other people or other groups" (293). "In the end," Gee says, "we run out of words, and meaning is rooted finally in judgment and action" (293).

To illustrate his points, Gee discusses two different stories written in an elementary classroom by two little girls, one white and middle-class, the other, black and working-class. He interprets the fluency of each story, illustrating how each is an exemplary literacy example of its specific social milieu. The little white girl is, however, rewarded with the label of "giftedness," while the little black girl's story is repressed by the teacher (the little girl finishes telling it, to the other children's delight, when the teacher is out of the room). Gee's narrative is illustrative of the role of just one incident in a classroom to mark a student as an outsider. It also well illustrates the social and political nature of the tacit rules and regulations that work to effectively silence nonconforming literacies, as what remains most disturbing in Gee's narrative is the teacher's seemingly innocent failure to recognize and validate the legitimacy of an alternative literacy.

[45] In "Literacy and the Politics of Difference," Henry Giroux recommends a specific version of literacy, a postmodern discourse of literacy that foregrounds difference. He seeks, he says, to emphasize the relationship between literacy and difference rather than the subjects and various approaches surrounding it. He wants, he says, "to develop a rationale, along with some pedagogical principles, for developing a politics of difference responsive to the imperatives of a critical democracy" (372).

First all levels of education must be situated within a moral and social context. Only then can a politics and pedagogy of difference effectively constitute a fundamental part of a critical democratic discourse. Next, it is imperative that the issues of education and difference be articulated as a crisis in citizenship and ethics. Indeed, the ethical imperative that connects difference, education, and democracy is education for assuming the responsibilities of governing. Additionally, educators, Giroux writes, must "link a politics of literacy and difference to a theory of social welfare and cultural democracy" (375). This entails the use of a curriculum informed by the notion of difference in order to reconceive ideas of justice and equality. Pedagogical practices, he says, must contribute to preparing students to critically negotiate and transform their worlds.

Giroux's brand of literacy may not appeal to all educators, but it is illustrative of a teacher's ethical obligation to practice reflexivity regarding his goals for students and to then explicitly articulate these goals.

[46] As media teachers, practitioners, and critics, David Sholle and Stan Denski critique the present state of critical media literacy and ultimately offer a new theory of it in their article "Reading and Writing the Media: Critical Media Literacy and Postmodernism." They recommend a critical media literacy project located within the larger sphere of critical theory and critical pedagogy and suggest the criteria by which to measure its success are that "it must seek out silenced voices, address the terror and terrorism of the other, and employ practices directed at the opening of new space for new voices" (302). To this end, Sholle and Denski offer three counterhegemonic practices. The first, rereading the media, involves the practice of ideology critique as a confrontation with the text. This would address the construction of reality, meaning, and subjectivity. The second is the practice of affective reflexivity, where we "attend to the *affective investments* that students bring to the text" (312). The third and last counterhegemonic practice is rewriting and the strategy of authorship, where reading is acknowledged to be a form of production, an active writing. In this way, the concepts of reader and writer are connected to those of audience and producer. This new media literacy, they conclude, enables "new relations to representation and new possibilities for reading and writing" (318). It is a literacy that would promote an ethical practice of alterity.

[47] The historical dimension John Trimbur offers in "Literacy and the Discourse of Crisis" contextualizes episodes of literacy crises and connects them with hegemonic forces. Literacy crises, he says, invoke various cultural, social, political, and economic anxieties among the middle-class that justify our practices and inform our self-image as teachers. As direct beneficiaries of this discourse, Trimbur says, writing programs and composition studies have flourished in a climate in which we have failed to question the cultural and political meanings associated with that inherited discourse. This crisis, he says, has been around at least since the mid-19th century. It reoccurs periodically in order to, as Gramsci puts it, reorganize cultural hegemony, which is defined by two processes: political authority by the state is consolidated through consent and the leadership of a particular class/political group is established that excludes "others." Two explanations of the crisis have prevailed, neither of which, Trimbur says, has deepened our understanding.

The first explanation is decline, that is, people no longer read and write as well as they once did, a narrative strategy used by "Why Johnny Can't Read," and a sentiment shared by those like Allan Bloom and E.D. Hirsch. In this scenario, crisis is produced by the results of standardized testing, which are claimed to provide empirical evidence but which, in reality, he says, are misinterpreted. The impulse of this explanation is antidemocratic, according to

Trimbur, in that it attacks educational reforms of the 1960s and 1970s such as affirmative action and remedial education. Effectively, this "firm[s] up the meritocracy in order to consolidate the privileges of middle-class and upper middle-class students" (283).

The second explanation is that skills have not declined but rather the demands for them have escalated due to social and economic factors, which Trimbur argues are not innocent and neutral. He does concede that with each successive literacy crisis, the standard of literacy has increased and this does represent a form of progress. However, it is the uses of an increased standard that must be considered, one of which has historically been a requirement of suffrage and thus political exclusion. These higher standards are also claimed to be necessary to the workforce, but Trimbur examines the changing demographics of this workforce and suggests the true impulse is the socialization of workers into the discipline of the workforce in order to guarantee productivity.

Literacy crises, then, are always strategic, a fact reinforced through Trimbur's tracing of its historical transformations in the common-school crusade of 1840–1870 and the rise of progressive education from 1890–1920. Both movements posited literacy as "a means of ameliorating class antagonisms, equalizing economic opportunity, and ensuring social cohesion and political integration" (286). As the movements played out historically, however, it became obvious that literacy posed a threat to political stability, so that the control of literacy became recognized as a means to "discipline and regulate habits and character" (289).

The common-school movement transformed literacy from "a tool for participation into an instrument of social control" (289), as linguistic propriety became associated with social status and literacy became a social marker for us/them distinctions. Here, literacy promised and ensured assimilation into middle-class culture. The second literacy transformation occurred in the rise of progressive education, which set in place testing and evaluation systems that changed the tenor of literacy from a moral to a cognitive measure of individuals. Again, Trimbur says, the middle-class viewed literacy as their best hope for achieving upward mobility, success, and social status.

Historically, then, the discourse that situates literacy in crisis is initiated by social/political crises experienced by the middle class. Trimbur argues that literacy is in crisis insofar as the fate of American democracy rests with citizens who place private, individual interests above those of the group. Trimbur calls upon academics to counter the privatization of education so that higher education can become available to everyone.

[48] I have elected to equate authorship to the textbook itself, due to the multiple editors *Writing with a Purpose* has enjoyed over its lifespan.

[49] Twenty-two pages later, however, a description of one of Ernest Hemingway's writing rituals reads "that when he had trouble starting a new

story he would squeeze orange peels into the fire, gaze out the window, and worry about whether he would ever write again" (25).

[50] The modes of discourse—exposition, description, narrative, argument—are discussed and critiqued in Robert Connors's 1981 article, "The Rise and Fall of the Modes of Discourse," while Benjamin Bloom's taxonomy of cognitive levels—knowledge, comprehension, application, analysis, synthesis, evaluation—is discussed in his 1956 book, *Taxonomy of Educational Objectives: The Classification of Educational Goals*.

[51] I do not intend to establish a dichotomy between the classroom and the world, but I do intend to distinguish them relative to the sort of exigency that characterizes the authoring which contributes to the architectonic of networked subjectivity. It is possible for the exigency of the classroom to issue merely from the institutional economy of the writing course, while the exigency of the authoring that contributes to the architectonic of networked subjectivity must issue from the individual's experience of felt dissonance, the only sort of answer that appropriately responds to the world's addressivity. So, rather than a dichotomy, the distinction as described here places the classroom and the world at absolute points on the continuum of authoring.

[52] The exception to my statement that there are no gradations to existence is, however, qualified by Bakhtin, who contends that madness is the only legitimate alibi in existence.

[53] See Scott McLemee's article, "Deconstructing Composition: The 'New Theory Wars' Break Out in an Unlikely Discipline."

[54] For a complex and nuanced study of rhetoric and composition, textbooks, and the textbook industry, see Libby Miles's 1998 award-winning dissertation, *Building Rhetorics of Production: A Critical Analysis of Composition Textbook Publishing*.

[55] James Porter, Patricia Sullivan, Stuart Blythe, Jeffrey Grabill, and Libby Miles make the case in their article, "Institutional Critique: A Rhetorical Methodology for Change," that "space itself is a major factor in achieving systemic change; [that] timely deployment and construction of space (whether it be discursive or physical) can be a key rhetorical action affecting institutional change, and once created, the space can operate independently of the sponsoring agents" (630).

[56] In her reader response to J. Hillis Miller, Patricia Harkin takes exception to Miller's characterization of composition studies as "so condescending and reductive (and widespread) that many compositionists want to leave their institutional 'homes' and strike out on their own" (150). Miller, not surprisingly, does not think this a good idea; he writes in "The Function of Rhetorical Study at the Present Time" that "the worst catastrophe that could befall the study of English literature would be to *allow* the programs in expository writing to become separate empires in the universities and colleges wholly cut off from the departments of English and American literature" (qtd. in Har-

kin 150–51). Harkin says that "in this interview, he describes a discussion at Irvine about 'whether composition ought *to be taken away* from the English Department and *given* to some dean, made a cross-school program" (emphasis added, qtd. in Harkin 151). One can't help noticing that in these sentences composition programs become objects to be given and taken away, allowed to go and come. Then, he asserts that 'composition ought to stay in English departments not to help composition but to help English departments. It's good for them to have the composition people'" (qtd. in Harkin 151).

That rhetoric and composition is routinely "othered" is also observed by Anne Ruggles Gere, who says that "as most of us know from our own experiences as well as from the observations of theorists, literature actually depends upon composition to provide the 'other' against which it can stand. Not surprisingly, those in literature resist any moves from composition colleagues that might change this hierarchical relationship" ("The Long" 125). Winterowd and Gillespie characterize our situation thusly: "compositionists reside in the literarist empire only as documented aliens, the courses they teach entitling them to green cards. The content of composition is, by and large, an institution so structured as to provide no territory for the discipline (as opposed to the practice)" (vii). Finally, in an article in *The Chronicle of Higher Education,* our role in English departments is characterized as "playing the part of the ugly stepsister" (Schneider).

[57] We understand from Antonio Gramsci's notion of hegemony that it can exist only with the consent of those it oppresses. Sidney Dobrin writes in *Constructing Knowledges* that Gramsci "argues that the cultural and ideological relationship between ruling and oppressed classes is less an issue of domination than it is of a push toward hegemony—the idea that control is not achieved through manipulation of the masses but that controlling classes must engage in negotiations with those who oppose their views, must legitimately accommodate opposing views, and that hegemony succeeds not by eliminating the opposition but by dissolving it through the *articulation* of assimilation" (122). It is not surprising, then, that we have been slow to act in the pursuit of change. Often, we genuinely like, respect, and sometimes even admire our oppressors, who are not evil people. Their flaw is that they do not "see" their own privilege and power and they have no vested interest, of course, in doing so. As Charles Schuster writes in "Seeking a Disciplinary Reformation," "English studies, for all its deconstruction and Marxism, its gender and cultural studies, is conservative—and one of its primary missions is to conserve its current privileges and procedures exactly as they are" (147).

[58] Humorous (and not-so-humorous) are the confused and confounded looks of too many literary scholars when confronted with news of their hegemonic status. The constellation of the universe of most English departments as ruled by literary studies, around which "other" English department planets revolve, is taken simply as a natural given. Thus, all is right with the

world of the English department when such commonsense prevails. At least, such is the case for those whose privilege it thereby maintains.

[59] Kurt Spellmeyer writes in "Education for Irrelevance? Or, Joining Our Colleagues in Lit Crit on the Sidelines of the Information Age" that "we may ridicule Matthew Arnold, but we still believe that our task is to remain above the fray and to save the Philistines from themselves through acts of heroic interpretation" (83).

[60] It is worth noting that most of us are likely less capable of countering the hegemony of the English department as effectively as Janice Lauer, as few of us share the strength and fortitude of her personality. I mention this only with the utmost respect and affection.

[61] For example, see Ellen Cushman's "Vertical Writing Programs in Departments of Rhetoric and Writing." Goggin and Beatty also remind us that Fred Newton Scott (University of Michigan) was the first to separate from the English department to form a department of rhetoric. The year was 1903. When he retired in 1930, the department was dismantled. "Had others followed his lead," they write, "it might have been more difficult for those in the English department at Michigan to have co-opted the rhetoric department Scott had built" (59). Another significant point to be made concerns the question of electing to migrate to discipline-dedicated programs and centers in lieu of departments. The problem of programs and centers entails the same issues involved with the first-year composition course and our historical myopic gaze upon it. Programs and centers, then, are unlikely to have the capacity to alter this situation, as they simply do not garner the same legitimacy and security that comes with the designation of departmental status.

[62] Kurt Spellmeyer humorously describes the situation thusly: "Our full professors now sit alongside gray-haired British Chaucerians and Frenchified senior modernists, and they have votes on the committees that choose graduate directors and hammer out degree requirements" ("Education" 78). Continuing in this vein, he writes that "new journals and new conferences get created every day. More than a few members of our profession have crossed the golden threshold of 100K. Some from our ranks have moved on to prestigious jobs as deans, provosts, and vice presidents. Some even chair the English departments that formerly looked down their noses at comp in much the same way as one used to look at one's poor, alcoholic uncle. Surely we have arrived" (79). (He goes on, however, to question if we really want to be where we have arrived.) Maureen Daly Goggin notes that in the 50 years since the establishment of the Conference on College Composition and Communication (CCCC), rhetoric and composition has developed into a legitimate discipline, with tenure-track faculty lines, Ph.D. programs, funded research projects, book series, scholarly journals, and professional conferences (1995, 1997, 2000). Tom Fox says there is "no longer need to argue about whether rhetoric and composition is a discipline, although our status is still low. We

sponsor journals, doctoral programs, conventions, and scholarship, as well as some newer departments and programs that are independent of literature departments" ("Working" 91).

[63] John Trimbur succinctly says that "the rise of English departments not only works out imaginary relations between reading and writing, literature and composition, white-collar and blue-collar labor—in terms of the struggle to distinguish the moral and intellectual leadership of the new professional middle classes from the working class, on one hand, and the older aristocratic families and the new plutocracy of capital, on the other—but also offers a forum to promote the mindedness among the classes around a national culture and the mission of the 'English speaking race' as a global power. This unifying impulse provides the warrant for the study of English literature" ("The Problem" 21).

[64] For example, see Janice Lauer's "Composition Studies: Dappled Discipline," Ross Winterowd's "Fragments of History, Personal and Institutional," Richard Lloyd-Jones's "Omnivorous Study," and John Warnock's "The Discipline and the Profession: *It's a Doggy Dog World.*"

[65] Keith Moxey in *The Practice of Theory* makes the point that "pluralism in intellectual matters is based on the premise that it is possible to consider more than one interpretation of the same subject as valid or true. The view depends on the notion of determinate meaning; that is, there are meanings that are epistemologically true or false. On this view, it is our incapacity ever to know the whole truth which enables us to recognize more than one account as affording us at least a partial truth about the subject in question. Our choice between competing accounts is said to depend on the persuasiveness of the interpretations in question. [. . .] the notion that competing interpretations depend for their success or failure on their powers of persuasion suggests a naive and unlikely paradigm of intellectual debate. There is, in other words, a politics of pluralism, a politics that has traditionally masked the ways in which cultural and social interests intersect with and determine the value we find in specific intellectual positions. Pluralism fails to acknowledge the role of power in the process of selecting and promoting the forms of interpretation which are considered legitimate by a particular culture at a particular moment. It suggests that all voices can be heard and that rational evaluation and debate determine which succeed and which fail" (14–15).

[66] Sharon Crowley asks: "If composition studies did not undergo a paradigm shift in the 1960s and 1970s, what did happen? What was it that felt so revolutionary then? [. . .] I will hazard that what changed was our professional identity" ("Around" 72). This conclusion regarding professional identity could just as well apply today.

[67] Lynn Bloom reminds us, too, that "process remains the default mode in much of our thinking about writing" (31).

Works Cited

Alcorn, Marshall W., Jr. "Changing the Subject of Postmodernist Theory: Discourse, Ideology, and Therapy in the Classroom." *Rhetoric Review* 13.2 (1995): 331–49.

Althusser, Louis. "Ideology and Ideological State Apparatuses (Notes towards an Investigation)." *Lenin and Philosophy and Other Essays.* Trans. Ben Brewster. London: New Left Books, 1971. 121–73.

Anderson, Gary L., and Patricia Irvine. Lankshear and McLaren 81–104.

Ashton-Jones, Evelyn, and Dene Kay Thomas. "Composition, Collaboration, and Women's Ways of Knowing: A Conversation with Mary Belenky." *JAC* 10.2 (1990): 275–92.

Austin, J. L. *How to Do Things with Words.* Cambridge, MA: Harvard UP, 1975.

Bakhtin, Mikhail. *Art and Answerability: Early Philosophical Essays by M. M. Bakhtin.* Trans. Vadim Liapunov. Ed. Michael Holquist and Vadim Liapunov. Austin, TX: U of Texas P, 1990.

—. *The Dialogic Imagination: Four Essays by M. M. Bakhtin.* Trans. Caryl Emerson and Michael Holquist. Austin, TX: U of Texas P, 1981.

—. *Speech Genres and Other Late Essays.* Ed. Michael Holquist and Caryl Emerson. Austin, TX: U of Texas P, 1986.

Baudrillard, Jean. "The Precession of Simulacra." Natoli and Hutcheon 342–75.

Bazerman, Charles. "The Case for Writing Studies as a Major Discipline." Olson, *Rhetoric and Composition* 32–38.

—. "A Rhetoric for Literate Society." Goggin, *Inventing a Discipline: Rhetoric Scholarship in Honor of Richard E. Young* 5–28.

Bee, Barbara. "Critical Literacy and the Politics of Gender." Lankshear and McLaren 105–32.

Benhabib, Seyla. *Situating the Self: Gender, Community, and Postmodernism in Contemporary Ethics.* New York, NY: Routledge, 1992.

Berkenkotter, Carol. "Paradigm Debates, Turf Wars, and the Conduct of Sociocognitive Inquiry in Composition." *College Composition and Communication* 42.2 (1991): 151–69.

Berlin, James A. "Composition Studies and Cultural Studies: Collapsing Boundaries." Gere 99–116.

—. "Contemporary Composition: The Major Pedagogical Theories." *College English* 44.8 (1982): 765–77.

—. "Rhetoric and Ideology in the Writing Class." *College English* 50 (1988): 477–94.

—. *Rhetoric and Reality: Writing Instruction in Nineteenth-Century American Colleges 1900–1985*. Carbondale: Southern Illinois UP, 1987.

—. *Writing Instruction in Nineteenth-Century American Colleges*. Carbondale: Southern Illinois UP, 1984.

Berlin, James A., and Robert P. Inkster. "Current-Traditional Rhetoric: Paradigm and Practice." *Freshman English News* 8.3 (1980): 1–14.

Berlin, James A., and Michael J. Vivion, eds. *Cultural Studies in the English Classroom*. Portsmouth, NH: Boynton/Cook, 1992.

Best, Stephen, and Douglas Kellner. *Postmodern Theory: Critical Interrogations*. London: Macmillan, 1991.

Bialostosky, Don H. "Mikhail Bakhtin." Enos, *Encyclopedia of Rhetoric and Composition* 64–66.

Bitzer, Lloyd F. "The Rhetorical Situation." *Philosophy and Rhetoric* 1.1 (1968): 1–14.

Bizzell, Patricia. *Academic Discourse and Critical Consciousness*. Pittsburgh, PA: U of Pittsburgh P, 1992.

—. "Commentary: Fredric Jameson and Composition Studies." *JAC* 16.3 (1993): 471–87.

—. Foreword. *Constructing Knowledges: The Politics of Theory-Building and Pedagogy in Composition*. Sidney Dobrin. Albany, NY: SUNY P, 1997. 1–4.

Bizzell, Patricia, and Bruce Herzberg, eds. *The Rhetorical Tradition: Readings from Classical Times to the Present*. Boston, MA: Bedford Books, 1990.

Bleich, David. *The Double Perspective: Language, Literacy, and Social Relations*. Baltimore: Johns Hopkins UP, 1988.

—. "The Materiality of Rhetoric, The Subject of Language Use." Petraglia and Bahri 39–60.

Blomley, Nicholas K. *Law, Space, and the Geographies of Power*. New York, NY: The Guilford Press, 1994.

Bloom, Benjamin. *Taxonomy of Educational Objectives: The Classification of Educational Goals*. New York: D. McKay Co., Inc., 1956.

Bloom, Lynn Z. "The Great Paradigm Shift and Its Legacy for the Twenty-First Century." Bloom, Daiker, and White, *Composition in the Twenty-First Century* 31–47.

Bloom, Lynn Z., Donald A. Daiker, and Edward M. White, eds. *Composition in the Twenty-First Century: Crisis and Change*. Carbondale: Southern Illinois UP, 1996.

—. *Rereading the Past, Rewriting the Future: Composition Studies in the New Millennium.* Carbondale: Southern Illinois UP, 2003.
Blyer, Nancy. "Research in Professional Communication: A Post-Process Perspective." Kent, *Post-Process Theory: Beyond the Writing Process Paradigm* 65–79.
Blyler, Nancy Roundy, and Charlotte Thralls, eds. *Professional Communication: The Social Perspective.* Newbury Park, CA: Sage, 1993.
Boehm, Beth, Debra Journet, and Mary Rosner, eds. *History, Reflection, and Narrative: The Professionalization of Composition, 1963–1983.* Norwood, NJ: Ablex, 1999.
Bourdieu, Pierre, and Jean-Claude Passeron. *Reproduction: In Education, Society, and Culture.* Trans. Richard Nice. Los Angeles: Sage, 1977.
Bowden, Darsie. "Literacy." Heilker and Vandenberg 140–44.
Brand, Alice G. "The Why of Cognition: Emotion and the Writing Process." *College Composition and Communication* 38.4 (1987): 436–43.
Brannon, Lil. "(Dis)Missing Compulsory First-Year Composition." Petraglia, *Reconceiving Writing* 239–48.
Brodkey, Linda. *Academic Writing as Social Practice.* Philadelphia, PA: Temple UP, 1987.
Brummett, Barry. "Some Implications of 'Process' or 'Intersubjectivity': Postmodern Rhetoric." *Philosophy and Rhetoric* 9.1 (1976): 21–51.
Budd, Malcolm. "Wittgenstein on Seeing Aspects." *Mind* 96 (Jan. 1987): 1–17.
Bulkin, Elly, Minnie Bruce Pratt, and Barbara Smith, eds. *Yours in Struggle: Three Feminist Perspectives on Anti-Semitism and Racism.* Brooklyn, NY: Long Haul Press, 1984.
Bullock, Richard, and John Trimbur, eds. *Politics of Writing Instruction.* Westport, CT: Heinemann, 1991.
Burke, Kenneth. *Language as Symbolic Action: Essays on Life, Literature, and Method.* Berkeley, CA: U of California P, 1966.
Cassam, Quassim. "Self-consciousness." Honderich 817.
Cauthen, Cramer R. "The Breadth of Composition Studies: Professionalization and Disciplinarity." Interview with Joseph Conprone, Lisa Ede, Peter Elbow, Janice Lauer, Andrea Lunsford, and Richard Young. *History, Reflection, and Narrative: The Professionalization of Composition, 1963–1983.* Ed. Beth Boehm, Debra Journet, and Mary Rosner. Norwood, NJ: Ablex, 1999. 205–13.
Cintron, Ralph. "Wearing a Pith Helmet at a Sly Angle or Can Writing Researchers Do Ethnography in a Postmodern Era?" *Written Communication* 10 (1993): 374–412.
Cixous, Helene. "The Laugh of the Medusa." Bizzell and Herzberg. 1232–45.

Clark, Katerina, and Michael Holquist. *Mikhail Bakhtin*. Cambridge, MA: Harvard UP, 1984.

Clark, H. H., and Susan H. Haviland. "Comprehension and the Given-New Contract." Freedle 1–40.

Clifford, John, and Elizabeth Ervin. "The Ethics of Process." Kent, *Post-Process Theory: Beyond the Writing Process Paradigm* 179–97.

"Codify." Merriam-Webster's Collegiate Dictionary. 10th ed. Springfield, MA: Merriam-Webster, Incorporated, 1994. 221.

Conners, Patricia E. "The History of Intuition and its Role in the Composing Process." *Rhetoric Society Quarterly* 20.1 (1990): 71–78.

Connors, Robert J. "The Abolition Debate in Composition: A Short History." Bloom, Daiker, and White, *Composition in the Twenty-First Century* 47–63.

—. *Composition-Rhetoric: Backgrounds, Theory, and Pedagogy*. Pittsburgh, PA: U of Pittsburgh P, 1997.

—. "The New Abolitionism: Toward a Historical Background." Petraglia, *Reconceiving Writing* 3–26.

—. "The Rise and Fall of the Modes of Discourse." *College Composition and Communication* 32.4 (1981): 444–63.

—. "Textbooks and the Evolution of the Discipline." *College Composition and Communication* 37.2 (1986): 178–194.

Consigny, Scott. "Rhetoric and Its Situations." *Philosophy and Rhetoric* 7.3 (1974): 175–86.

Cooper, Marilyn. "The Ecology of Writing." *College English* 48 (1986): 364–75.

Cooper, Marilyn M., and Michael Holzman, eds. *Writing as Social Action*. Postsmouth, N.H.: Boynton Cook, 1989.

Couture, Barbara. "Modeling and Emulating: Rethinking Agency in the Writing Process." Kent, *Post-Process Theory: Beyond the Writing Process Paradigm* 30–48.

Covino, William A. *The Art of Wondering: A Revisionist Return to the History of Rhetoric*. Portsmouth, NH: Boynton/Cook Publishers, 1988.

Crary, Jonathan. *Techniques of the Observer: On Vision and Modernity in the Nineteenth Century*. 6th. ed. Cambridge, MA: MIT P, 1995.

Crowley, Sharon. "Around 1971: Current-Traditional Rhetoric and Process Models of Composing." Bloom, Daiker, and White, *Composition in the Twenty-First Century* 64–74.

—. "Communications Skills and a Brief Rapporachement of Rhetoricians." *Rhetoric Society Quarterly* 34.1 (2004): 89–103.

—. "Composition's Ethic of Service, the Universal Requirement, and the Discourse of Student Need." *JAC* 15.2 (1995): 227–40.

—. *The Methodical Memory: Invention in Current-Traditional Rhetoric*. Carbondale: Southern Illinois UP, 1990.

Cushman, Ellen. "Beyond Specialization: The Public Intellectual, Outreach, and Rhetoric Education." Petraglia and Bahri 171–85.
—. "Vertical Writing Programs in Departments of Rhetoric and Writing." Bloom, Daiker, and White 121–25.
Dasenbrock, Reed Way. *Inquiries into Truth and Interpretation.* Oxford: Clarendon Press, 1984.
—. "J. L. Austin and the Articulation of a New Rhetoric." *College Composition and Communication* 38.3 (1987): 291–305.
—. *Literary Theory After Davidson.* Pittsburgh, PA: Pennsylvania State UP, 1989.
—. "The Myths of the Subjective and of the Subject in Composition Studies." *JAC* 13.1 (1993): 21–32.
—. *Redrawing the Lines: Analytic Philosophy, Deconstruction, and Literary Theory.* Minneapolis: U of Minnesota P, 1989.
—. "A Response to 'Language Philosophy, Writing, and Reading: A Conversation with Donald Davidson'" *JAC* 13.2 (1993): 523–28.
—. "A Rhetoric of Bumper Stickers: What Analytic Philosophy Can Contribute to a New Rhetoric." Enos and Brown 191–206.
—. *Truth and Consequences: Intentions, Conventions, and the New Thematics.* Pittsburgh, PA: Pennsylvania State UP, 2000.
Dear, Michael, Derek Gregory, and Nigel Thrift, eds. *Indifferent Boundaries: Spatial Concepts of Human Subjectivity.* New York, NY: Guilford Press, 1996.
DeJoy, Nancy. "I Was a Process-Model Baby." Kent, *Post-Process Theory: Beyond the Writing Process Paradigm* 163–78.
de Lauretis, Teresa. *Feminist Studies/Critical Studies.* Bloomington: Indiana UP, 1986.
—. "The Violence of Rhetoric: Considerations on Representation and Gender." *Technology of Gender: Essays on Theory, Film, and Fiction.* Bloomington, IN: Indiana UP, 1987. 31–50.
de Saussure, Ferdinand. *Course in General Linguistics.* New York, NY: McGraw Hill Book Co., 1966.
Derrida, Jacques. *Margins of Philosophy.* Trans. Alan Bass. Chicago: U of Chicago P, 1981.
—. *Positions.* Trans. Alan Bass. Chicago: U of Chicago P, 1981.
—. "Signature Event Context." *Glyph* 1 (1977): 172–97.
—. "Structure, Sign, and Play in the Discourse of the Human Sciences." *Writing and Difference.* Trans. Alan Bass. Chicago: U of Chicago P, 1978. 278–293.
—. *Writing and Difference.* Trans. Alan Bass. Chicago: U of Chicago P, 1978.
Dewey, John. *Logic: The Theory of Inquiry.* New York, NY: H. Holt and Company, 1938.

Dixon, Kathleen. "Gendering the 'Personal.'" *College Composition and Communication* 46.2 (1995): 255–75.

Dobrin, Sidney I. *Constructing Knowledges: The Politics of Theory-Building and Pedagogy in Composition.* Albany, NY: SUNY P, 1997.

—. "Paralogic Hermeneutic Theories, Power, and the Possibility for Liberating Pedagogies." Kent, *Post-Process Theory: Beyond the Writing Process Paradigm* 132–48.

Dreyfus, Hubert L., and Paul Rabinow. *Michel Foucault: Beyond Structuralism and Hermeneutics.* 2nd ed. Chicago: U of Chicago P, 1983.

Ebert, Teresa. "The 'Difference' of Postmodern Feminism." *College English* 53 (1991): 886–904.

Emig, Janet. *The Composing Process of Twelfth Graders.* NCTE Research Report No. 13. Urbana, IL: National Conference of Teachers of English, 1971.

—. "Inquiry Paradigms and Writing." Goswami and Butler 157–70.

—. "Literacy and Freedom." Goswami and Butler 171–78.

—. "The Origins of Rhetoric: A Developmental View." Goswami and Butler 55–60.

—. "The Relation of Thought and Language Implicit in Some Early American Rhetoric and Composition Texts." Goswami and Butler 1–43.

—. "The Uses of the Unconscious in Composing." Goswami and Butler 44–53.

—. "Writing as a Mode of Learning." Goswami and Butler 123–31.

Enos, Theresa, ed. *Encyclopedia of Rhetoric and Composition: Communication from Ancient Times to the Information Age.* Vol. 1389. Garland Reference Library of the Humanities. New York: Garland Publishing, Inc., 1996.

Enos, Theresa, and Stuart C. Brown, eds. *Defining the New Rhetorics.* Newbury Park, CA: Sage, 1993.

Ewald, Helen Rothschild. "A Tangled Web of Discourses: On Post-Process Pedagogy and Communicative Interaction." Kent, *Post-Process Theory: Beyond the Writing Process Paradigm* 116–31.

Faigley, Lester. "Competing Theories of Process: A Critique and a Proposal." *College English* 48.6 (1986): 527–42.

—. *Fragments of Rationality : Postmodernity and the Subject of Composition.* Pittsburgh, PA: U of Pittsburgh P, 1992.

Feyerabend, Paul. *Against Method.* New York: Verso, 1988.

Flannagan, Owen. "Consciousness." Honderich 152–53.

Fleischer, Cathy. "Forming an Interactive Literacy in the Writing Classroom." Berlin and Vivion 182–99.

Fleming, David. "Rhetoric as a Course of Study." *College English* 61.2 (1998): 169–91.

—. "The End of Composition-Rhetoric." Williams, *Visions and Re-Visions* 109–30.

Flower, Linda. "Three Comments on 'Rhetoric and Ideology in the Writing Class.'" *College English* 51.7 (1988): 765–69.
Flower, Linda, and John R. Hayes. "A Cognitive Process Theory of Writing." *College Composition and Communication* 32.4 (1981): 365–87.
Foster, David. "The Challenge of Contingency: Process and the Turn to the Social in Composition." Kent, *Post-Process Theory: Beyond the Writing Process Paradigm* 149–62.
Foucault, Michel. *The Archaeology of Knowledge.* Trans. A M. Sheridan Smith. New York, NY: Harper, 1976.
—. *Discipline and Punish: The Birth of the Prison.* Trans. Alan Sheridan. New York, NY: Vintage, 1979.
—. "Of Other Spaces." *Diacritics* 16 (1986): 22–27.
—. "Practicing Criticism." *Politics, Philosophy, Culture: Interviews and Other Writings, 1977–1984.* Ed. Lawrence D. Kritznar. New York, NY: Routledge, 1988. 152–58.
—. "Space, Knowledge, and Power." *The Foucault Reader.* Ed. Paul Rabinow. Trans. Christian Hubert. New York, NY: Pantheon Books, 1984. 239–56.
—. *Space, Knowledge, Power.* New York, NY: Pantheon, 1984.
—. "The Subject and Power." *Critical Inquiry* 8 (1982): 777–95.
—. *Truth and Power.* New York, NY: Pantheon, 1984.
—. "Two Lectures." *Power/Knowledge: Selected Interviews and Other Writings, 1972–1977.* Ed. and trans. Colin Gordon. New York, NY: Pantheon, 1980. 78–108.
Fox, Tom. "Working Against the State: Composition's Intellectual Work for Change." Olson, *Rhetoric and Composition* 91–100.
Freedle, Roy O., ed. *Discourse Production and Comprehension.* Norwood, NH: Ablex, 1977.
Freedman, Aviva. "The What, Where, When, Why, and How of Classroom Genres." Petraglia, *Reconceiving Writing* 121–44.
Freire, Paulo. *Education for Critical Consciousness.* New York, NY: Continuum Publishing Co., 1973.
Fulkerson, Richard. "Four Philosophies of Composition." *College Composition and Communication* 30 (1979): 343–48.
—. "Of Pre- And Post-Process: Reviews and Ruminations." *Composition Studies* 29.2 (2001): 93–119.
Fuss, Diana. *Essentially Speaking.* New York, NY: Routledge, 1982.
Gale, Fredric G. *Political Literacy: Rhetoric, Ideology, and the Possibility of Justice.* Albany, NY: SUNY P, 1994.
Gale, Xin Liu. *Teachers, Discourses, and Authority in the Postmodern Composition Classroom.* Albany, NY: SUNY P, 1996.

Gebhardt, Richard. "Writing Processes, Revision, and Rhetorical Problems: A Note on Three Recent Articles." *College Composition and Communication* 34.3 (1983): 294–96.

Gee, James Paul. "Postmodernism and Literacies." Lanskshear and McLaren 271–95.

George, Diana, and Diana Shoos. "Issues of Subjectivity and Resistance: Cultural Studies in the Composition Classroom." Berlin and Vivion 200–10.

Gere, Anne Ruggles, ed. *Into the Field: Sites of Composition Studies.* New York: Modern Language Association, 1993.

—. "The Long Revolution in Composition." Bloom, Daiker, and White, *Composition in the Twenty-First Century* 119–32.

—. "Public Opinion and Teaching." Bullock and Trimbur 263–75.

Giroux, Henry. "Literacy and the Politics of Difference." Lankshear and McLaren 367–78.

Giroux, Henry A., and Roger I. Simon. "Critical Pedagogy and the Politics of Popular Culture." *Cultural Studies* 2.3 (1988): 294–320.

Godzich, Wlad, and Jochen Schulte-Sasse, eds. *Mikhail Bakhtin: The Dialogical Principle.* By Tzvetan Todorov. Trans. Wlad Godzich. Vol. 13. Minneapolis: U of Minnesota P, 1984.

Goggin, Maureen Daly. "Composing a Discipline: The Role of Scholarly Journals in the Disciplinary Emergence of Rhetoric and Composition Since 1950." *Rhetoric Review* 15.2 (1997): 322–48.

—. "The Disciplinary Instability of Composition." Petraglia, *Reconceiving Writing* 27–48.

Goggin, Maureen Daly, and Steve Beatty. "Accounting for Well-Worn Grooves: Composition as a Self-Reinforcing Mechanism." Goggin 29–66.

Goggin, Maureen Daly, ed. *Inventing a Discipline: Rhetoric Scholarship in Honor of Richard E. Young.* Urbana, IL: National Council of Teachers of English, 2000.

Goswami, Dixie, and Maureen Butler, eds. *The Web of Meaning: Essays on Writing, Teaching, Learning and Thinking.* Montclair, NJ: Boynton/Cook Publishers, Inc., 1983.

Graves, Richard L., ed. *Rhetoric and Composition: A Sourcebook for Teachers and Writers.* Upper Montclair, New Jersey: Boynton, 1984.

Grossberg, Lawrence. "Putting the Pop Back into Postmodernism." *Universal Abandon.* Ed. Andrew Ross. Minneapolis: U of Minnesota P, 1988. 167–90.

Grossberg, Lawrence, Cary Nelson, and Paula Treichler, eds. *Cultural Studies.* New York, NY: Routledge, 1992.

Hamlyn, D. W. "The History of Epistemology." Honderich 242–45.

Haraway, Donna J. "A Cyborg Manifesto: Science, Technology, and Socialist-Feminism in the Late Twentieth Century." *Simians, Cyborgs, and Women: The Reinvention of Nature.* New York, NY: Routledge, 1991. 149–81.
Harkin, Patricia. "Ideology." Heilker and Vandenberg 119–24.
—. "On Transforming the English Department: A Response to J. Hillis Miller." *JAC* 15.1 (1995): 147–54.
Harkin, Patricia, and John Schilb, eds. *Contending with Words: Composition and Rhetoric in a Postmodern Age.* New York, NY: Modern Language Association, 1991.
Harris, Joseph. *A Teaching Subject: Composition Since 1966.* Upper Saddle River, NJ: Prentice Hall, 1996.
Hebdige, Dick. *Subculture: The Meaning of Style.* London: Methuen, 1979.
Heilker, Paul, and Peter Vandenberg, eds. *Keywords in Composition Studies.* Portsmouth, NH: Boynton/Cook Publishers, 1996.
Helmers, Marguerite H. *Writing Students: Composition, Testimonials, and Representations of Students.* Albany, NY: SUNY P, 1994.
Hermogenes. "Hermogenes *On stasis:* A Translation with an Introduction and Notes." Trans. R. Nadeu. *Speech Monographs* 31.4 (1964): 361–424.
Holquist, Michael, and Vadim Liapunov. "Introduction: The Architectonics of Answerability." *Art and Answerability: Early Philosophical Essays by M. M. Bakhtin.* Trans. Vadim Liapunov. Ed. Michael Holquist and Vadim Liapunov. Austin, TX: U of Texas P, 1990. ix-xlix.
Holzman, Michael. "Nominal and Active Literacy." *Writing as Social Action.* Ed. Marilyn M. Cooper and Michael Holzman. Portsmouth, NH: Boynton Cook, 1989. 151–73.
—. "Observations on Literacy: Gender, Race, and Class." Bullock and Trimbur 297–305.
Honderich, Ted, ed. *The Oxford Companion to Philosophy.* Oxford, NY: Oxford UP, 1995.
hooks, bell. "Postmodern Blackness." Natoli and Hutcheon 510–18.
—. "Representing Whiteness in the Black Imagination." Grossberg, Nelson, and Treichler 338–46.
—. *Talking Back: Thinking Feminist, Thinking Black.* Boston, MA: South End Press, 1989.
Jacobs, Debra. "Disrupting Understanding: The Critique of Writing as Process." *JAC* 21.3 (2001): 662–74.
Jameson, Fredric. *Postmodernism, or, The Cultural Logic of Late Capitalism.* Durham, NC: Duke UP, 1995.
Jarratt, Susan C. "The First Sophists and Feminism: Discourses of the 'Other.'" *Hypatia* 5.1 (1990): 27–41.
—. "The First Sophists and the Uses of History." *Rhetoric Review* 6.1 (1987): 67–78.

—. "Sapphic Pedagogy: Searching for Women's Difference in History and in the Classroom." *Learning from the Histories of Rhetoric: Essays in Honor of Winifred Bryan Horner.* Ed. Theresa Enos. Carbondale: Southern Illinois UP, 1993. 75–90.

Jay, Martin. *Downcast Eyes: The Denigration of Vision in Twentieth-Century French Thought.* Berkeley, CA: U of California P, 1993.

Jensen, George H., and John K. DiTiberio. "Personality and Individual Writing Processes." *College Composition and Communication* 35.3 (1984): 285–99.

Johnson, Barbara. Introduction. *Dissemination.* By Jacques Derrida. Chicago: U of Chicago P, 1981. 7–33.

Jolliffe, David. "Discourse, Interdiscursivity, and Composition Instruction." Petraglia, *Reconceiving Writing* 197–216.

Journet, Debra. "Writing Within (and Between) Disciplinary Genres: The 'Adaptive Landscape' as a Case Study in Interdisciplinary Rhetoric." Kent, *Post-Process Theory: Beyond the Writing Process Paradigm* 96–115.

Kaufer, David, and Patricia Dunmire. "Integrating Cultural Reflection and Production in College Writing Curricula." Petraglia, *Reconceiving Writing* 217–38.

Kemp, Fred. "Writing Dialogically: Bold Lessons From Electronic Text." Petraglia, *Reconceiving Writing* 179–94.

Kent, Thomas. "Beyond System: The Rhetoric of Paralogy." *College English* 51.5 (1989): 492–507.

—. "Externalism and the Production of Discourse." *JAC* 12.1 (1992): 57–74.

—. "Formalism, Social Construction, and the Problem of Interpretive Authority." Blyler and Thralls 79–91.

—. "The Hope of Communication." *JAC* 12 (1992): 427–30.

—. "Language Philosophy, Writing, and Reading: A Conversation with Donald Davidson." *JAC* 13.1 (1993): 1–20.

—. "On the Very Idea of a Discourse Community." *College Composition and Communication* 42 (1991): 425–45.

—. "Paralogic Hermeneutics and the Possibilities of Rhetoric." *Rhetoric Review.* 8.1 (1989): 24–42.

—. "Paralogic Rhetoric: An Overview." Olson, *Rhetoric and Composition as Intellectual Work* 143–52.

—. *Paralogic Rhetoric: A Theory of Communicative Interaction.* Cranbury, NJ: Associated U Presses, 1993.

—, ed. *Post-Process Theory: Beyond the Writing Process Paradigm.* Carbondale: Southern Illinois UP, 1999.

Killingsworth, M. Jimmie. "Discourse Community." Enos, *Encyclopedia of Rhetoric and Composition* 194–96.

Kinneavy, James L. "*Kairos:* A Neglected Concept in Classical Rhetoric." *Rhetoric and Praxis: The Contribution of Classical Rhetoric to Practical Reasoning.* Ed. Jean Dietz Moss. Washington, DC: Catholic UP, 1986. 79–105.

—. "The Process of Writing: A Philosophical Base in Hermeneutics." *JAC* 7.1–2 (1987): 1–9.

Kirby, Kathleen M. *Indifferent Boundaries: Spatial Concepts of Human Subjectivity.* New York, NY: Guilford Press, 1996.

Kitzhaber, Albert Raymond. *Rhetoric in American Colleges 1850–1900.* Dallas, TX: Southern Methodist UP, 1990.

Knoblauch, C. H. "Intentionality in the Writing Process: A Case Study." *College Composition and Communication* 31.2 (1980): 153–59.

Knoblauch, C. H., and Lil Brannon. *Critical Teaching and the Idea of Literacy.* Portsmouth, NH: Boynton/Cook, 1993.

Kostelnick, Charles. "Process Paradigms in Design and Composition: Affinities and Directions." *College Composition and Communication* 40.3 (1989): 267–81.

Kritznar, Lawrence D., ed. *Politics, Philosophy, Culture: Interviews and Other Writings, 1977–1984.* New York, NY: Routledge, 1988.

Kroll, Barry M. "Some Developmental Principles for Teaching Composition." Graves 258–62.

Krupnick, Mark, ed. *Displacement: Derrida and After.* Bloomington: Indiana UP, 1983.

LaCapra, Dominic. "Marxism in the Textual Maelstrom: Fredric Jameson's *The Political Unconscious.*" *Rethinking Intellectual History: Texts, Contexts, Language.* Ithaca, NY: Cornell UP, 1983.

Lankshear, Colin, and Peter L. McLaren, eds. *Critical Literacy: Politics, Praxis, and the Postmodern.* Albany, NY: SUNY P, 1993.

Lauer, Janice. "Composition Studies: Dappled Discipline." *Rhetoric Review* 3.1 (1984): 20–29.

—. "Instructional Practices: Toward an Integration." *Focuses* 1 (1988): 3–10.

—. *Invention in Rhetoric and Composition.* West Lafayette, IN: Parlor Press, 2004.

—. "Issues in Rhetorical Invention." *Essays on Classical Rhetoric and Modern Discourse.* Ed. Robert J. Connors, Lisa S. Ede, and Andrea A. Lunsford. Carbondale: Southern Illinois UP, 1984. 127–39.

—. "Rhetoric and Composition Studies: A Multimodal Discipline." Enos and Brown 44–54.

Lefebvre, H. "Reflections on the Politics of Space." *Antipode* 8.2 (1979): 30–37.

Lindemann, Erika. *A Rhetoric for Writing Teachers.* New York, NY: Oxford UP, 1982.

Lloyd-Jones, Richard. "Omnivorous Study." Williams, *Visions and Re-Visions* 13–32.

Lowe, E. J. "Self." Honderich 816–17.

Lynch, Kevin. *The Image of the City*. Cambridge, MA: MIT P, 1960.

Lyotard, Jean-Francois. *The Postmodern Condition: A Report on Knowledge*. Minneapolis: U of Minnesota P, 1984.

Mahala, Daniel, and Jody Swilky. "Remapping the Geography of Service in English." *College English* 59.6 (1997): 625–46.

Mannheim, Karl. *Ideology and Utopia*. Trans. Louis Wirth and Edward Shils. New York, NY: Harcourt Brace, 1936.

Matsuda, Paul Kei. "Process and Post-Process: A Discursive History." *Journal of Second Language Writing* 12.1 (2003): 65–83.

May, Todd. *Between Genealogy and Epistemology: Psychology, Politics, and Knowledge in the Thought of Michel Foucault*. University Park, PA: The Pennsylvania State UP, 1993.

McLemee, Scott. "Deconstructing Composition: The 'New Theory Wars' Break Out in an Unlikely Discipline." *The Chronicle of Higher Education* 49.28 (March 21, 2003): A16.

McComiskey, Bruce. *Teaching Composition as a Social Process*. Logan, UT: Utah State UP, 2000.

McCormick, Kathleen. "Using Cultural Theory to Critique and Reconceptualize the Research Paper." Berlin and Vivion 211–30.

McLaren, Peter. "Critical Literacy and Postcolonial Praxis: A Freirian Perspective." *College Literature* 19 (1992): 7–27.

McLeod, Susan. "Some Thoughts about Feelings: The Affective Domain and the Writing Process." *College Composition and Communication* 38.4 (1987): 426–34.

Miles, Elizabeth. "Building Rhetorics of Production: An Institutional Critique of Composition Textbook Publishing." Diss. Purdue University, 1998.

Miller, J. Hillis. "The Function of Rhetorical Study at the Present Time." *Theory Now and Then*. Durham, NC: Duke UP, 1991. 201–16.

Miller, Nancy K. "Arachnologies: The Woman, the Text, and the Critic." *Poetics of Gender*. New York: Columbia, 1986. 270–95.

Miller, Susan. *Textual Carnivals*. Carbondale: Southern Illinois UP, 1991.

—. "Why Composition Studies Disappeared and What Happened Then." Bloom, Daiker, and White, *Composition Studies in the New Millennium* 48–56.

—. "Writing Studies as a Mode of Inquiry." Olson, *Rhetoric and Composition as Intellectual Work* 41–54.

Moxey, Keith. *The Practice of Theory: Poststructuralism, Cultural Politics, and Art History*. Ithaca, NY: Cornell UP, 1994.

Murphy, Michael. "After Progressivism: Modern Composition, Institutional Service, and Cultural Studies." *JAC* 13.2 (1993): 345–64.

Natoli, Joseph, and Linda Hutcheon, eds. *A Postmodern Reader.* Albany, NY: SUNY P, 1993.

North, Stephen M. *The Making of Knowledge in Composition: Portrait of an Emerging Field.* Portsmouth, NH: Heinemann, 1987.

Odell, Lee. "Measuring Changes in Intellectual Processes As One Dimension of Growth in Writing." *Evaluating Writing: Describing, Measuring, Judging.* Ed. Charles R. Cooper and Lee Odell. Urbana, IL: National Council of Teachers of English, 1977. 107–34.

Ohmann, Richard. *English in America: A Radical View of the Profession.* New York, NY: Oxford UP, 1976.

Olson, Gary A. *Rhetoric and Composition as Intellectual Work.* Carbondale: Southern Illinois UP, 2002.

—. "Toward a Post-Process Composition: Abandoning the Rhetoric of Assertion." Kent, *Post-Process Theory: Beyond the Writing Process Paradigm* 7–15.

Ong, Walter J. *Orality and Literacy: The Technologizing of the Word.* London: Methuen, 1982.

Peirce, Charles Sanders. "Logic as Semiotic: The Theory of Signs." *Semiotics: An Introductory Anthology.* Ed. Robert Innis. Bloomington, IN: Indiana UP, 1985. 1–23.

Penticoff, Richard, and Linda Brodkey. "'Writing About Difference': Hard Cases for Cultural Studies." Berlin and Vivion 123–44.

Perkins, Jane M. "Donald Davidson." Enos, *Encyclopedia of Rhetoric and Composition* 160–61.

Perl, Sondra. "Composing Processes of Unskilled College Writers." *Research in the Teaching of English.* 13 (1980): 317–36.

—. "Understanding Composing." Graves 304–10.

Petraglia, Joseph. "Is There Life after Process? The Role of Social Scientism in a Changing Discipline." Kent, *Post-Process Theory: Beyond the Writing Process Paradigm* 49–64.

—, ed. *Reconceiving Writing, Rethinking Writing Instruction.* Mahwah, NJ: Lawrence Erlbaum Associates, 1995.

—. "Writing as an Unnatural Act." Petraglia, *Reconceiving Writing* 79–100.

Petraglia, Joseph, and Deepika Bahri, eds. *The Realms of Rhetoric: The Prospects for Rhetoric Education.* Albany, NY: SUNY P, 2003.

Petruzzi, Anthony. "Kairotic Rhetoric in Freire's Liberatory Pedagogy." *JAC* 21 (2001): 349–81.

Phelps, Louise Wetherbee. "Composition Studies." Enos, *Encyclopedia of Rhetoric and Composition* 123–33.

—. "Practical Wisdom and the Geography of Knowledge in Composition." *College English* 53 (1991): 863–85.

Porter, James E. "Developing a Postmodern Ethics of Rhetoric and Composition." Enos and Brown 207–26.

Porter, James E., Patricia Sullivan, Stuart Blythe, Jeffrey Grabill, and Libby Miles. "Institutional Critique: A Rhetorical Methodology for Change." *College Composition and Communication* 51 (2000): 610–42.

Porter, Kevin. "Review: *Post-Process Theory: Beyond the Writing-Process Paradigm*, Thomas Kent, ed." *JAC* 20.3 (2000): 710–15.

Poulakos, John. "Toward a Sophistic Definition of Rhetoric." *Philosophy and Rhetoric* 16 (1983): 35–48.

Pratt, Minnie Bruce. "Identity: Skin Blood Heart." *Yours in Struggle: Three Feminist Perspectives on Anti-Semitism and Racism*. Ed. Elly Bulkin, Minnie Bruce Pratt, and Barbara Smith. Brooklyn, NY: Long Haul Press, 1984. 11–63.

Pullman, George. "Stepping Yet Again Into the Same Current." Kent, *Post-Process Theory: Beyond the Writing Process Paradigm* 16–29.

Rickert, Thomas. "'Hands Up, You're Free': Composition in a Post-Oedipal World." *JAC* 21 (2001): 287–316.

Ritchie, Joy S. "Confronting the 'Essential' Problem: Reconnecting Feminist Theory and Pedagogy." *JAC* 10.2 (1990): 249–74.

Rodby, Judith, and Tom Fox. "Basic Work and Material Acts: The Ironies, Discrepancies, and Disjunctures of Basic Writing and Mainstreaming." *The Journal of Basic Writing* 19.1 (2000): 84–99.

Rohman, D. Gordon. "Pre-Writing: The Stage of Discovery in the Writing Process." *College Composition and Communication* 16 (1965): 106–12.

Rorty, Richard. *Philosophy and the Mirror of Nature*. Princeton, NJ: Princeton UP, 1979.

Rose, Mike. *Lives on the Boundary: The Struggles and Achievements of America's Underprepared*. New York, NY: Free Press, 1989.

Rosenblatt, Louise M. "The Transactional Theory: Against Dualisms." *College English* 55.4 (1993): 377–86.

Ross, Andrew. *Universal Abandon*. Minneapolis: U of Minnesota P, 1988.

Royer, Dan. "Lived Experience and the Problem With Invention on Demand." Petraglia, *Reconceiving Writing* 161–78.

Russell, David. "Activity Theory and Its Implications for Writing Instruction." Petraglia, *Reconceiving Writing* 51–78.

—. "Activity Theory and Process Approaches: Writing (Power) in School and Society." Kent, *Post-Process Theory: Beyond the Writing Process Paradigm*, 80–95.

—. *Writing in the Academic Disciplines, 1870–1990: A Curricular History*. Carbondale: SIUP, 1991.

Schilb, John. "Reprocessing the Essay." Kent, *Post-Process Theory: Beyond the Writing Process Paradigm* 198–214.

—. "Three Comments to 'Rhetoric and Ideology in the Writing Class.'" *College English* 51.7 (1988): 769–70.
Schneider, Alison. "Bad Blood in the English Department: the Rift Between Composition and Literature." *The Chronicle of Higher Education.* 13 February 1998. 6 pars. 18 June 2004. <http://chronicle.com/prm/che-data/articles/dir/art-44.dir/issue-23.dir/23a00101.htm>
Schriner, Delores K. "One Person, Many Worlds: A Multi-Cultural Composition Curriculum." Berlin and Vivion 95–111.
Schuster, Charles. "Seeking a Disciplinary Reformation." Bloom, Daiker, and White, *Composition in the Twenty-First Century* 146–49.
Scott, Joan Wallach. *Gender and the Politics of History.* New York: Columbia UP, 1988.
Scriven, Karen. "Three Comments to 'Rhetoric and Ideology in the Writing Class.'" *College English* 51.7 (1988): 764–65.
Selzer, Jack. "Exploring Options in Composing." *College Composition and Communication* 35.3 (1984): 276–84.
Sharpley-Whiting, T. Denean. "The Dawning of Racial-Sexual Science: A One Woman Showing, A One Man Telling, Sarah and Cuvier." *French Literature Studies* 23 (1996): 115–28.
Shoemaker, Sydney. *Identity, Cause, and Mind.* Cambridge: Oxford UP, 1984.
Sholle, David, and Stan Denski. "Reading and Writing the Media: Critical Media Literacy and Postmodernism." Lankshear and McLaren 297–322.
Smith, Paul. "A Course in Cultural Studies." Berlin and Vivion 169–81.
Soja, Edward. *Postmodern Geographies: The Reassertion of Space in Critical Social Theory.* London: Verso, 1989.
Spellmeyer, Kurt. *Common Ground: Dialogue, Understanding, and the Teaching of Composition.* Englewood Cliffs, NJ: Prentice Hall, 1993.
—. "Education for Irrelevance? Or, Joining Our Colleagues in Lit Crit on the Sidelines of the Information Age." Bloom, Daiker, and White, *Composition Studies in the New Millennium* 78–87.
—. "Foucault and the Freshman Writer: Considering the Self in Discourse." *College English* 51 (1989): 715–29.
—. "Travels to the Heart of the Forest: Dilettantes, Professionals, and Knowledge." *College English* 56.7 (November 1994): 788–809.
Spigelman, Candace. "What Role Virtue?" *JAC* 21 (2001): 321–48.
Spivak, Gayatri Chakravorty. "Displacement and the Discourse of Woman." Krupnick 169–95.
Stewart, Donald. Foreword. *Writing Instruction in Nineteenth-Century American Colleges.* By James A. Berlin. Carbondale: Southern Illinois UP, 1984. ix-x.

Tagg, John. *The Burden of Representation: Essays on Photographies and Histories*. Amherst, MA: U of Massachusetts P, 1988.

Takayoshi, Pamela, ed. "Watson Conference Oral Histories." *History, Reflection, and Narrative: The Professionalization of Composition 1963–1983*. Ed. Beth Boehm, Debra Journet, and Mary Rosner. Norwood, NJ: Ablex Press, 1999. 6 interviews. 205–213.

Taylor, Mark C. *The Moment of Complexity*. Chicago: U of Chicago P, 2001.

Taylor, Todd. "A Methodology of Our Own." Bloom, Daiker, and White, *Composition Studies in the New Millennium* 142–50.

Therborn, Goran. *The Ideology of Power and the Power of Ideology*. London: Verso, 1980.

Thrift, Nigel. "On the Determination of Social Action in Space and Time." *Environment and Planning: Society and Space* 1 (1983): 23–57.

Tobin, Lad. "Introduction: How the Writing Process Was Born—And Other Conversion Narratives." Tobin and Newkirk 1–14.

—. "Process Pedagogy." *A Guide to Composition Pedagogies*. Ed. Gary Tate, Amy Rupiper, and Kurt Schick. New York: Oxford UP, 2001. 1–18.

Tobin, Lad, and Thomas Newkirk. *Taking Stock: The Writing Process Movement in the '90s*. Ed. Lad Tobin and Thomas Newkirk. Portsmouth, NH: Boynton/Cook, 1994.

Todorov, Tzvetan. *Mikhail Bakhtin: The Dialogical Principle*. Trans. Wlad Godzich. Ed. Wlad Godzich and Jochen Schulte-Sasse. Vol. 13. Minneapolis: U of Minnesota P, 1984.

Trimbur, John. "Literacy and the Discourse of Crisis." Bullock and Trimbur 227–96.

—. "Taking the Social Turn: Teaching Writing Post-Process." *College Composition and Communication* 45 (1994): 108–18.

—. "The Problem of Freshman English (Only): Toward Programs of Study in Writing." *Writing Program Administration* 22.3 (1999): 9–30.

Vandenberg, Peter. "Discourse Community." Heilker and Vandenberg 67–70.

Van Dijk, Teun A. "Principles of Critical Discourse Analysis." *Discourse & Society* 4.2 (1993): 249–83.

Vatz, Richard E. "The Myth of the Rhetorical Situation." *Philosophy and Rhetoric* 6.3 (1973): 154–61.

Villanueva, Victor. "Considerations for American Freireistas." Bullock and Trimbur 247–62.

Warnock, John. "The Discipline and the Profession: *It's a Doggy Dog World*." Williams, *Visions and Re-Visions* 69–86.

Weedon, Chris. *Feminist Practice and Poststructuralist Theory*. New York, NY: B. Blackwell, 1987.

Williams, James D., ed. *Visions and Re-Visions: Continuity and Change in Rhetoric and Composition.* Carbondale: Southern Illinois UP, 2002.

Williams, Raymond. *Keywords: A Vocabulary of Culture and Society.* New York, NY: Oxford UP, 1983.

Winterowd, Ross. "Fragments of History, Personal and Institutional." Williams, *Visions and Re-Visions* 33–48.

Winterowd, F. Ross, and Vincent Gillespie, eds. *Composition in Context: Essays in Honor of Donald C. Stewart.* Carbondale: Southern Illinois UP, 1994. 180–95.

Yagelski, Robert P. "Who's Afraid of Subjectivity? The Composing Process and Postmodernism or a Student of Donald Murray Enters the Age of Postmodernism." Tobin and Newkirk 203–18.

Young, Iris Marion. *Justice and the Politics of Difference.* Princeton, NJ: Princeton UP, 1991.

Young, Richard, and Maureen Daly Goggin. "Some Issues in Dating the Birth of the New Rhetoric in Departments of English: A Contribution to a Developing Historiography." Enos and Brown 22–43.

Young, Richard. "Concepts of Art and the Teaching of Writing." *Landmark Essays on Rhetorical Invention in Writing.* Ed. Richard E. Young and Yameng Liu. Davis, CA: Hermagoras Press, 1994. 193–202.

Zavarzadeh, Mas'ud, and Donald Morton. "Theory, Pedagogy, Politics: The Crisis of 'The Subject' in the Humanities." *Boundary* 2.15 (1987): 1–22.

Zuboff, Shoshana. *In the Age of the Smart Machine: The Future of Work and Power.* New York, NY: Basic Books, 1988.

Index

agency, 23, 59, 62-63, 65–68, 71–78, 89–90, 99, 107–108, 110–112, 117, 120, 129, 163-164, 174–175, 179, 203, 206
Alcorn, Marshall, 77, 203
alterity, 99, 102-104, 107-108, 111, 132, 137, 142-49, 151, 160, 163-164, 173, 175-177, 220
Althusser, Louis, 67, 72–73, 77, 115
Ashton-Jones, Evelyn, 96
audience, 14, 21, 45–47, 49, 50–52, 55–56, 58, 61, 63–64, 107–108, 142-148, 150, 159, 161–162, 182, 202, 220
Austin, J. L., 83-94, 217–218; speech-act theory, 83

Bakhtin, Mikhail, 80, 81, 84-88, 91-95, 99-108, 110, 116-118, 120, 130-132, 143, 148, 150, 156, 173, 204, 214, 222; addressivity, 93, 104, 108-109, 112, 140, 143, 156, 157, 160-162, 164-165, 174-175, 177, 179, 222; answerability, 93, 104-109, 112, 143, 156, 157, 160-165, 173, 175, 177, 179, 204; dialogism, 85, 86, 88, 90, 92, 94, 100, 104, 131, 143, 149, 151, 156, 175; heteroglossia, 85, 87-88, 92, 101, 103, 116-118, 151, 214; horizon, 33, 102-103, 107, 123, 132, 143, 153-155, 158-159, 164
Baudrillard, Jean, 72

Bazerman, Charles, 189-190
Beatty, Steve, 181, 193, 224
Bee, Barbara, 216-217
Benhabib, Seyla, 74, 203
Berkenkotter, Carol, 35
Berlin, James A., xiii, 38, 42-70, 77, 85, 182, 194, 201-203; and Robert Inkster, 43-44, 46-48, 62-63; cognitive map, xiii, 43, 47, 52, 54-55, 58, 59, 61-67, 70, 200-201
Bialostosky, Don H., 80
Bitzer, Lloyd F, 109
Bizzell, Patricia, 9, 11, 38, 115, 200
Bleich, David, 137, 192
Blomley, Nicholas K., 122, 123
Bloom, Allan, 220
Bloom, Benjamin, 160, 222
Bloom, Lynn Z., 4, 225
Blyer, Nancy, 22, 25
Blythe, Stuart, 222
Bourdieu, Pierre, and Jean-Claude Passeron, 126
Bowden, Darsie, 136
Brand, Alice G., 36
Brannon, Lil, 9, 10, 14, 16, 129, 137, 181
Brodkey, Linda, 77, 217-218
Brummett, Barry, 78
Budd, Malcolm, 98
Burke, Kenneth, 108, 131-132

California State University, Chico, 141, 166-167, 172, 177, 179
Cassam, Quassim, 99

Cauthen, Cramer R., 186-187
Cintron, Ralph, 36
cognitive map(s), xiii, 43, 47, 52, 54-55, 58-59, 61-67, 70, 200-201
composition, xi, xiv, 3-5, 9, 11, 14, 16-17, 20-22, 24, 26-28, 30-33, 35, 43-44, 47-48, 51, 53, 61-64, 76-79, 82, 104, 108, 115, 122, 129, 154, 156, 160, 167, 181-185, 187-191, 193-194, 196-197, 199-200, 202, 211, 217-218, 220, 222-225; abolition of, 5, 17, 181, 195; and rhetoric, xii, 3-5, 12, 14, 30-31, 38, 43, 71, 77-79, 82, 113, 128, 135-136, 138, 182-183, 185-191, 193-197, 200, 222-224; reform of, xiv, 5-6, 15, 17, 23-24, 26, 166, 170-171, 178, 181, 195, 214
Connors, Robert J., 17, 181, 184, 194, 200, 222
Consigny, Scott, 109
Cooper, Marilyn, 77
Couture, Barbara, 21, 23
Covino, William A., 201
Crary, Jonathan, 98
Crowley, Sharon, 82, 181-184, 191-192, 194, 225
culture, xi-xii, xiv, 5, 6, 10, 12-13, 15, 17, 25, 27, 29, 31-32, 37-38, 40-44, 52-54, 57-59, 61, 64, 68, 72-73, 75-77, 83-84, 88-90, 96-98, 104, 106, 112-113, 120-124, 126, 128, 135-136, 140, 157, 161-162, 168, 174, 177, 179, 189, 191-193, 197, 199-203, 205, 207, 209- 213, 216, 218-221, 223, 225; turn, 5, 6, 13, 17, 29, 31, 38
Cushman, Ellen, 191-192, 224
cyborg, 26, 76

Dasenbrock, Reed Way, 77, 83, 200

Davidson, Donald, 6-7, 39-40, 199-200; intersubjectivity, 39-40
de Lauretis, Teresa, 75, 84, 88
de Saussure, Ferdinand, 83, 84, 116
DeJoy, Nancy, 21, 26
Denski, Stan, 124, 126, 137, 220
Derrida, Jacques, 42, 72, 83, 87-88, 91-92, 201, 206, 214
Dewey, John, 35-36
différance, 87-88
difference, 9, 25-26, 49, 50, 72, 74-75, 83, 85, 88, 99, 125, 151-152, 158-159, 181-182, 202, 206, 213, 215-217, 219
disciplinarity, 17, 28, 31, 43, 78, 180, 183-184, 186, 188, 191, 194-197
discipline, xiii, 9, 14, 16, 20, 29, 30, 34, 46, 55-56, 68, 112, 140, 166, 182, 185-186, 188-196, 204, 218, 221, 223-224
discourse, xiii, 5-9, 11, 15, 24, 26, 28, 31, 36-38, 46-47, 52, 56-57, 61-62, 65, 67-68, 71, 74-75, 77, 79, 82-87, 89, 94, 97, 102-104, 107-110, 112, 114, 116, 118-121, 124-125, 130, 133, 137, 142-143, 148, 151, 156, 162-164, 176-178, 180, 185, 189, 192, 194, 196, 202, 206, 207-209, 212-214, 218-222
discourse community, 56-57, 65, 133, 178, 218
discursive formation, xiii, 37-38, 56-57, 112, 133-136, 138-142, 165-166, 178, 217
discursive relations, 112-116, 118-124, 127, 130, 134, 136, 138, 165
Dixon, Kathleen, 128
Dobrin, Sidney I., 24, 28-29, 91, 136, 199, 223
doxa, 12, 189
Dreyfus, Hubert L., and Paul Rabinow, 133

Ebert, Teresa, 73
Economy, 123, 166, 168-171, 175, 177-79, 222
Emig, Janet, 31-32
English department(s), 14, 20, 47-48, 55, 185-188, 190, 194, 195, 217, 223-225
environment, 29, 70, 102-103, 117, 122, 136, 154-155, 164, 168-169, 173, 187
epistemology, xiii, 44, 46-47, 50-51, 55-57, 59, 61-63, 65-68, 79, 114, 131-134, 136, 138-140, 163, 175, 179, 214
ethic(s), 25, 29, 87, 89, 107-108, 110, 128, 157, 163, 165, 179, 182, 202, 213, 219
existence, xii, 25, 59, 73, 91-92, 100-101, 103, 104-106, 109-110, 116, 120, 143, 156, 157, 177, 207, 222

Faigley, Lester, 34, 38, 78, 115, 127, 200, 204
feminism, 206, 213
feminist, xi, 26, 40, 74-75, 97, 124, 205-207, 213-216
Feyerabend, Paul, 37
Flannagan, Owen, 91
Fleischer, Cathy, 140
Fleming, David, 181, 183, 190-192
Flower, Linda, 8, 35, 60
Foster, David, 25
Foucault, Michel, 58, 66-67, 73, 112, 118-121, 133, 135, 165-166, 204, 208, 214; discourse community, 56-57, 65, 133, 178, 218
Fox, Tom, 166, 168, 171-174, 176, 225
Freedman, Aviva, 15-16, 17
Freire, Paulo, 11, 76, 128, 210, 211
Fulkerson, Richard, 30, 128
Fuss, Diana, 97

Gale, Fredric G., 137,
Gale, Xin Liu, 126-127, 211
Gebhardt, Richard, 34
Gee, James Paul, 125, 137, 218-219
George, Diana, and Diana Shoos, 76
Gere, Anne Ruggles, 138, 197, 223
Gillespie, Vincent, 223
Giroux, Henry, 124-125, 137, 219-220
Goggin, Maureen Daly, 181, 190, 192-193, 224
Grabill, Jeffrey, 222
Grossberg, Lawrence, 125
GWSI, 5, 11, 13-17, 19, 21-27, 30, 36, 38, 42-43, 66, 74, 76-77, 88, 91, 97, 120, 142, 165-167, 172, 174-176, 189, 200-201, 210, 214, 218, 220
GWSI (general writing skills instruction), 14, 16-17, 27

Hamlyn, D. W., 130
Haraway, Donna, 26, 75-76
Harkin, Patricia, 115, 137, 222
Harris, Joseph, 182, 204
Hayes, John R., 8, 35
Hebdige, Dick, 120
Helmers, Marguerite H., 78-79
Hermogenes, 109
heuristic, 47, 50-51, 61-62, 64, 70, 112, 116, 132, 141, 143, 148, 151, 153, 163, 198-199
Holquist, Michael, 204
Holzman, Michael, 138, 208-209
hooks, bell, 74-75, 96, 124, 127, 172, 175, 207-208, 213

identity, xi-xiv, 3-4, 13, 20, 27, 41, 73-75, 127, 180, 182, 185, 187, 191-192, 194, 196-197, 216, 225
ideology, 50, 55-60, 63-68, 72-73, 77, 114-118, 120-121, 136, 138, 163, 204, 209, 211, 220
invention, 15, 21, 33, 45, 49, 52, 218

Jacobs, Debra, 11-13
Jameson, Fredric, 43, 70, 73, 200-201
Jarratt, Susan C., 123, 205-207, 212-216
Jay, Martin, 97-99
Jensen, George H., 35
Johnson, Barbara, 42, 194
Jolliffe, David, 15
Journet, Debra, 23

Kaufer, David, 15, 17
Kemp, Fred, 15
Kent, Thomas, 5-9, 12-13, 18-19, 21, 23-26, 28-29, 37, 39-40, 199
Killingsworth, M. Jimmie, 218
Kinneavy, James L., 33, 46, 108
Kirby, Kathleen M., 96, 200-201
Kitzhaber, Albert R., 194
Knoblauch, C. H., 9, 10, 35, 129, 137
Kostelnick, Charles, 34
Kroll, Barry M., 8, 35

labor, 4, 168, 171, 182-184, 195, 214, 225
LaCapra, Dominic, 73
language, 6-8, 10-11, 15, 18-19, 31, 45-46, 48-52, 55-56, 58, 62-64, 66-67, 72, 74, 77, 80, 82-89, 91-93, 96-98, 100-101, 103-104, 107-108, 110, 112, 116-118, 120, 122, 132-133, 137, 142-143, 151-153, 162-164, 169, 190, 192, 202, 208
Lauer, Janice, 33, 109, 187-188, 199, 218, 224-225
Lefebvre, H., 121-122
Lindemann, Erika, 34
literacy, xiii, 9-10, 16, 32, 55-57, 59, 65-67, 114, 125, 127, 136-140, 163, 167, 172-175, 179, 182, 185, 192, 194, 208-210, 212, 214, 216, 218-221
Lloyd-Jones, Richard, 225
logos, 206
Lowe, E. J., 90

Lynch, Kevin, 70
Lyotard, Jean-Francois, 26, 72, 133

Mahala, Daniel, 182
Mannheim, Karl, 97
map(s), xii, 43, 55, 62-63, 65, 67, 70-71, 79-80, 90, 107, 110, 113, 200-201, 204, 217-218
Matsuda, Paul Kei, 36, 200
May, Todd, 121
McComiskey, Bruce, 200
McCormick, Kathleen, 127
McLaren, Peter, 76
McLemee, Scott, 184-185, 222
McLeod, Susan, 36
Miles, Elizabeth, 222
Miles, Libby, 222
Miller, J. Hillis, 222
Miller, Nancy K., 207
Miller, Susan, 30, 189, 192
monologism, 85, 204
Morton, Donald, 214
Moxey, Keith, 116, 119, 225
Murphy, Michael, 202

naming, 180, 191-92
networked process, xii-xiv, 41, 43, 68, 70-71, 79, 84, 88-89, 108, 110, 112-114, 141, 163, 165, 166, 191, 197-198, 201
networked subjectivity, xiii-xiv, 71, 79-81, 89, 108, 110, 112-113, 115-116, 132, 141, 163, 167, 173, 175, 177, 222
noetic field, 52-55, 57, 64-65
North, Stephen M., 20, 194

Odell, Lee, 35, 187
Ohmann, Richard, 137
Olson, Gary A., 21, 26, 30
Ong, Walter J., 53-54, 65
other, 36, 85, 88, 93-94, 98, 100-101, 103, 106-107, 115, 120, 126, 131, 137, 143, 148, 154, 157, 205, 220, 222, 225

paralogic hermeneutics, 5-7, 9, 13, 26, 29, 39, 199
passive understanding, 131
Penticoff, Richard, 217-218
Perkins, Jane M., 7
Perl, Sondra, 33, 35
Petraglia, Joseph, 13-14, 16-17, 19, 27-28, 181
Petruzzi, Anthony, 11-12
Phelps, Louise Wetherbee, 129, 196
Porter, James E., 196-197, 222
Porter, Kevin, 30
postmodernism, xi, 4, 10, 15, 26, 40-41, 73-74, 77, 125, 137, 166, 200, 202, 214, 218-219
post-process, xi- xiii, 3-6, 9-13, 17-19, 21, 23-27, 29-31, 37-38, 40, 43, 180-181, 184-185, 194-197, 200; reform, 23; strand one, 5, 13; strand two, 5, 6, 18-19, 23, 27
Poulakos, John, 108
power, xii-xiii, 19, 22, 25, 29-30, 32, 34, 51, 56-59, 66-67, 73, 75, 79, 87, 98, 112, 115, 118-128, 131, 134, 136-137, 142, 156, 161-163, 166, 168, 170, 179, 189, 195-196, 206, 212, 214-216, 218, 223, 225
Pratt, Minnie Bruce, 122
process, xi-xiv, 3-6, 8-13, 17-31, 33-38, 40-52, 57, 60-62, 64, 67-70, 77-78, 82-84, 86, 89, 93-94, 97, 100, 102-103, 107-108, 110, 112-113, 124-126, 128-129, 133, 135-138, 140-155, 157-159, 162-167, 170, 172-173, 177, 179-181, 184-185, 195-197, 199-201, 203-204, 206, 208, 211, 213, 215-216, 218, 225; critique, 5, 11, 13-15, 17, 19, 21-26, 30, 36, 38, 42-43, 66, 74, 76-77, 88, 91, 97, 120, 142, 165-167, 172, 174-176, 189, 200-201, 210, 214, 218, 220

Pullman, George, 19, 21

reality, 27, 39-40, 45-52, 54, 56-58, 61, 63, 66-67, 76, 78, 85, 89, 96, 101, 107-110, 114-115, 123, 161, 175, 181-183, 195, 198, 202, 207, 209, 220-221
reform, xiv, 5-6, 15, 17, 23-24, 26, 166, 170-171, 178, 181, 195, 214
responsive understanding, 94, 148-153, 160, 164, 173, 175
rhetoric, xii, 3-5, 10, 12, 14, 19-21, 23, 25, 30-32, 36, 38, 40-43, 45-46, 48, 50-59, 61-66, 71, 77-80, 82-83, 89, 99, 107, 109, 113, 124, 128, 130, 180, 193-197, 200-201, 205-206, 218, 222-224; and composition, 6, 9, 135-136, 138, 182-191, 199, 218; social epistemic, 40, 58-59, 61
Rickert, Thomas, 11, 12
Ritchie, Joy S., 128
Rodby, Judith, 166, 168, 171-174, 176
Rohman, D. Gordon, 34
Rorty, Richard, 50, 64, 203
Rose, Mike, 217
Rosenblatt, Louise M., 83
Ross, Andrew, 225
Royer, Dan, 15
Russell, David, 15, 20, 22, 27, 181, 191

Schilb, John, 24, 60, 137
Schneider, Alison, 223
Schriner, Delores K., 211-212
Schuster, Charles, 182, 223
Scott, Joan Wallach, 215
Scriven, Karen, 60
seeing, surplus of, 101, 143
self, 3, 5-6, 9, 11, 13, 18-19, 21, 23, 25-27, 33, 36, 42, 54, 58, 66, 71-72, 74-75, 77-78, 89-101, 104, 107-108, 110, 112, 117, 120-121,

127, 132, 137, 142-143, 157, 163-164, 169, 176, 194, 199, 202-204, 208, 211-213, 216, 220
Selzer, Jack, 35
Sharpley-Whiting, T. Denean, 205
Shoemaker, Sydney, 99-100
Sholle, David, 124, 126, 137, 220
Shoos, Diana, 76
Simon, Roger I., 124
social construction(ist), 5, 8, 27-28, 40, 123, 131, 200
social/cultural turn, 5-6, 13, 17, 29, 31, 38
Soja, Edward, 121
space, xii, xiv, 4, 10-14, 28-29, 36, 41, 48, 53, 59, 79, 81, 90-92, 95-96, 99, 101, 104-106, 108, 115-117, 120-124, 128, 131, 143, 151, 154, 156, 158, 163, 170, 172-176, 178-179, 185, 190, 195, 197, 201, 205, 207, 213, 220, 222
Spellmeyer, Kurt, 9, 11, 188, 224
Spigelman, Candace, 11-12
Spivak, Gayatri Chakravorty, 206-208
stasis, xii, xiii, 4, 37, 38, 40, 108-109, 110, 153
Stewart, Donald, 51
subjectivity, xiii-xiv, 7, 26, 31-34, 37, 39-41, 43, 58-59, 61, 66-68, 70-79, 81-82, 84, 86-88, 89-93, 95-96, 99-110, 112, 114-118, 120, 122-123, 127-129, 131-133, 134-136, 138-139, 141-142, 144-147, 149-150, 154, 156-162, 164-167, 169-171, 175, 177-178, 184, 200, 203-208, 214, 216, 218, 220, 222, 225
Sullivan, Patricia, 222
Swilky, Jody, 182

Tagg, John, 118, 120
Taylor, Mark, 199
Taylor, Todd, 188
Thomas, Dene Kay, 96
Thrift, Nigel, 121
time, 4, 17, 27, 34, 38, 51, 54, 56-58, 74-75, 79, 81-82, 92, 101, 105-108, 121-122, 124, 144-145, 151, 155-156, 159, 171-173, 181, 190, 193, 196, 205-206, 213-214
Tobin, Lad, 37, 199, 200
Todorov, Tzvetan, 85, 91, 94-95, 100, 102-104, 106, 131, 204
triangulation, 7, 29, 39-40
Trimbur, John, 9-12, 137, 182, 191, 200, 220, 221, 225

Vandenberg, Peter, 218
Vatz, Richard E., 109
Villanueva, Victor, 125, 210-212

Warnock, John, 225
Weedon, Chris, 112
Williams, Raymond, 114, 197
Winterowd, W. Ross, 223, 225
writer, xiv, 11, 14, 18, 20-21, 29, 32-36, 41, 45-52, 54, 61, 63-64, 67, 77-79, 82, 89, 104, 107, 142, 144-146, 149-150, 152-160, 163-164, 169, 170-171, 177, 202, 220
writing major, 190-191
Writing with a Purpose (McKrimmon), 141-145, 147, 149-155, 157, 160, 162-164, 221

Yagelski, Robert P., 77
Young, Iris Marion, 130
Young, Richard, 35, 46, 186

Zavarzadeh, Mas'ud, 214
Zuboff, Shoshana, 123

About the Author

Helen Foster holds a PhD in Rhetoric and Composition from Purdue University and is currently associate professor of English at the University of Texas El Paso, where she serves as director of the Rhetoric and Writing Studies Program. She has presented papers at numerous conferences and is published in various journals. Her research areas include the history and theory of composition studies; rhetorical and cultural studies theory, particularly regarding issues of power, knowledge, marginalization, and legitimacy; and the emerging area of undergraduate rhetoric and writing studies.

www.ingramcontent.com/pod-product-compliance
Lightning Source LLC
Chambersburg PA
CBHW030132240426
43672CB00005B/116